The Truth Option

THE
TRUTH
OPTION

A Practical Technology
for Human Affairs

by Will Schutz

1 TEN SPEED PRESS

Text copyright © 1984 by Will Schutz
Illustrations copyright © 1984 by Nancy Austin

1⊙ TEN SPEED PRESS
P O Box 7123
Berkeley, California 94707

Library of Congress Catalog Number: 83-40025
ISBN: 0-89815-107-4 (paper)
ISBN: 0-89815-108-2 (cloth)

Cover Design by Brenton D. Beck
Book Design and Illustrations by Nancy Austin
Typesetting by Accent & Alphabet

Printed in the United States of America
4   5   6   7   8   —   95   94   93   92   91

TO MY TEACHERS:

Ed Feigon, who taught me how to be — when we were 10.

Sheldon Courshon, who introduced me to Dostoevski — when we were 11.

Mrs. McIlvain, who convinced me that it was OK to be creative — in a high school geometry class.

Lou Gehrig, who demonstrated the meaning of quiet determination.

Abraham Kaplan, who introduced me to the excitement of precise thinking.

Elvin Semrad, who unveiled the fascinating underworld of group interaction.

Louis Guttman, who showed me that numbers can be human.

Alexander Lowen, who revealed to me the body-mind connection.

Ida Rolf, who taught me that when I touch someone they should be better for it.

Moshe Feldenkrais, who illustrated how self-awareness makes living more graceful.

ACKNOWLEDGMENTS

To the original trainees, supporters and colleagues: Jorge Diaz, Ed Hahn, Rick Martin, Rob Nelson, Tony Reilly, Mark Rocchio, David Simmons, Peter Taylor, Ron Tilden, Bruce Tuck, Russ Volckmann and Geoff Williams.

To the original risk-takers: Logan Cockrum, John Collins, Sister Corita, Wayne Counts, the AHP staff and Fran Macy, Bricca Prestridge, Colonel Sherburne, Fran Ulschak, Bernard Warner, Keith Yates.

To the first helpers: Madelyn Burley-Allen, Davida Cohen, Joyce Feddon, Sean O'Byrne, Rhoda Rosenbaum, Cheryl Schutz, Sukey Waller.

To the sage advice givers: Caroline Andrew, Thompson Barton, Judi Bell, David Bradford, Irene Herrold, Chris Iosbaker, Gail Kelley, Michael Phillips, Linda Potter, Caleb Schutz.

To the manuscript preparers: Judith Abrahms, Estela Contreras, Libby Patterson, Naomi Steinfeld.

To the artist and the publisher: Nancy Austin and George Young.

To the one who cleared the way: Ailish Mellard.

And to the original inspiration—Claudia.

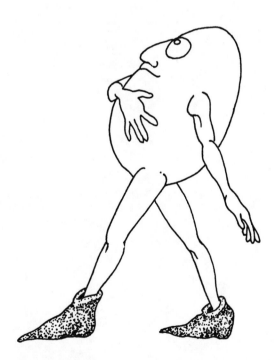

CONTENTS

INTRODUCTION

In virtually all successful science fiction movies of the past decade, from "2001" to "Return of the Jedi," there is a common theme, an inadvertent and revealing contrast: The technology of the future is breathtakingly elegant, precise, and powerful; improvements over modern technology are stupendous and glittering. But in this future people relate to each other in exactly the way they do now. The same duplicity, superficiality, withholding, hostility, strategizing, competing. No improvement whatsoever.

The world stumbles when people negotiate with people. Peace talks are a vast, grotesque network of scheming, evasion, bluffing, and conning. Black–white confrontations, labor–management mediation, generation conflicts—all are marked by the same assumption about people: A strategy must be devised to get them to do what you want. Machiavelli survives as the most profound influence on human interaction.

Perhaps it is time to take a look at another approach, the truth option. It seems quite possible that the truth does make you free. Why not explore the consequences of telling the truth to each other?

If a country's negotiations are marked by deception and diplomacy, it may be because that is the way its people deal with each other. Public policy is related directly to private affairs. If a nation spends half its energies on national defense, it is probably because that is the amount of energy its people spend on personal defensiveness. Public ills reflect private ills. Therefore, exploring the truth option for individuals also has profound implications for issues on a larger scale. The book provides a technology for this exploration.

SOCIAL CONTEXT

Although this could probably be said of any era, it appears that now is a propitious time for us to make breakthroughs in understanding the human condition. Now is the time we are able to devise methods for improving the human side of society as effectively as we have improved the technological side.

Trend analyzers have pointed to two strong social trends in the 1980s. One is a strong conservative pull, centered around the Reagan philosophy and strongly supported by the John Wayne image of strength and independence, and by the emergence of professional football as a national totem. This trend emphasizes self-determination through reduction of big government and encouragement of competition and private enterprise.

The other trend appears contradictory, on the surface. It is a continuation and growth of the human potential, social liberation, hippie, humanistic values of the 1960s and 1970s, which have matured into a heightened sensitivity to human feelings, fairness, and compassion. Politically, it leads to increases in welfare programs, social security, child care, and other projects based on human compassion.

Each trend—the conservative and the liberal, the Republican and the Democratic—contains an important ingredient of a method for improving the human condition.

Here is a paradigm of social change that incorporates some values from each of these positions and synthesizes them in a way that human beings can use to function more effectively:

social change

```
┌─────────────┐                        ┌──────────────┐
│ PRESENT     │                        │    SELF      │
│ SITUATION   │ ─────────────────────▶ │ DETERMINATION│
│             │      transition        │              │
└─────────────┘                        └──────────────┘
```

Enlightened conservatives point to autonomous, independent, self-determining individuals as an end result of their policies. If we are all empowered, we will be more of what we are capable of. Our human energy problems will be solved, and we will be able to function more effectively, with more joy, and with less government.

Thoughtful liberals understand that many people now require support and assistance to survive during the period of transition to increased self-determination. We must not allow our fellow humans to suffer unduly.

When we combine the insights of both, a clearer picture emerges: *We want to go toward a world of self-determining people. We recognize that many people need to make a major transition, and that they will arrive there faster if given outside support.*

PROBLEM

Conservatives understand the goal, but they are not clear about the compassionate support that helps create the transition to self-determination. Therefore, they are often accused of being heartless and uncaring as they reduce supportive social programs.

Liberals understand the desirability of human support, but they do not realize that this support is only a temporary aid, to be given while people are in the process of achieving self-determination. Liberals are accused of being profligate — of spending more and more money on social programs, because they are never-ending if the goal of self-determination is not incorporated into the supportive programs.

RESOLUTION

The Truth Option is aimed at combining the strengths of these two views. Individual empowerment is enhanced through learning and examining the truth, through increasing self-awareness, and through recognizing the ability of each of us to choose our own life. This aim is accomplished while supporting the humanness of us all. There is no blame, no imposition of morality, no humiliation or shame implied in the path to autonomy. Instead, we recognize how each of us functions, and how similar we are at a deep level. We are interested in understanding, not in evaluating. In this context we flourish.[1]

TECHNOLOGY

A crucial factor in the timeliness of this human breakthrough is the tremendous increase in the understanding of human behavior, human consciousness, and human interaction that has developed over the last several decades. In terms of theory, objective test instruments, and educational and therapeutic techniques, the explosion of knowledge and experience has been extraordinary. Methods from all over the world and from many points in time have converged, and new and more powerful syntheses have arisen. These new approaches are just now beginning to be applied to social issues.[2]

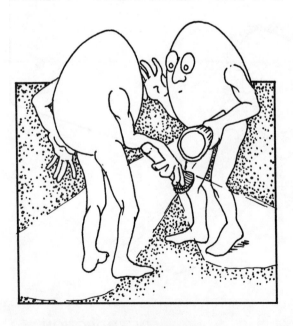

DESIGN

This book is designed to guide you through a journey of discovering yourself and of how to live your life the way you want to. It is different from most "you can do it!" books in that it also deals with those parts of you that you are now unaware of — your unconsciousness. *The Truth Option* helps you bring this part of yourself to awareness.

The book deals with you as an individual, as a person in relation to others, and as a person in the context of a job and an organization. It is aimed at helping you deal more effectively with yourself, your friendships, your love relations and your work.[3]

Appendix A presents background and development of this book. Appendix D suggests several possibilities for continuing the process begun in the book.

The examples presented in this book come from both personal and work experiences. All the examples are true — they are embellished a bit for literary clarity, but they are taken from actual personal experiences of the author, of his friends and acquaintances, or of people in various workshops aimed at growth for individuals, couples or organizations.

USE

To gain the most from the book, it is suggested that you skim through it as a whole first to get a sense of the entire journey, without going into detail. (But if you enjoy surprises, don't skim — just start in.) Then begin at the beginning and work your way through the book step by step. Do not hurry. If you find something puzzling, stay with it until it becomes clear. If it is too difficult, make a note of it — it probably has particular personal significance. Then proceed through the book and come back to that point.

This book may be completed over a long period of time. You may want to carry it with you and read and react to new material or review material you have already done, as you feel the desire. Here are some reading suggestions to help you get the most from this style:

1. Read an idea: then put down the book and free-associate to it. That is, let whatever images or thoughts or feelings come to mind. Write them down.

2. When you run out of associations, go over the list and think about them. See if you can derive the logical connection among them. Think of experiences in your life relevant to the idea.

3. Complete all the activities related to the idea, and notice how your understanding evolves.

4. Discuss the idea with friends.

5. Use the notes at the back of the book to pursue written material relevant to the idea.

STYLE

In order to avoid sexist locutions and to speak directly to you, the reader, I will use the device of writing in the first person. "I" will mean everyone, the universal person. "You" will be used to represent everyone else, in either the singular or the plural forms, depending on the situation. For example, "In my job, it is desirable that I control you" means "It is desirable that anyone who holds this job controls everyone whom they meet on the job."

The hope is that at some point you will identify yourself with "I," and experience reading the book as a personal journey. When I, the author want to talk to you, the reader, I will indicate it by the presence of my symbol.

chapter one

POINT OF VIEW:
Truth, Choice, Self-Regard

This book is based on a point of view that was developed over the last twenty years. This viewpoint emerged from experiences in organizations; psychological and group theory; the human potential movement; scientific and experiential investigations of the human side of organizations; and a great deal of practical experience.[4]

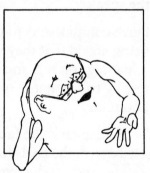

The aim of this book is to help me be aware of myself and function with all my parts — intellectual, physical, emotional, and spiritual[3] — in harmony. When this happens I will be a happy, productive, and fulfilled person.

These are the basic principles of this point of view:

- *Self-regard.* The ultimate basis for my personal and professional success is for me to understand, respect, and like myself.

- *Truth.* Truth is the great simplifier of personal and interpersonal difficulties.

- *Choice.* I empower myself when I take responsibility for myself.

SELF-REGARD

Self-regard is "the bottom line."[5] If I do not feel good about myself and I am not aware of it, I often will blame other people or circumstances for my bad feeling. I may, for example, act rushed as a way of hiding my feelings of incompetence — as if to say, "Of course I could do better if only I had the time." Or I may be furious with myself when I miss a shot on the tennis court, as if to tell observers, "I usually hit shots like that," when, in fact, I probably have never hit a shot like that in my life. Or if I do not feel that I am very likeable, I may act harsh and demanding so that I can attribute my lack of popularity to "dedication to the job." I have devised ingenious ways of covering my feelings of inadequacy.

On the other hand, when I feel good about myself, it is almost certain that my activities will be successful and that I will derive great joy[6] from them. When I feel good about myself:

- I take risks with confidence. I am neither foolhardy nor overcautious.

- I am not shattered by lack of support or by not being liked. I keep on being who I am, confident and likeable.

- I follow directions without resentment. I give directions without guilt or fear of punishment.

- I accept criticism and make constructive use of it.

- I speak directly and honestly to people with whom I have a problem, instead of talking behind their backs.

- I accept a compliment graciously, without suspecting the sincerity of the speaker.

- I give compliments to people without being afraid that they will gain an advantage on me, and without first testing to see that they feel the same about me.

As I understand the factors involved in self-regard, the tools for a more successful and productive life will become evident. I shall return to this issue as I progress through the book.

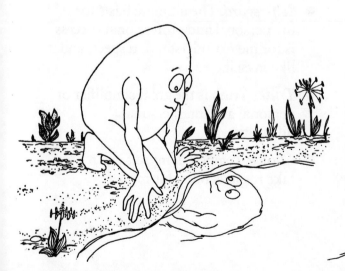

TRUTH

One of the most obvious and yet the most neglected keys to improved relationships and to self-awareness is the concept of truth.[7] "The truth shall make you free" is a phrase I have heard all my life but only recently have I understood how fundamental it is. I find that at every level — body, individual, couple, group, organization, nation — the more truth, the more success.

This discovery was shocking, because I always assumed that I had to be strategic, judicious, discreet, and selective about the truth I tell. But to my surprise, I found that not telling the truth is the source of most problems. My personal relations are more vital when I am totally honest. When I go to work, at my job, it seems that about 80 percent of all my problems are not real problems at all. They are simply the result of not telling the truth, of lying or withholding.

Definition

Truth simply means what *is,* whether I know it or not. *My truth* is my experience — the state of every cell of my body, my memories, my thoughts, my feelings, my sensations.

As I understand it, truth has nothing to do with morality. I do not pursue truth because it is good or moral or spiritual or right. I observe what happens to me and to my relationships when I tell more truth than usual. I regard truth as a problem-solving tool; then I see how useful it is for finding better solutions to my life situations.

To profit most from this book, I assume that knowing the truth about human behavior and feelings is valuable.

Awareness

How much I let myself know of my own truth is called my *awareness.* I am aware of some things about myself that I am afraid of, or ashamed of, or feel guilty about. I let myself know my truth to certain levels, depending on how comfortable I am about knowing it.

That truth which I do not choose to let myself know about may be called my *unaware* part, or my unconscious. When I am aware of a truth, I can decide consciously what I want to do. When I am not aware of some of my truth, it may control me in a way that I do not understand. Therefore, bringing that which I am not aware of to my awareness is one of the objectives of this journey, and is a key to a self-fulfilling life.

Honesty

If I choose to tell you what I am aware of, I am being *honest*. If I choose to tell you something contrary to my awareness, I am lying. If I choose not to tell you something I am aware of, I am withholding.

To communicate my truth to you, I must be both aware and honest.

To be honest and not aware is what may be called the Sincere Politician Syndrome. When I am sincerely honest but have not allowed myself much self-awareness, then what comes out usually is boring. I do not present myself fully because I am not aware of my total experience.

Honesty is often the key to simplifying relationships and to reducing tension.

One of the difficulties encountered by many of the thirty employees of a scientific company during *The Human Element** training was not trusting the division leader, who wanted to reorganize the division. After several sessions, most members felt free enough to speak out: "Simon, I think you want to rise in this organization, and that you feel a reorganization will make you more powerful. That's why we are resisting." After a long interchange, Simon acknowledged that he did have ambitions, but that he believed if he let them be known he would be punished for them.

After this acknowledgement, tensions relaxed. Simon realized that his fear was groundless, and that everyone knew about his ambitions anyway. The employees made it clear to him that having ambitions was fine (they had them, too), but that they did not like his denial of his ambition. Once he had acknowledged his ambition, then they could all work to help Simon attain his aspirations and to plan a sensible reorganization. Honesty had eased the relationships and simplified the situation.

* (the name given to *The Truth Option* when used in organizations)

Body

When I tell the truth, my body feels good. When I lie or withhold the truth, the lie or the withhold expresses itself in my body as some form of discomfort, such as shortened breath, neck pain, tight stomach, sweaty palms, dry throat, or headache. I also get clues to my own truth through feedback from other people about how they sense my behavior.

The more I tell the truth, the healthier I am. Lies and withholds lead me not only to body tensions but also to distancing in relationships, to loss of motivation, to burn-out, to illness and absenteeism, and to declining productivity on the job.

Helen had just contracted a life-threatening disease and had decided that she should understand herself better. So she entered a Human Element workshop. Helen had kept a big secret from her husband of twenty-five years: One of their children was not his. Her guilt had led her to abandon work on her doctorate and to devote herself almost slavishly to her husband and children. She had sacrificed her own career and interests to a large extent, in an effort to make up for her transgression. In the course of the group session, she decided that it would be best to tell her husband the truth and to take the consequences, since withholding had not brought her what she had expected. To her amazement, she learned that her husband already knew her secret — and always had. In an extended discussion, he revealed that he had dealt with the situation long ago and had forgiven her at that time; he had had virtually no thoughts about it for years. She was struck with the realization that her excessive self-sacrifice for twenty-five years had been pointless and unnecessary.[8]

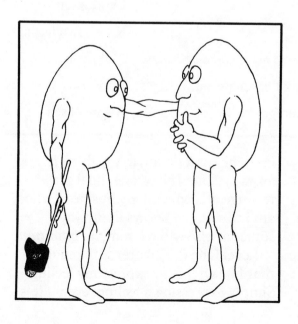

Levels

One common objection to telling the truth is: "If I ever told my bosses what I really think of them, I'd be fired."

However, as I reflect on it, the firing (or the leaving) would not be the result of telling the truth, but rather of not telling *enough* truth.

Usually when I say "the truth," I mean "telling you what you really are" — which usually translates into something like "You're a bastard!" Consider, however, that this statement is not a very deep truth. (Depending on the facts of your ancestry, it may not even be accurate.) This most superficial level of truth is about you.

Something becomes true on a deeper level when it has more to do with what I experience directly and less to do with my speculations about what is happening outside of my experience. In other words, my truth deepens as I move from talking about what *you* are like toward paying attention to what *I* experience.

Here are the steps involved in the truth process, from the most superficial level to the deepest.

TABLE 1. Levels of Truth

Level	Statement	Example	Skill Required
0	(Silence)	. . . (withholding)	Aware of sensations
1	"You are . . .	. . . a bastard."	Express self
2	"About you I feel . . .	. . . dislike."	Know own feelings
3	"Because . . .	. . . you don't reward my accomplishments."	Make connections
4	"Which means . . .	. . . you don't think I'm competent."	Know own defenses
5	"About me I fear . . .	. . . that I'm not competent."	Aware of self

Level Zero of truth occurs when I am feeling something and not expressing it. This level accounts for the overwhelming proportion of all feelings. I have many rationalizations for withholding: it's not tactful, it's not diplomatic, it wouldn't do any good, it will only hurt her feelings, I might get fired, he can't do anything about it anyway, I may be wrong, he'll get revenge, it's none of my business, who am I to say, she knows it anyway, someone else will tell him, *ad infinitum*.

Level One ("You are . . .") requires that I be willing to express my feeling. Simply expressing a feeling, even if it is name-calling, is a considerable step toward truth. For example, I tell my boss he is a bastard. However, if I stop at that level, my fears of being fired or rejected will probably be realized. To find deeper levels of truth I switch my focus from you to me.

Level Two ("About you I feel . . .")— for example, expressing my dislike for you or for your actions — requires a greater awareness of my feeling state. In most cases, if I express my dislike I will be less likely to run into difficulty with you than if I call you a name.

Level Three is reached when I realize which behaviors have led to my feeling. This requires another level of skill that I must acquire in order to deepen my truth. I may realize, for example, that my feeling of dislike began when you did not compliment me on my report ("Because . . ."). Most often the connection between event and feelings is not realized, and the resulting interaction is off the point and fruitless. When I realize which events led me to feel as I do, then we are on the way to

resolving our difficulties, and our chances of coming to a bad end diminish further.

Level Four ("Which means . . .") requires a knowledge of which defense (or coping) mechanisms I use to avoid feeling bad. In the example, I interpret your behavior as indicating that you do not feel I am competent (projection).

Level Five ("About me, I fear . . .") arrives when I recognize how I feel about myself—in this case, that I do not feel competent. That is why I perceive you as feeling the same way I do about myself. If I have this much awareness, I will not get in any difficulty with you, because I probably will not even mention it(since it has to do primarily with me and very little with you).

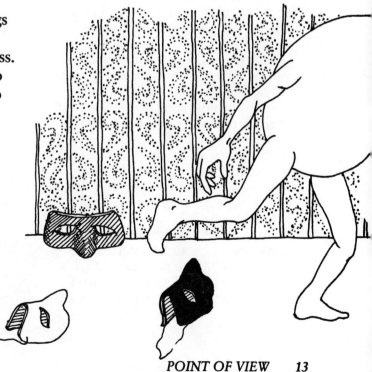

Here's something that happened to me that illustrates the point:

Our tradition was to talk about serious issues within our relationship in the large bathtub at night, by candlelight and incense. This night I began: "You bitch [Level One: "You are . . ."]! You know it bothers me when you spend a whole evening with your old boyfriend. You're not finished with him yet."

"You're so insecure [Level One]," she replied, "I can't even see an old friend. I feel suffocated [Level Two: "About you I feel . . ."]."

"When you do that I feel that you don't care about my feelings. I feel shitty [Level Two]. I feel the same when you wouldn't meet my plane at the gate because you were having dinner with your friends [Level Three: Because . . ."]."

"I'm afraid to stay at a girlfriend's house one night even if it's late [Level Three]," she said. "I'm afraid you'll think I don't love you. I feel stifled."

After the bickering, I felt a wave of sadness. "I think I'm just covering up my feeling that you don't really love me. I seize on any little thing you do that I can interpret that way [Level Four: "Which means . . ."]."

"Well," she said, "I hate to admit it but I think I want to make sure I have someone to go to in case you get tired of me [Level Four]. I feel that eventually you will leave me."

"Of course," I said. "I'm afraid you don't love me because *I* don't love me [Level Five: "About me I fear . . ."]. It's hard for me to feel loved by anyone. I just don't see why they would love me."

"I feel I'm boring [Level Five]," she reflected. "I think I don't have enough to keep a man interested."

This condensed report of a five-hour discussion illustrates the successive levels through which truth can travel if it is pursued thoroughly, without stopping prematurely because of fear of what may emerge.

Exceptions

Exploring the consequences of telling the truth all the time may appear to sound absurd. Telling the truth does not mean that I am required to stop everyone on the street and tell them my reaction to their appearance. It does not mean that I must spend an hour telling a waitress my feelings about her competence instead of being on time for an important meeting. Even though I may be willing to tell the waitress my feelings, I choose instead to spend my time elsewhere.

The question is how to decide what is relevant and what is irrelevant to tell. The best rule of thumb is this: *If I am trying to decide whether I should or should not tell something — I should.* The dilemma is that I know it is important to tell, and I want to think of a reason for *not* telling. If the issue were really irrelevant, it probably never would have entered my mind. This rule does not always work, but it seems to cover the vast majority of cases.

A large division of a finance company was in trouble. The division's productivity and morale were very low. So management called in a consultant.

The major complaint of the vice president heading this division was the salary procedure. Each year, the seven managers under him would parade into his office, one at a time, and present evidence to show why they should receive a higher salary. He, in turn, would marshal his forces to show them why their raises should be somewhat lower. This process spread over several months, frequently ending with bitterness and resentment on the part of some. "Truly," said the vice president, "this whole process is a nightmare, probably the worst part of my job."

Since everyone agreed that this was their major problem, the consultant decided to focus on resolving it in the three days allotted for the consultation. He began by asking them to tell the truth about their salaries. "Would everyone be willing to tell the group how much you make?"

The response was a resounding "no." This request violated one of the cardinal rules of organizational life: "It's a private matter"/"It's nobody's business"/"I don't even tell my wife."

After two and a half days, the consultant suggested a compromise. Everyone knew the total amount of money available for salaries for the seven managers and the vice president. The consultant asked everyone to write down privately how he or she would divide the total amount among the eight people. All agree to do that. The consultant then collected these papers, mixed them up, and wrote the results on the board for all to see. All were astonished: with two minor differences, everyone had agreed almost exactly on how much salary each person should get.

After a brief discussion, they adjusted the salary of a modest manager upward and that of an overambitious one downward. The group stared at the board for several minutes. Slowly they began to realize what they had accomplished.

In thirty minutes, through being open about their attitudes toward salaries, they had solved their horrendous, months-long, annual problem. In the process, they found that:

● revealing their salaries was not so threatening;

● everyone knew everyone else's salary anyway (within a few thousand dollars); and

● revealing how they felt about their own worth and that of others led to very productive discussions.

Telling the truth had the effect of releasing a huge amount of company time and energy, and of all but eliminating resentment and deception. Their "horrendous" problem actually required only thirty minutes per year, if they were willing to tell the truth.

Truth is the grand simplifier.

Here's an activity to help you understand the ideas better.

You might find it valuable to write your answer on the facing page. This gives you an opportunity to see if and how you change as you proceed through the book.

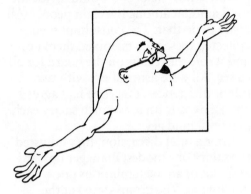

ACTIVITY 1. Truth

1. Do you feel that it is always good to tell the truth? Why? Under what circumstances, if any, do you think it is not a good idea to tell the truth?

2. Think of an example from your personal life or from your organization when it was or was not good to tell the truth.

3. Would you like your friends to be more honest with you? Less honest? How about the people you work with?

4. When your close friends are not truthful, do you think it is because of lack of honesty or lack of awareness? Elaborate.

5. How do you feel about your own honesty? Would you like to be more or less honest than you are?

6. How do you feel about your own awareness? Are there things that you hide from yourself? Do you know why?

7. Think of one thing you are not being honest about right now. Are you willing to tell it to yourself?

RESPONSES: Activity 1. Truth

CHOICE

It is important for me to realize that I have the power to change. To profit most from this book, I shall assume that I am running my own life and that I have the capability to make any changes that I wish in myself, in my relationships, and in my work situation. To assume that some things are unchangeable is to impose limitations before even trying. If I do not believe that I can change, I have little reason to acquire increased personal awareness.

Like truth, the concept of choice—(or self-responsibility)—has nothing to do with morality. I am not now considering whether it is good or proper or moral or responsible or right to take responsibility for my own life. Those are interesting questions, but I am concerned here only with the practical consequences of the concept: What happens in my life as a result of my assumption that I am choosing what happens? If choice does not prove a useful assumption, I can simply revert back to the belief I have now.

Following is the view of choice[9] that I shall explore.

I choose my whole life, and I always have. I choose my behavior, my feelings, my thoughts, my illnesses, my body, my reactions, and my spontaneity.

Conscious and Unconscious

Some of these choices I choose to be aware of, and some I choose not to be aware of. I often choose not to be aware of feelings I do not want to deal with, of unacceptable thoughts, and of some connections between events. I may feel lustful or vengeful, for example, but my social or religious beliefs deplore these feelings. I may deal with this dilemma by acting as if I were highly moral and quite forgiving. I may even hide my true feelings from myself.

According to this formulation, what has been called the unconscious is simply all those things of which I choose not to be aware. I choose my unconscious, too; therefore it follows that since I created my unconscious, I also can choose to make it conscious.

Self-Responsibility

There are no accidents. Events occur because I choose them to occur. However, I am not always aware that I am choosing them.

Once I accept responsibility for choosing my life, everything is different. I accept my power. I decide. I am in control of my life.

If I accept the concept of choice, I must alter my understanding of many key ideas about people — ideas such as "group pressure," "manipulation," "using people," "brainwashing," and "scapegoating." All these terms imply that something is being done to me; but according to the choice principle, I am *allowing* something to be done to me. I use these terms to blame others for what I do myself. In fact, I cannot be "pressured" or "brainwashed" or "manipulated" or "used" unless I allow myself to be.[10]

Fear

Likewise, things do not frighten me. I may say that I am afraid of a person, such as my boss; or of an action, such as rejection; or of a thing, such as a shark. But, to be consistent with the choice point of view, I am not really afraid of those things out there; I am only afraid of my inability to cope with my boss, or to cope with rejection, or to cope with sharks. If I am swimming about and see a shark, I may feel fear. But if I am standing inside a shark cage under the water, I may not feel fear. The shark has not changed, only my ability to cope with it.

As long as I see you as the cause of my fear, I spend my time trying to change, criticize, avoid, or destroy you. But once I see that my fear is in me, I may work on improving my ability to cope — a much more useful undertaking.

I have only one fear: the fear of not being able to cope — of my own uncopability.

Suppose I dread seeing you come into my office because I have these fears: "You talk all the time;" "I will have to listen to all the problems you have with your wife and your kids;" "You take up my time;" "I never get anything done when you are around;" "You intrude on my privacy."

In truth, I dread your visit because I do not feel able to *cope*. As soon as I learn to ask you to leave when I do not want you around any more, I do not dread your approach. When I feel that I can cope with you in that situation, I lose my fear.

No judgment

The choice principle is neither good nor bad. Sometimes you may assume that if I say "You chose it," I am being callous and uncaring. Being compassionate has nothing to do with the principle. I can choose to be caring and helpful to you regarding a thing you chose, or I can choose to be hard and uncaring. These also are choices.

If I wish, I can feel guilty or wicked or evil or immoral for having chosen something. When I do, I realize that feeling those ways is also something I choose. There is nothing inherently guilt-inducing in the act. I am just choosing to feel bad. I could also choose to not feel bad.[11]

Payoff

The reason for making a particular choice is because I get a particular payoff. I may feel guilty because that makes me appear responsible— as, for example, when I take a vacation and leave my children with a relative. By feeling guilty, especially publicly, I may appear to be a conscientious and caring parent. Or, for example, I may choose to feel confused because I am thereby relieved of the responsibility of making a decision.

The value of the choice principle is that it reorients my search for solutions. Before, when things went bad I blamed you, and cursed my fate that I was so victimized by circumstance. Now that I accept that I chose the situation, I look for the payoff I get for creating the situation in which I find myself. I do not *blame* myself, I simply look for my personal rewards— and usually have no trouble finding them. Typical payoffs in a work situation are: sympathy from others; lower expectations for work; justification for being sick (therefore earning sick leave); and putting down my boss so that I look better.

Choice is not a judgmental concept. It is simply a concept that helps me to figure out what is happening. It is an idea that helps me solve problems rather than assign blame.

This Book

One implication of choice is: I will benefit from reading this book exactly to the degree that I choose. I can make it the most valuable experience of my life; I can choose to be bored with it or depressed by it; I can find it useless; I can use it to do the things I have always wanted to do; I can resist the exercises; I can participate fully; I can ridicule; I can enjoy; I can cooperate; I can complain; I can compete with the author; or I can be inspired. In short, I can react any way I wish. I choose what and how much benefit I derive from this book.

Preprograms

Further, my state of mind in approaching this book has already started to determine how much I am getting from it. I may have decided that this is exactly what I need to take the next big step in life and be completely ready to use all my creative forces to make important advances. Or I may have decided that I will learn nothing from this book because:

- I already know what is in it;

- I know more than the author;

- this is California flake, and there couldn't be anything of substance in it;

- it is too theoretical and has nothing to offer a practical person;

- it is too extremist, too radical;

- and so on.

I have innumerable ways to block myself from deriving the maximum benefit from learning situations.

Again, this is not good or bad — it is simply an important factor to be aware of. And being aware of it puts me in a position to change it, if I wish.

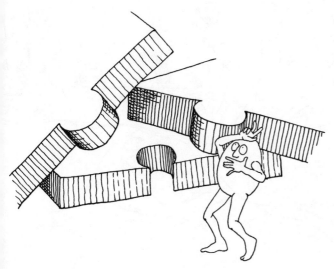

STRESS

"Stress" and "stress management" are concepts that currently are popular. Confusions about the concepts of truth, self-regard, and choice are the main reasons for feeling stress.

Truth

Not telling the truth induces stress. This stress includes the energy required for lying; the induction of body tensions; the need to remember the lie, as well as to whom I told it; the concern over being caught; the worry that someone will reveal my lie; the tension of facing someone who knows I am lying; the anxiety over whether or not someone else is lying; and the conflict with my moral or religious beliefs. For these reasons and many more, I commonly experience a feeling of relaxation when I have just told a long-withheld truth.

Self-Regard

Similarly, if I have a low self-regard, chances are that I feel much tension as a result. I may be concerned that you will ignore me, or that you will discover that I am not as competent as I appear — that I am a phony. I may fear being rejected; or being disliked; or that I said something wrong; or that I failed to speak up when I should have; or that I failed to be loyal to a friend. The worse my self-concept, the more my life will be filled with stress related to anticipating being ignored, humiliated, or rejected.

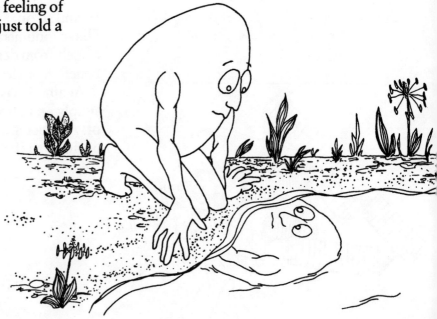

Choice

Failure to understand self-responsibility or choice also leads to stress. If I feel that I am responsible for everyone around me, then I quickly reach burn-out. I have difficulty delegating, or letting my children decide for themselves. I keep all decisions to myself, even those I am not aware of. Understanding clearly where responsibility resides in each situation is one of the surest ways to reduce stress.

Choice also implies that I choose to feel pressure or stress. There is nothing inherent in my life situation that requires me to feel pressure. I choose to interpret what I experience as stress. Whatever my circumstances are, they just are. I am the one who labels them as stressful. The concept of a "stressor" — something in the environment that is responsible for my stress — is misleading. Nothing is stressful to me unless I interpret it as stressful.[12]

Eddie Murray, the fine batter for the Baltimore Orioles baseball team, was asked by a reporter how he handled the stress and pressure of the pennant race and World Series.

"Everyone is counting on you, Eddie, to come through for the team," urged the reporter. "You know that if you don't, your job, your salary, your career may be in jeopardy. When it comes down to September and October, every game, every time you are at bat may make the difference between winning the championship and being a loser."

"I make my own pressure," he replied.

Apparently he understands the choice principle in that situation.

ACTIVITY 2. Choice

 You might want to ponder #3 especially.

PART A

1. Define the concept of choice as you understand it. How much do you now take responsibility for your own life?

2. Do you agree that there is only one fear (uncopability)?

3. Discuss this implication of choice: "I will benefit from reading this book exactly to the degree that I choose. I can make it the most valuable experience of my life; I can choose to be bored with it or depressed by it; I can find it useless; I can use it to do the things I have always wanted to do; I can resist the exercises; I can participate fully; I can ridicule; I can enjoy; I can cooperate; I can complain; I can compete with the author; or I can be inspired. In short, I can react any way I wish. I just need to be aware that I am responsible for my choice."

   Do you believe it?

4. List the preprograms you had before you started this book which you think will help you to get the most from it.

5. How did you preprogram yourself to prevent yourself from profiting fully? Write these ways down and check them periodically as you proceed through the book.

PART B

1. Write a short autobiography based on the assumption that you chose how you were brought up — or, more specifically, that it was a collusion between yourself and your parents. One way to start is to think of how you tortured your parents.

   Keep in mind that this way of looking at your life has nothing to do with blaming. It is simply an attempt to understand what happened.

2. Does this exercise help you to understand anything about yourself? (Bear in mind that this is just an exploration. If you do not find it useful, you may drop it.)

RESPONSES: Activity 2. Choice

After each chapter there is a Segue which summarizes the essence of the chapter, reflects on its content, and serves as a transition to the next chapter.

SEGUE

The bases for the approach described in *The Truth Option* are truth, choice, and self-regard. *These principles are offered as ideas for me to explore, to see whether I find them useful.*

If I achieve the aims of this book for myself, my relationships, and my working life, I will be in the following state:

- I feel good about myself. I am fully present in what I do. I am spontaneous, yet in control. I am aware of myself—of my strengths, of my weaknesses, and of how personal issues in my life affect my work.

- I feel significant, and I do not ask you to pay excessive attention to me. I feel competent, and I do not demand constant praise for my work. I feel likeable, and I am not afraid of rejection. I appreciate personal acknowledgement, but I do not depend on it for my feeling of self-worth.

- I know myself better and am motivated to take care of myself better, both physically and psychologically. I am more aware of the condition of my body and of the relation between my feelings of physical well-being and the rest of my life.

- My increase in self-acceptance expresses itself in my home life. I have new insight and pleasure in my relations with my family and friends.

- My relations are characterized by an atmosphere of truth. I know that any time I ask a question I get a straight answer, and I always respond truthfully.

- I find more personal pleasure at my job. It is an important source of personal enjoyment. The "Thank God it's Friday" club has died.

- I take responsibility for myself. When you and I are involved in a project, there is no question of accountability. We both assume full responsibility for success of the project.

- Since I feel secure in myself, I am free to experience you as you really are, and to appreciate and support you.

- Since my job relations and my personal relations are characterized by lessened anxiety and by increased personal growth, my absenteeism, illness, and lateness are reduced dramatically.

- My creativity and productivity are greatly increased because I am living much nearer my full capacity.

The first step toward understanding myself so that I can start on the road to achieving these aims is to understand my behavior. For this I need a framework to help me make sense of the whole complicated field of human behavior.

chapter two

BEHAVIOR:
Inclusion, Control, Openness

If I understand behavior I may gain increased understanding of: myself and other people; how and why I behave as I do; why I sometimes have trouble working and being with you; and how to use my full energies to achieve whatever goal I desire most effectively.

I want to become more aware of how I function. I am *not* concerned with evaluating myself, with deciding what is good or bad, or with blaming myself for anything. I want to understand what is, and to learn how to change what I want to change.

These are some questions I want to answer:

- Why do I act as I do?

- How are you and I alike? How do we differ?

- How can I understand myself better?

- How can I understand you better?

- How can I have more awareness, enjoyment, and effectiveness in my work and my life?

THE BASIC BEHAVIORS

From the time I was a child, I functioned in three areas of behavior: inclusion, control, and openness. When fully expressed, these dimensions are popularly called fame, power, and love. Understanding each of these areas is a key to understanding my own behavior.[13]

Inclusion

Inclusion is the area concerned with achieving just the right amount of contact with you and with others. Sometimes I like a great deal of inclusion. I am outgoing, I like to go to parties, I like to do things with a group, I like to start conversations with strangers.

At other times, I prefer to be alone. I like to be by myself, I am more reserved, I seldom start conversations, I avoid parties.

You and I differ as to how much we wish to be with other people and how much we wish to be alone, as to how much we want to be in groups with other people and how much we want to avoid groups.

Inclusion has to do with *in* or *out*.

Control

The second area is concerned with achieving just the right amount of *control* over you and other people. Sometimes I am more comfortable when I am in charge of you. I like to be the boss, to give orders, to make decisions both for myself and for you.

At other times, I prefer to have no control over you. I am content never to tell you what to do. I even seek out situations where I have no responsibility.

You and I both have some desire to control other people and some desire to be free from controlling. We vary in the amount we like to be on top and the amount we want to be free of controlling others.

Control has to do with *top* or *bottom*.

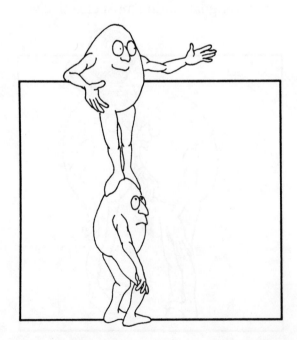

Openness

The third area is concerned with achieving just the right amount of *openness*.[14] Sometimes I enjoy a relationship with you where we talk about our feelings, our secrets, and our innermost thoughts. I enjoy having one person, or at most a few people, in whom I confide.

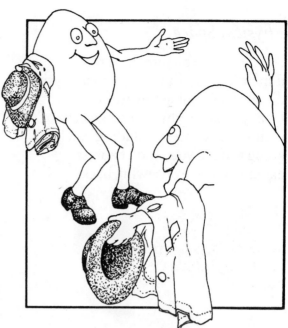

Openness has to do with *open* or *closed*.

It is neither good nor bad to prefer any of these behaviors. It is helpful to be aware of what I prefer and to be aware of my preferences.

At other times, I prefer to avoid being open with you. I would rather keep things impersonal, and I prefer to have acquaintances rather than a few close friends.

You and I both have some desire for open relations and some desire to keep our relations more private. We differ in how much we like to be open and how much we like to be closed.

Physical Space

One way to picture these three dimensions is to imagine actual physical dimensions. Going toward or away from you is the physical equivalent of inclusion. I express including you by going toward you, and I express excluding you by drawing back.

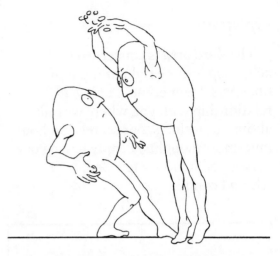

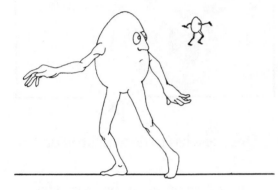

Rising above you or falling below you is the physical equivalent of control. I express control over you by being over you, and I express being controlled by being below you.

Reaching my arms out to the side is the physical equivalent of being open with you, while closing my arms around myself is the physical equivalent of being closed to you. I express being open by inviting you in, and I express being closed by keeping you out.

QUESTIONS. Behavior

Understanding behavior does not require an expert. In my own life, I have had a great deal of experience with people, and I already know a great deal about them. I probably know more about people than I am aware of knowing.

The following questions will help me to check my understanding of the ideas presented on pages 28 and 29.

I place the letter of my answer (I, C, or O) on the line at the left. The letters mean:

(I) Inclusion
(C) Control
(O) Openness

_____ 1. Workers who are worried that the boss is not honest with them are concerned about ?

_____ 2. Bosses who are not sure how much they want to delegate responsibility are concerned about ?

_____ 3. Which area is described by these words: sociable, outgoing, gregarious?

_____ 4. If I try to be popular with all my coworkers but avoid getting close with any one of them, I am low on ?

_____ 5. Which area is described by these words: authoritarian, influential, organizer, supervisor, laissez-faire, democratic?

_____ 6. A worker who avoids all office picnics and parties is low on ?

_____ 7. Which area is described by these words: self-disclosing, confiding, secretive, aloof, businesslike, impersonal?

_____ 8. A secretary who is "the power behind the throne" is high on ?

Answers: OCI OCI OC

ACTIVITY 3. Behavior Imagery[15]

Using your imagination helps to understand the ideas. Everyone can do it — eventually — and it's fun.

PART A

Inclusion

1. Find yourself a comfortable place to lie or sit. Shut your eyes. (You may read directions 2, 3, 4 ahead of time or record them or have someone read them to you. This applies to all imagery that follows.)

2. Imagine yourself climbing a mountain. As you approach the top, you see a large group of people coming over the mountain from the far side. Watch and see what happens. What do you do?

3. (Pause 60 seconds.) How does it feel to be in that position? Are the people friendly or hostile? Do they come toward you, avoid you, walk away from you or ignore you? Do they all act the same? What do they look like? Is there any contact, verbally or physically? How does your body feel?

4. (Pause 60 seconds.) Open your eyes and sit up. Reflect on what you saw and how you feel about what you experienced. Write this on the following page.

Control

5. Shut your eyes and relax. Imagine that you are much larger than everyone around you. See what happens. (Pause 60 seconds.) Now see yourself become much smaller than everyone else. See what happens.

6. (Pause 60 seconds.) How does it feel to be much larger? Much smaller? Which do you prefer? Is it comfortable, powerful, frightening? How do you look? What is the setting? How do the other people look? How does your body feel?

7. (Pause 60 seconds.) Open your eyes and sit up. Reflect on what you saw and how you felt. Write this on the following page.

Openness

8. Shut your eyes and relax. Imagine yourself revealing all your secrets to a group of people. See what happens.

9. (Pause 60 seconds.) Is it a frightening or a comfortable thing to do? Are you really telling everything? What are you omitting? Who are the people in the group? How do they react? How does your body feel?

10. (Pause 60 seconds.) Open your eyes and sit up. Reflect on what you saw and how you felt. Write this on the following page.

11. How does your imagery help you to understand your feelings about inclusion, control, and openness, respectively? Write your final reflections.

12. Take a short break, then continue with Part B.

PART B

1. Using the descriptions on pages 28 and 29 and your imagery, define each dimension. Is it clear? Continue until you are sure that you understand inclusion, control, and openness. Describe the difference between inclusion and openness.

2. Give some words that mean almost the same thing as inclusion; the same thing as control; the same thing as openness.

3. Read each question on page 31. Reread any question where you disagree with the answer given, until you are sure you understand.

RESPONSES: Activity 3. Behavior Imagery

ASPECTS OF BEHAVIOR

For each of the three behavioral areas — inclusion, control, and openness — two aspects will be distinguished and measured: Do–Get and Is–Want.

Do–Get

I may describe what I Do toward you (my behavior toward you), and what I Get from you (your behavior toward me).

I Do behavior toward you in each area, respectively, when I include you, control you, and am open with you.

I Get behavior from you in each area, respectively, when you include me, control me, and are open with me.

Is–Want

I may also describe the behavior that Is happening (the behavior that I perceive to be actually happening), and the behavior that I Want to have happen (my ideal behavior).

In the three behavioral areas, respectively, I may perceive (Is) that I include, I control, and I am open with you; and that you include me, you control me, and you are open with me. I may also Want to include you, to control you, and to be open with you, and Want you to include me, to control me, and to be open with me.

These two aspects, Do–Get and Is–Want, are summarized in Table 2 below. Each statement in the table becomes the name of the dimension measured by Element B (Behavior).[12]

TABLE 2. Aspects of Behavior

		IS	WANT
	Inclusion	I include people.	I want to include people.
DO	*Control*	I control people.	I want to control people.
	Openness	I am open with people.	I want to be open with people.
	Inclusion	People include me.	I want people to include me.
GET	*Control*	People control me.	I want people to control me.
	Openness	People are open with me.	I want people to be open with me.

QUESTIONS. Aspects of Behavior

I place the letter of my answer on the line at the left. The letters mean:

(a) I include people.
(b) I control people.
(c) I am open with people.
(d) People include me.
(e) People control me.
(f) People are open with me.
(g) I want to include people.
(h) I want to control people.
(i) I want to be open with people.
(j) I want people to include me.
(k) I want people to control me.
(l) I want people to be open with me.

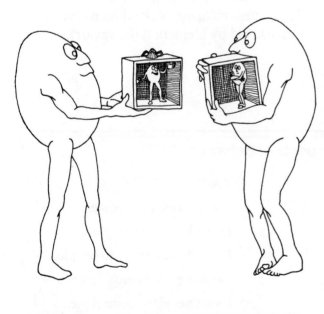

Answers: ghd cjk abl

_____ 1. A vice president who wants to call many meetings so he has people to talk to is high on ?

_____ 2. A highly qualified senior employee who consistently refuses promotions to executive positions is probably low on ?

_____ 3. An employee who is not invited to a company picnic is low on ?

_____ 4. An employee who is attracted to another employee but who does not tell him about it is exhibiting low ?

_____ 5. Employees who are disappointed when they are not invited to social events are high on ?

_____ 6. An employee who wants to be told what to do is high on ?

_____ 7. A boss who invites all 100 of his employees to his house for a Sunday barbecue by putting a notice on the bulletin board is high on ?

_____ 8. A company that has a job requirement that all male employees must wear dark suits at all times is high on ?

_____ 9. A boss who wants each employee to talk to her individually about personal problems is showing high ?

ACTIVITY 4. Aspects of Behavior

1. Define each Do dimension until you are convinced that you understand them.

2. Give examples from your work situation and from your personal life of high or low "I include people," "I control people," "I am open with people."

3. Define each Get dimension until you are convinced that you understand it.

4. Give examples from your work situation and from your personal life of high and low "People include me," "People control me," "People are open with me."

 Thinking of examples is especially valuable.

5. Give examples of each for both Is and Want.

6. Give examples from your personal life and from your work situation of each for both Is and Want.

7. Read each question on page 36. Reread any question where you disagree with the answer given, until you are sure you understand.

A word about the five Elements, the first of which appears on the next few pages. The Elements are meant to help you understand what is presented in the book. Each is instructive on its own and can be scored on the page opposite. To fully use the information, complete the interpretation of each Element and the combination of all five Elements in the back of the book.

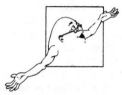

The small numbers next to the boxes on pages 41 to 43 are the scale code numbers. You use them to ensure accuracy when you transfer scores between pages or to the Scoring Summary in the back of this book. When two numbers are subtracted from each other, the Difference is designated by the Greek delta, Δ.

Measurement

Element B[16] measures my preferences on all the aspects of inclusion, control, and openness listed in Table 2 on page 35.

Prediction

Before I fill out Element B, I will record how I perceive myself. Turning to pages 42 and 43 in the circles marked "P", I will put a score from 0 to 9 indicating how much I agree with each of the twelve statements. Nine means "most agreement," and zero means "least agreement."

Disagree 0 1 2 3 4 5 6 7 8 9 **Agree**

After the predictions are recorded, I fill out and score Element B.

ELEMENT B

There are no "right" answers. The more honest I am, the more accurate will be the information I receive from Element B.

First, I complete the column "The way it IS" for all items.

For each statement, I place a number from 1 to 6 on the line to the left of the item, in the appropriate column. The numbers indicate how much I agree with the statement.

Disagree 1 2 3 4 5 6 **Agree**

When I have finished, I return to the top of the column and respond to the same items for "The way I WANT it to be."

The Way It IS	The Way I WANT It to Be	
1	___	I seek out people to be with.
2	___	People decide what we do when we are together.
3	___	I am totally honest with my close friends.
4	___	People invite me to do things.
5	___	I am the dominant person when I am with people.
6	___	My close friends tell me their real feelings.
7	___	I join social groups.
8	___	People strongly influence my actions.
9	___	I confide in my close friends.
10	___	People invite me to join their activities.
11	___	I get other people to do the things I want done.
12	___	My close friends tell me about private matters.
13	___	I join social organizations.
14	___	People control my actions.
15	___	I am more comfortable when people do not get too close.
16	___	People include me in their activities.
17	___	I strongly influence other people's actions.
18	___	My close friends do not tell me everything about themselves.
19	___	I am included in informal social activities.
20	___	I am easily led by people.
21	___	People should keep their private feelings to themselves.
22	___	People invite me to participate in their activities.
23	___	I take charge when I am with people socially.
24	___	My close friends tell me their real feelings.
25	___	I include other people in my plans.
26	___	People decide things for me.
27	___	There are some things that I do not tell anyone.
28	___	People include me in their social affairs.
29	___	I get people to do things the way I want them done.
30	___	My closest friends keep secrets from me.
31	___	I have people around me.
32	___	People strongly influence my ideas.
33	___	There are some things I would not tell anyone.
34	___	People ask me to participate in their discussions.
35	___	I take charge when I am with people.
36	___	My friends confide in me.
37	___	When people are doing things together, I join them.
38	___	I am strongly influenced by what people say.
39	___	I have at least one friend to whom I can tell everything.
40	___	People invite me to parties.
41	___	I strongly influence other people's ideas.
42	___	My close friends keep their feelings a secret from me.
43	___	I look for people to be with.
44	___	Other people take charge when we work together.
45	___	There is a part of myself that I keep private.
46	___	People invite me to join them when we have free time.
47	___	I take charge when I work with people.
48	___	I have at least two friends who tell me their true feelings.
49	___	I participate in group activities.
50	___	People often cause me to change my mind.
51	___	I have close relationships with a small number of people.
52	___	People invite me to do things with them.
53	___	I see to it that people do things the way I want them done.
54	___	My friends tell me about their private lives.

ELEMENT B: Scoring

I *compare* my two responses to each item of Element B to the "Scored Responses" printed beside the number.

If my response is the *same as* any one of the Scored Responses, I place a check mark (✔) on the line under IS or WANT or both.

I *add* the checks in each column and record the total (0 to 9) in the box at the bottom of the column.

I *transfer* scores to pages 42 and 43.

Item	Scored Responses	Column IS	WANT
1	4,5,6		
7	3,4,5,6		
13	3,4,5,6		
19	4,5,6		
25	5,6		
31	5,6		
37	5,6		
43	6		
49	6		

I include people. ☐ 11

I want to include people. ☐ 12

Item	Scored Responses	Column IS	WANT
4	5,6		
10	5,6		
16	5,6		
22	5,6		
28	5,6		
34	6		
40	5,6		
46	5,6		
52	4,5,6		

People include me. ☐ 13

I want people to include me. ☐ 14

Item	Scored Responses	Column IS	WANT
5	4,5,6		
11	5,6		
17	5,6		
23	4,5,6		
29	5,6		
35	4,5,6		
41	4,5,6		
47	5,6		
53	4,5,6		

I control people. ☐ 21

I want to control people. ☐ 22

Item	Scored Responses	Column IS	WANT
2	3,4,5,6		
8	3,4,5,6		
14	3,4,5,6		
20	4,5,6		
26	2,3,4,5,6		
32	4,5,6		
38	4,5,6		
44	3,4,5,6		
50	3,4,5,6		

People control me. ☐ 23

I want people to control me. ☐ 24

Item	Scored Responses	Column IS	WANT
3	5,6		
9	6		
15	1,2,3		
21	1,2,3		
27	1,2,3,4		
33	1,2,3,4		
39	6		
45	1,2,3,4		
51	6		

I am open with people. ☐ 31

I want to be open with people. ☐ 32

Item	Scored Responses	Column IS	WANT
6	5,6		
12	5,6		
18	1,2		
24	6		
30	1,2,3		
36	5,6		
42	1		
48	5,6		
54	4,5,6		

People are open with me. ☐ 33

I want people to be open with me. ☐ 34

ELEMENT B: Interpretation

I transfer scores from page 41 to appropriate boxes below (using identification codes).

I include people ☐ ○
                  11 P11

High Score
I usually invite people to parties, I start conversations, and I am outgoing.

Low Score
I do not include people. I tend to stay alone or to wait to be invited by others.

I want to include people ☐ ○
                  12 P12

High Score
I want to invite people to parties and to start conversations with people.

Low Score
I do not want to include people. I want to make no overtures toward other people.

Difference (11 minus 12) ☐
                                  ▲11

Positive Score
I include people more than I want to.

Negative Score
I want to include people more than I do.

I control people ☐ ○
                  21 P21

High Score
I tend to take charge, provide direction, give orders, and make decisions.

Low Score
I do not control people. I am not a leader and do not tell people what to do.

I want to control people ☐ ○
                  22 P22

High Score
I want to take charge of people, to give them orders and directions, and to make decisions.

Low Score
I do not want to control people. I do not want to make decisions or to be influential.

Difference (21 minus 22) ☐
                                  ▲21

Positive Score
I control people more than I want to.

Negative Score
I want to control people more than I do.

I am open with people ☐ ○
                  31 P31

High Score
I am open with people. I express my feelings; I confide in and am honest with my friends.

Low Score
I am closed. I keep secrets. I do not express everything I feel. I do not tell my friends private things about myself.

I want to be open with people ☐ ○
                  32 P32

High Score
I want to be open with people. I would like to be honest and to tell them my feelings.

Low Score
I do not want to be open. I want to keep secrets and to keep my personal life private.

Difference (31 minus 32) ☐
                                  ▲31

Positive Score
I am open with people more than I want to be.

Negative Score
I want to be open with people more than I am.

Scores range from 0 to 9. Zero (lowest score) means that I strongly disagree with the statement; nine (highest score) means that I strongly agree with the statement.

For each pair of scales I enter the Difference score.

People include me □ ○
13   P13

High Score
People invite me into their activities. They include me in their lives.

Low Score
I am not invited by people to their affairs. I am frequently ignored socially.

I want people to include me □ ○
14   P14

High Score
I want people to include me in their activities. I want them to invite me to join them.

Low Score
I do not want to be invited. I want people to leave me alone.

Difference (13 minus 14) □
Δ13

Positive Score
People include me more than I want them to.

Negative Score
I want people to include me more than they do.

People control me □ ○
23   P23

High Score
People tell me what to do. They influence my actions. I am easily led.

Low Score
Nobody tells me what to do. People do not influence me.

I want people to control me □ ○
24   P24

High Score
I want people to tell me what to do. I want them to make decisions for me.

Low Score
I do not want anyone to tell me what to do. I want no one to make my decisionsfor me.

Difference (23 minus 24) □
Δ23

Positive Score
People control me more than I want them to.

Negative Score
I want people to control me more than they do.

People are open with me □ ○
33   P33

High Score
People confide in me their personal thoughts. They are open and do not hesitate to tell me their true feelings.

Low Score
People do not tell me how they feel. They are not open with me.

I want people to be open with me □ ○
34   P34

High Score
I want people to tell me how they really feel. I want to hear the things they keep secret.

Low Score
I do not want to hear people's private affairs. They should keep them to themselves.

Difference (33 minus 34) □
Δ33

Positive Score
People are open with me more than I want them to be.

Negative Score
I want people to be open with me more than they are.

ACTIVITY 5. Behavior Measures

PART A

1. Compare your scores with your predictions. For those that are less accurate, how would you explain the difference?

2. Among the explanations you give yourself, include this possibility: "There is a part of me that I am not entirely aware of. That is the part that filled out Element B." See if you can find any truth in this possibility.

3. Do your Difference (Δ) scores fit with how well you see yourself? Do the differences indicate (a) that you are dissatisfied with yourself, or (b) simply that you recognize the difference but are not dissatisfied?

4. Do your scores help you to understand anything about yourself or your relationships?

Here's another way to learn about your behavior.

PART B

1. Look at the figure below. In each box, which circle would you be? Place an "X" in one circle in each box. (It works best if you do it without thinking too much; just feel the circle that is you.)

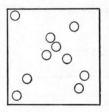 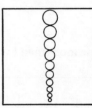 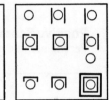

2. Refer to the diagrams below. Place the number of the circle you chose in the box above each diagram.

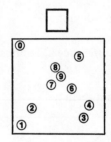 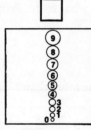 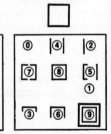

3. How are your three scores—I, C, O—related to your Element B scores on inclusion, control, and openness?

4. How are they both related to your imagery in Activity 3 (page 32)?

SELF-UNDERSTANDING

Now that I have seen how I respond to three different situations related to behavior, I can understand myself better. Element B allowed me to state how I believe I am and how I would like to be. Since I am assuming the choice principle—in particular, that I choose my *behavior*—the instrument tells me how I think I have chosen to be right now.

This does not mean that I cannot change. Indeed, if I have made myself that way, obviously I can learn to change myself if I choose to.

I now have a new interpretation of Element B and of all psychological questionnaires. They measure traits that are permanent only if I choose them to be permanent. So Element B, for example, presents a still photograph of the way I have chosen to be right now.

The behavior imagery gives me another way to look at myself. If I am not totally aware of the way I am (perhaps because I do not like myself in some ways), then I hide those ways from myself; I may distort myself on Element B. I may, for example, give myself a low score on "I want to include people" when, in fact, I am afraid of people and would rather be alone. Since I may not want to admit my fear to myself, I write down a high score.

However, on the first imagery, I may see the people coming over the hill as threatening and see myself getting a gun and hiding behind a rock. I notice that the imagery often goes its own way no matter what I want. It is not in my conscious control.

When I place myself in the first diagram in Activity 5, by following how my body feels as I place my mark, I may find that I select the remote circle numbered "2".

These three sources of information—conscious, imaginative, and bodily—provide me with a richer picture of how I see myself. I may compare for consistency (1) the information provided by my unconscious via two techniques (imagery and picture) that elicit responses from my unconscious, with (2) my conscious view of myself (as elicited by Element B).

I must remind myself that nothing that I discover is inherently good or bad. My discovery is merely whether or not I am consistent or congruent. Whatever the outcome, now I am more aware of what I am like than before. I am discovering more truth, and I am beginning to see some of the implications of choice.

Once again, I shut my eyes, reflect on the issues of inclusion, control, and openness, my scores on Element B, the imagery, and the three diagrams. Then I write down my most significant reactions.

PERSONAL MEANING OF BEHAVIOR

SEGUE

I can understand human behavior with the aid of three dimensions: inclusion, control, and openness. I achieve a more precise understanding when I consider two aspects of these dimensions: (1) what I initiate toward others (Do) and what I receive from them (Get), and (2) what is actually happening now (Is) and what I want to have happen (Want). I may understand my behavior toward people by using: (1) imagery, to see what emerges when I do not consciously control my thoughts; (2) a questionnaire (Element B), where I describe how I think I am; and (3) a graphic expression. Comparing these sources of information provides me with a rounded impression of how I am on these dimensions.

If my conscious description of my behavior matches the results of these indirect measures, I feel that I am aware of myself in these areas. If it does not match, then I have an opportunity to look into some areas of myself that I am not aware of.

I am beginning to see that I need have little fear in knowing myself better, and that as I allow this self-knowledge I begin to understand my behavior better. I also am seeing how I choose to behave the way I do.

chapter three

Let's take a look
at the feelings underlying
behavior.

FEELINGS:
Significance, Competence, Likeability

I know feelings affect my personal and work effectiveness. Cultural stereotypes have led me to have several attitudes toward feelings. Sometimes I think of feelings as feminine: women are emotional, men are logical. Sometimes I look at feelings as a sign of weakness, as if crying, being upset, and feeling anything but cool and under control is soft or weak.

On the other hand, I recognize that feelings are one of the major differences between robots and human beings. Feelings of love and compassion, even of jealousy and anger, are the traits that have been developed more fully by human beings than by probably other animals.

Whether I see them as strong or weak, as human or inhuman, feelings play a very large part in human behavior. An understanding of feelings helps me to understand and to choose my own life, so that I live the way I want to and function more efficiently.

Here, as with behavior, I have no interest in evaluating feelings as good or as bad. I simply recognize that feelings *are,* and that being aware of them is better than being ignorant of them. When I am not aware of feelings, I let them run my life without knowing it.

These are the questions I want to answer in this chapter:

- How do feelings affect my personal life and my work efficiency?

- What effect does not expressing feelings have on productivity?

- How do feelings underlie problems of communication?

- How can my communication of feelings improve effectiveness?

- How can I know my feelings better and use them to be more cooperative, productive, and happy?

A group of army men was meeting to discuss their productivity. When they received orders that seemed poor, they said nothing, "out of respect" for their superiors. When subordinates did not do their jobs, the norm was not to criticize them publicly but rather to do it one-on-one (although in fact this one-on-one rarely was done). More typically, the subordinates were told off at the next performance appraisal or they were transferred. Negative feelings went unexpressed out of a feeling of "loyalty" to their coworkers and to the army. Another reason for their reticence was that many had only a year or two to go before retirement and did not want to risk a bad rating.

There was an uncomfortable feeling in the group, a feeling that the men experienced as tension. Their belief was that they were doing a good job, remaining task-oriented, and not letting feelings interfere with their work. As the group progressed, it became clear that there was an unspoken agreement that productivity would be allowed to fall as low as it could become while still remaining satisfactory. Everyone did exactly as much as he had to do, and no more. Each person made sure that he could not be blamed; so if he received an order he would carry it out no matter how counterproductive he knew it to be, since he was "only following orders." He felt that if he raised questions he would have to share responsibility for the outcome, and he certainly did not want that.

Creativity in the group was virtually nonexistent. One of the chief symptoms of the men's unwillingness to be truthful was that they had put themselves on a work schedule that was destructive to family life, and which 80 percent of them despised. Yet because they were reluctant to express their feelings, no one had been able to change this schedule, even though the men all agreed on what would be a better one.

As discussion progressed, it became clear that contrary to what they originally had assumed, the failure to express their feelings had resulted in very low productivity.

THE BASIC FEELINGS

There are three basic feelings: *significance, competence,* and *likeability*. They parallel, respectively, *inclusion, control,* and *openness* that I explored on pages 28 and 29).

With respect to significance, competence, and likeability, this chapter examines:

● How I feel about you (people in general).

● How I *want* to feel about you.

● How I think you feel about me.

● How I *want* you to feel about me.

Significance

I feel that you are significant when you exist for me, mean something to me, are important to me; when I pay attention to you, notice your absence, and take account of you.

When I was a young child, being paid attention to and being touched communicated to me that my parents felt I was important. As a person and as a worker, I may feel significant when you consider me, talk to me, recognize me, and acknowledge and act toward me as if I make a difference.

Being significant does not mean necessarily being competent or being likeable. For example, there is such a thing as an unpleasant, ineffective executive.

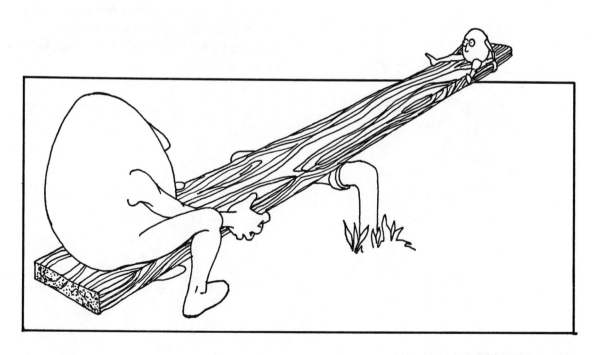

Competence

To me, you are competent if I feel that you have the capacity to cope with the world, to use your abilities to satisfy your wants, to avoid tragedy, and to be able to handle problems that arise in the course of living. "Competence" refers to the capacity to hold a job, to be self-sufficient, and to achieve something substantial in the way of material goods. Competence typically has to do with the ability to make decisions and to solve problems.

As a child, I usually felt competent when I was given responsibility and was allowed to undertake difficult tasks on my own. When I was severely restricted and had everything done for me, I received the message that my parents felt I was not able to make my own decisions.

Being competent does not necessarily mean being significant or likeable. There are, for example, obnoxious but efficient clerks.

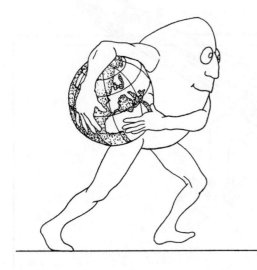

Likeability

Your likeability is based on your ability to create an atmosphere within which I like myself. I find you likeable if I like how I behave and feel in your presence. Paradoxically, my liking of you has very little to do with you. It depends on how I perceive you. I like you if I like myself when I am with you.[17]

When my parents reject me, I get the message that they do not find me likeable. They convey this feeling by not being happy when they are with me. I often get the feeling, "There must be something wrong with me."

Being significant and competent does not necessarily mean being likeable. For example, there are a successful criminals.

Likeability is sometimes called "loveability," but that term often is given several meanings that are not meant here.

QUESTIONS. Feelings

The following questions will help me to check my understanding of the ideas just presented. I place the letter of my answer (S, C, or L) on the line at the left. The letters mean:

(S) Significance
(C) Competence
(L) Likeability

___ 1. Workers who are concerned that their jobs are beyond their abilities are bothered about ?

___ 2. People who are silent because they "do not want to take up the committee's time" are concerned about ?

___ 3. Which area is described by these words: worthy of attention, forgettable, unimportant, ignorable, worthy of knowing?

___ 4. If I feel comfortable having people know all about my private life and feelings, I am showing confidence in my ?

___ 5. People who always brag about their achievements are probably concerned about their ?

___ 6. Which area is described by these terms: capable, phony, stupid, accomplished, weak, potent?

___ 7. When a friend forgets your name, it could give you concern about your ?

___ 8. Which area do these words describe: evil, nasty, caring, good person, warm, obnoxious?

___ 9. Bosses who keep their door shut and who do not want anyone to know them well may be concerned about their ?

Answers: CSS LCC SLL

ACTIVITY 6. Feelings Imagery

Get comfortable and let your imagination go wherever it wants to go.

PART A

Significance

1. Find a comfortable place to lie or sit. Shut your eyes. Imagine yourself the center of attention of a large group of people. They regard you as significant and important. They do not necessarily feel that you are competent or like you, but they feel that you are someone they should take notice of. They pay attention to you and are aware of your presence. Watch what happens.

2. (Pause 60 seconds.) How does it feel to be in this position? Do you see yourself enjoying this, or feeling uncomfortable and leaving the situation? Do you believe their sincerity? Do you regard *them* as significant and important? How does your body feel?

3. (Pause 60 seconds.) Open your eyes. Reflect on what you saw and how you feel about what you experienced. Pay special attention to your body: changes in breathing, feelings of lightness or heaviness, tensions in jaw or face, stomach or neck, or other body parts.

Competence

4. Shut your eyes. Imagine yourself in a situation where everyone feels that you are extremely competent. They do not necessarily feel that you are significant or likeable. Watch what happens.

5. (Pause 60 seconds.) How do you feel in this position? Are you confident that you will satisfy their desires? Do you see yourself answering their questions, or do you see yourself removing yourself from the situation? Do you believe their sincerity? Do you regard *them* as competent? How does your body feel?

6. (Pause 60 seconds.) Open your eyes. Reflect on what you saw and how you feel about what you experienced. Pay special attention to your body: changes in breathing, feelings of lightness or heaviness, tensions in jaw or face, stomach or neck, or other body parts.

Likeability

7. Shut your eyes. Imagine yourself being liked by everyone. Everywhere you go people like you. They do not necessarily feel that you are significant or competent. Picture this situation and watch what happens.

8. (Pause 60 seconds.) How does it feel to be in this situation? Do you see yourself enjoying it, or does it make you uncomfortable? Do you believe their sincerity? Do you like *them*? How does your body feel?

9. (Pause 60 seconds.) Open your eyes. Reflect on what you saw and how you feel about what you experienced. Pay special attention to your body: changes in breathing, feelings of lightness or heaviness, tensions in jaw or face, stomach or neck, or other body parts.

10. Take a short break, then continue with Part B.

PART B

1. Using the descriptions on pages 51 to 53 and your imagery, define each of the three feelings: significance, competence, likeability. Are they clear?

2. Describe the difference between significance and competence. Give an example from your own experience.

3. Give an example of your own for the difference between significance and likeability; between competence and likeability.

4. How do your images help you understand significance, competence, and likeability?

RESPONSES: Activity 6. Feelings Imagery

ASPECTS OF FEELINGS

Just as with the behavioral dimensions, each of the feelings dimensions has two aspects: Do–Get and Is–Want. The aspects are summarized in Table 3 below. The statement in each cell becomes the name of a dimension measured by Element F (Feelings).

TABLE 3. Aspects of Feelings

		IS	WANT
	Significance	I feel that people are significant.	I want to feel that people are significant.
DO	*Competence*	I feel that people are competent.	I want to feel that people are competent.
	Likeability	I like people.	I want to like people.
	Significance	People feel that I am significant.	I want people to feel that I am significant.
GET	*Competence*	People feel that I am competent.	I want people to feel that I am competent.
	Likeability	People like me.	I want people to like me.

QUESTIONS. Aspects of Feelings

I place the letter of my answer on the line at the left. The letters represent these attitudes:

(a) I feel that people are significant.
(b) I feel that people are competent.
(c) I like people.
(d) People feel that I am significant.
(e) People feel that I am competent.
(f) People like me.
(g) I want to feel that people are significant.
(h) I want to feel that people are competent.
(i) I want to like people.
(j) I want people to feel that I am significant.
(k) I want people to feel that I am competent.
(l) I want people to like me.

_____ 1. Bosses who do not delegate because they do not feel that their subordinates can do the job adequately are low on ?

_____ 2. People who are offended when their names are forgotten, or when they are left out of a meeting, are probably high on ?

_____ 3. Bosses who include all employees in weekly meetings are probably high on ?

_____ 4. A person who knows he will lose no friends when he acts obnoxious is confident that ?

_____ 5. People who frequently tell hero stories — that is, stories in which they turn out to be right — are high on ?

_____ 6. Bosses who walk directly through an office filled with employees, looking at no one unless they have business with them, are probably low on ?

_____ 7. Someone who enjoys giving compliments, giving presents, and doing things for people regardless of their response is probably high on ?

_____ 8. A person who would like to turn over the authority for an important function to a group of employees is high on ?

_____ 9. A person who donates time to charitable causes such as visiting sick children, and who does it in such a way that no one knows about it, is low on ?

_____ 10. People who assume that people care about what they say are high on ?

Answers: bja fka chl d

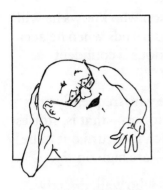

Just to make sure you are clear . . .

ACTIVITY 7. Aspects of Feelings

1. Define each of the twelve aspects listed on page 58. Are they clear? Give examples from your work situation and from your personal life.

2. Read each question on page 59. Reread any question where you do not agree with the answer given, until you are sure you understand.

RESPONSES: Activity 7. Aspects of Feelings

Measurement

Element F measures my preferences on all the aspects of significance, competence, and likeability listed in Table 3 on page 58.

Prediction

Before I fill out Element F, I will record how I perceive myself. Turning to pages 64 and 65, in the twelve circles marked "P", I will put a score from 0 to 9, indicating how much I agree with each of the twelve statements. Nine means "most agreement"; zero means "least agreement."

Disagree 0 1 2 3 4 5 6 7 8 9 **Agree**

After the predictions are recorded, I fill out and score Element F.

ELEMENT F

There are no "right" answers. The more honest I am, the more accurate will be the information I receive from Element F.

First, I complete the column "The way it IS" for all items.

For each statement, I place a number from 1 to 6 on the line to the left of the item, in the appropriate column. The numbers indicate how much I agree with the statement.

Disagree 1 2 3 4 5 6 **Agree**

When I have finished, I return to the top of the column and respond to the same items for "The way I WANT it to be."

The Way It IS	The Way I WANT It to Be	
1	____	I feel that each person is important.
2	____	I feel that people have confidence in my abilities.
3	____	I feel warm toward people.
4	____	I feel that people take an interest in me.
5	____	I can rely on people's judgment.
6	____	I feel that people feel affectionate toward me.
7	____	I feel that each person is a significant individual.
8	____	I feel that people feel that they can rely on my judgment.
9	____	I feel affectionate toward people.
10	____	I feel that people feel that I am an important person.
11	____	I am skeptical of people's abilities.
12	____	I feel that people feel personally close to me.
13	____	People do not mean anything to me.
14	____	I feel that people have doubts about my abilities.
15	____	I feel personally close to people.
16	____	I feel that people feel that I am of no importance.
17	____	I admire people's competence.
18	____	I feel that people are warm toward me.
19	____	I feel neutral toward people.
20	____	I feel that people are skeptical of my abilities.
21	____	I feel personally distant from people.
22	____	I feel that people feel concern for me.
23	____	I admire people's abilities.
24	____	I feel that people feel friendly toward me.
25	____	I am unconcerned about people.
26	____	I feel that people have reservations about my competence.
27	____	I feel bitter toward people.
28	____	I feel that people are interested in me.
29	____	I trust in people's abilities.
30	____	I feel that people like me.
31	____	I feel indifferent toward people.
32	____	I feel that people respect my competence.
33	____	I feel cordial toward people.
34	____	I feel that people feel neutral toward me.
35	____	I am suspicious of people's competence.
36	____	I feel that people do not like me.
37	____	I am interested in people.
38	____	I feel that people do not trust my abilities.
39	____	I feel friendly toward people.
40	____	I feel that people feel that I am significant.
41	____	I trust people's competence.
42	____	I feel people dislike me.
43	____	I am fascinated by people.
44	____	I feel that people do not have confidence in my abilities.
45	____	I feel cool toward people.
46	____	I feel that people feel indifferent toward me.
47	____	I have confidence in people's abilities.
48	____	I feel that people feel hostile toward me.
49	____	I am stimulated by people.
50	____	I feel that people feel they can depend on my abilities.
51	____	I hate people.
52	____	I feel that people feel that I am a significant person.
53	____	I feel that I can depend on people's judgment.
54	____	I feel that people are attracted to me.

ELEMENT F: Scoring

I *compare* my two responses (IS and WANT) to each item of Element F to the Scored Responses printed beside the item number.

If my response is the *same as* any one of the Scored Responses, I place a check mark (✔) on the line under IS or WANT or both.

I *add* the checks in each column and record the total (0 to 9) in the box at the bottom of the column.

I *transfer* scores to pages 64 and 65.

Item	Scored Responses	Column IS	WANT
1	6		
7	6		
13	1		
19	1,2,3		
25	1		
31	1,2,3		
37	5,6		
43	5,6		
49	6		

I feel that people are significant. ☐ 15

I want to feel that people are significant. ☐ 16

Item	Scored Responses	Column IS	WANT
4	6		
10	5,6		
16	1,2		
22	5,6		
28	5,6		
34	1,2		
40	4,5,6		
46	1,2		
52	4,5,6		

People feel that I am significant. ☐ 17

I want people to feel that I am significant. ☐ 18

Item	Scored Responses	Column IS	WANT
5	5,6		
11	1,2		
17	5,6		
23	6		
29	5,6		
35	1,2		
41	5,6		
47	5,6		
53	5,6		

I feel that people are competent. ☐ 25

I want to feel that people are competent. ☐ 26

Item	Scored Responses	Column IS	WANT
2	5,6		
8	6		
14	1,2		
20	1,2		
26	1,2		
32	6		
38	1,2		
44	1,2		
50	6		

People feel that I am competent. ☐ 27

I want people to feel that I am competent. ☐ 28

Item	Scored Responses	Column IS	WANT
3	5,6		
9	5,6		
15	5,6		
21	1		
27	1,2		
33	5,6		
39	5,6		
45	1		
51	1		

I like people. ☐ 35

I want to like people. ☐ 36

Item	Scored Responses	Column IS	WANT
6	4,5,6		
12	5,6		
18	5,6		
24	5,6		
30	5,6		
36	1,2		
42	1,2		
48	1,2		
54	5,6		

People like me. ☐ 37

I want people to like me. ☐ 38

ELEMENT F: Interpretation

I transfer scores from page 63 to appropriate boxes below.

For each pair of scales I enter the Difference score.

I feel that people are significant ☐ ◯
15   P15

High Score
I take care to notice each person. I may or may not like them, but I believe that they are significant and worthy of attention.

Low Score
I am not so concerned about each individual. I feel no obligation to have contact with everyone.

I want to feel that people are significant ☐ ◯
16   P16

High Score
I want to feel that each person is significant and important, and that each individual is a human being who is worth my attention.

Low Score
It is not important that I feel that everyone is important. I do not care whether I feel that way or not.

Difference (15 minus 16) ☐
Δ15

Positive Score
I feel that people are more significant than I want to feel.

Negative Score
I want to feel that people are more significant than I do feel.

I feel that people are competent ☐ ◯
25   P25

High Score
I feel that people are capable of dealing effectively with the world without my help. I have no trouble delegating because I assume it will be done well.

Low Score
Delegation is something that I rarely do. My tendency is to do things myself if I want them done right.

I want to feel that people are competent ☐ ◯
26   P26

High Score
I want to feel that people are competent, that I can rely on their ability to do a competent job, and that I can count on them.

Low Score
I do not want to feel that people are competent. It is not important for me to feel that I can count on other people.

Difference (25 minus 26) ☐
Δ25

Positive Score
I feel that people are more competent than I want to feel.

Negative Score
I want to feel that people are more competent than I do feel.

I like people ☐ ◯
35   P35

High Score
I assume that people mean well, want to do good, and are not out to get me. I can trust them in any business dealings.

Low Score
I feel that people will take advantage of me if given a chance. People are often not trustworthy.

I want to like people ☐ ◯
36   P36

High Score
I want to like people. I want to feel that they are basically good and that I have a warm feeling for people.

Low Score
I have no desire to like people. It does not matter to me whether I like people or not.

Difference (35 minus 36) ☐
Δ35

Positive Score
I like people more than I want to like them.

Negative Score
I want to like people more than I do.

I transfer the eighteen scores on these pages to Scoring Summary (using scale code numbers).

People feel that I am significant □ ○
17   P17

High Score
In my opinion, people feel that I am a significant, important person, worthy of attention, concern, and interest, and of equal importance to anyone else.

Low Score
In my opinion, people do not see me as a significant person.

I want people to feel that I am significant □ ○
18   P18

High Score
I want people to feel that I am a significant, important person, worthy of attention, concern and interest, and of equal importance to anyone else.

Low Score
I do not care whether people see me as significant or not.

Difference (17 minus 18) □
△18

Positive Score
People feel that I am more significant than I want them to.

Negative Score
I want people to feel that I am more significant than they do.

People feel that I am competent □ ○
27   P27

High Score
In my opinion, people feel that I am a competent, capable person who is able to cope with life and who is intelligent, strong, and attractive.

Low Score
In my opinion, people do not find me competent.

I want people to feel that I am competent □ ○
28   P28

High Score
I want people to feel that I am a competent, capable person who is able to cope with life and who is intelligent, strong, and attractive.

Low Score
I do not care whether people find me competent.

Difference (27 minus 28) □
△27

Positive Score
People feel that I am more competent than I want them to.

Negative Score
I want people to feel that I am more competent than they do.

People like me □ ○
37   P37

High Score
In my opinion, people feel that I am a likeable person who is decent, kind, considerate, and capable of loving.

Low Score
In my opinion, people do not find me likeable.

I want people to like me □ ○
38   P38

High Score
I want people to feel that I am a likeable person who is decent, kind, considerate, and capable of loving.

Low Score
I do not care whether people like me or not.

Difference (37 minus 38) □
△37

Positive Score
People like me more than I want them to.

Negative Score
I want people to like me more than they do.

ACTIVITY 8. Feelings Measures

PART A

1. Compare your scores with your predictions. For those that are less accurate, how would you explain the difference?

2. Among the explanations you give yourself, include this possibility: "There is a part of me that I am not entirely aware of. That is the part that filled out Element F." See if you can find any truth in that possibility.

3. Do your Difference (△) scores fit with you you see yourself? Do the differences indicate (a) that you are dissatisfied with yourself, or (b) simply that you recognize the difference but are not dissatisfied?

4. Do your scores help you to understand anything about yourself or your relationships?

PART B

1. Compare each of your scores with the corresponding imagery on pages 55 and 56.

2. Keeping in mind the comments on self-understanding (page 46), do you have a deeper sense of your feelings about significance, competence, and likeability?

3. Shut your eyes and reflect on the concepts of significance, competence, and likeability, your Element F scores, and the imagery. Write down your most significant reactions.

#3 is especially important.

PERSONAL MEANINGS OF FEELINGS

SEGUE

The feelings of significance, competence, and likeability underlie the behaviors of inclusion, control, and openness. I can measure how I feel toward others (Do) and how they feel toward me (Get). I also can compare how things are (Is) with how I want them to be (Want), and thereby obtain a measure of how close I am to the way I want to be. Comparing my imagery about feelings with my responses to the questionnaire items (Element F) again gives me a fuller picture of myself and helps me to recognize that how I think I am is not always how I actually feel and behave.

Now that I have a better insight into my behavior and feelings toward and from other people, I am in a good position to understand a large aspect of my life: work. I can explore how I fit into my present work situation and how I can better choose my career to fit the way I am.

Now that we know more about behavior and feelings, let's see what we can learn about job and career.

chapter four

JOB AND CAREER FIT:
True Livelihood

There is no reason for work not to be a source of great pleasure and satisfaction. The reasons I am not happier in my job may be summarized in one word — *Fit*. Understanding behavior and feelings allows me to understand better the factors that contribute to a good fit.[14]

Any worker may be effective when put in the right job with the right people and the right training. Trouble begins when I do not fit my job, or when we who work together do not fit each other.

Questions to be answered in this chapter are:

- How may I define jobs so that the human element is included?

- How satisfied am I with the job I have selected?

- How can I improve my job satisfaction?

- What is the best procedure for selecting the right job?

- How can I analyze my problems on the job more quickly and accurately?

- What is the best procedure for selecting a career?

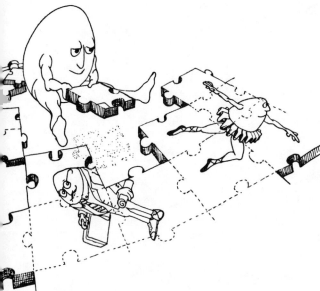

FIT

Here are some typical problems of Fit between me and jobs:

- Job requirements are not clear to me. I am never sure what I am expected to do.

- My original understanding of the job did not include many requirements that appeared only later.

- I thought I would have more autonomy than I do or I thought I would get more direction than I do, or I thought I would get more support or recognition than I do.

- My duties overlap with some other job, so it is not clear who is supposed to do what.

- I am not included in making decisions that affect my job.

- I would like to do more but I am not sure if it is allowed.

- I wonder if this is the best job for me. Perhaps I have more talent for something else.

- I am bored with work. It is no longer challenging.

When issues of fit are not resolved, I feel a loss of energy, a loss of desire to do the job. Coming to work is drudgery, and leaving work is a relief. What is lacking is a feeling of aliveness, of vitality, of excitement. Solving the problem of fit goes a long way toward arousing this alive, vital, excited feeling in me.

JOB DESCRIPTION

It is estimated that the personal and relational aspects of the job account for as much as 90 percent of firings and quittings on the job. Troubles that stem from actual lack of job competence are relatively small compared with troubles that stem from personal relationships. This fact suggests that job descriptions should include consideration of personal factors as well as of task factors.

Jobs typically describe how much accounting is required, how many people are to be supervised, what goals are to be achieved, and what budget may be used. Rarely do they say how important I, the job holder, am to the operations or whether my competence will be recognized, or how open the organization wants me to be. Yet these are just the areas that are crucial for job satisfaction, for turnover, and, ultimately, for efficiency.[18]

The Job Form (page 79) covers personal and interpersonal factors that are desirable for performing well on the job. This technique of job description is meant to supplement rather than replace the usual job descriptions, which cover such required work skills as accounting, engineering, and typing.

DIMENSIONS

To make the descriptions of jobs most usable, I shall define the terms of the interpersonal dimensions used to describe my own behavior and feelings: inclusion, control, and openness, and significance, competence, and likeability.

Behavior Dimensions

To succeed in some jobs it is desirable for me to include you in my activities. If I am a door-to-door sales representative and I do not enjoy initiating contact with people, I probably will not be successful. Similarly, if I am an army private and I am not willing to follow orders and to be controlled, I probably will not go very far. If I am a social worker and I do not enjoy being open with people, I probably will not succeed.

Below are the crucial questions to ask in order to define the *behavioral* elements of a job, along with some examples of occupations that illustrate the extremes of each.

- In the following descriptive method, a scale of 0 to 9 is used to describe how important these behaviors are on the job.

  Scores of 0 and 9 are end points of a continuum from "disagree" to "agree."

- Recall that in the statements below, "I" refers to the job holder.

TO DO THIS JOB BEST, IT IS DESIRABLE THAT I INCLUDE PEOPLE.

Disagree (0): Bridge-toll taker, bank teller
Agree (9): Traveling sales representative, fund raiser

TO DO THIS JOB BEST, IT IS DESIRABLE THAT I CONTROL PEOPLE.

Disagree (0): Laborer, waiter
Agree (9): Military officer, supervisor

TO DO THIS JOB BEST, IT IS DESIRABLE THAT I BE OPEN WITH PEOPLE.

Disagree (0): CIA Agent, diplomat
Agree (9): Nursery-school teacher, priest

TO DO THIS JOB BEST, IT IS DESIRABLE THAT PEOPLE INCLUDE ME.

Disagree (0): Lumber jack, farmer
Agree (9): Complaint-department employee, therapist

TO DO THIS JOB BEST, IT IS DESIRABLE THAT PEOPLE CONTROL ME.

Disagree (0): Artist, consultant
Agree (9): Secretary, army private

TO DO THIS JOB BEST, IT IS DESIRABLE THAT PEOPLE ARE OPEN WITH ME.

Disagree (0): Lie-detector operator, poker player
Agree (9): Mother, rabbi

QUESTIONS: Behavior

The following questions will help me to check my understanding of the behavioral job descriptions.

- On the line to the left of each of the following occupations, place the letter of the behavioral job description (A, B, C, D, E), given in the table below, which best describes that occupation. (Suggestion: Look down each column and get an overall impression for each job before examining each score.)

___ 1. Accountant

___ 2. Administrative Assistant

___ 3. Fund Raiser

___ 4. Highway Patrol Officer

___ 5. Military Officer

- The numbers mean:

  Disagree 0 1 2 3 4 5 6 7 8 9 **Agree**

	Job A	Job B	Job C	Job D	Job E
TO DO THIS JOB BEST, IT IS DESIRABLE THAT I . . .					
. . . *include people.*	2	0	6	4	9
. . . *control people.*	9	5	7	4	3
. . . *be open with people.*	1	0	1	3	8
TO DO THIS JOB BEST, IT IS DESIRABLE THAT PEOPLE . . .					
. . . *include me.*	2	1	2	5	8
. . . *control me.*	6	4	4	8	6
. . . *be open with me.*	1	0	1	2	7

Answers: bde   ca

Feelings Dimensions

In virtually any job, it is important for me to be aware of the feelings that I want expressed toward me and the feelings that others want me to express toward them. If I want people to like me, for example, then it is not wise for me to spend my work day handing people traffic tickets. If I desire fame, then being an unknown ghostwriter would leave me dissatisfied.

If the feelings that I enjoy expressing and receiving do not occur on my job, I will not be happy. People go where they are appreciated. I probably will seek gratification elsewhere — at home, at school, with friends — and merely tolerate my working hours.

As employees of a food company began to be open about their feelings, all the employees of one division agreed that they each felt satisfied with how their jobs fit them, except for one dimension: None of these employees felt *significant* in the eyes of their employers. They felt ignored, unimportant, unnecessary to the company, easily forgotten and seldom missed. This discovery was especially valuable since their supervisor was in the same workshop and had had no idea of the employees' feelings. He expressed surprise that they cared that much about how *he* felt. A discussion generated by this discovery cleared up a great deal of misunderstanding quite simply. The people just did not realize how important they were to each other.

Just as jobs can be defined in terms of behavior, so can they be described in terms of feelings. Here are statements, with examples, for describing the feelings aspects of a job.

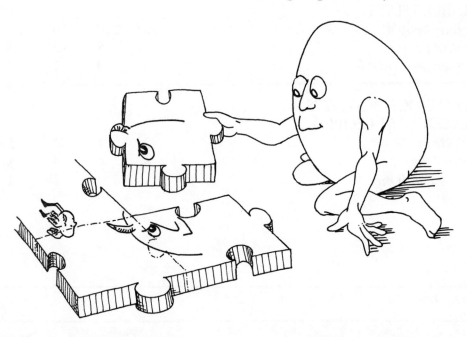

- In the following descriptive method, a scale of 0 to 9 is used to describe how important these feelings are on the job. Scores of 0 and 9 are end points of a continuum from "disagree" to "agree."

- Recall that in the statements below, "I" refers to the job holder.

TO DO MY JOB BEST, IT IS DESIRABLE THAT I FEEL THAT PEOPLE ARE SIGNIFICANT.

Disagree (0): Bank examiner, efficiency expert
Agree   (9): Nurse, judge

TO DO MY JOB BEST, IT IS DESIRABLE THAT I FEEL THAT PEOPLE ARE COMPETENT.

Disagree (0): Job inspector, driver-test examiner
Agree   (9): Parachute jumper, flight attendant

TO DO MY JOB BEST, IT IS DESIRABLE THAT I LIKE PEOPLE.

Disagree (0): Customs inspector, loan officer
Agree   (9): Poverty worker, teacher of retarded

TO DO MY JOB BEST, IT IS DESIRABLE THAT PEOPLE FEEL THAT I AM SIGNIFICANT.

Disagree (0): Custodian, assembly-line worker
Agree   (9): Building inspector, governor

TO DO MY JOB BEST, IT IS DESIRABLE THAT PEOPLE FEEL THAT I AM COMPETENT.

Disagree (0): Messenger, unskilled laborer
Agree   (9): Computer programmer, mechanic

TO DO MY JOB BEST, IT IS DESIRABLE THAT PEOPLE LIKE ME.

Disagree (0): Bill collector, bouncer
Agree   (9): Fund raiser, minister

QUESTIONS: Feelings

The following questions will help me to check my understanding of the feelings job description.

- On the line to the left of each of the following occupations, place the letter of the feelings job description (A, B, C, D, E), given in the table below, which best describes that occupation. (Suggestion: Look down each column and get an overall impression for each job before examining each score.)

____ 1. Financial Officer

____ 2. Grocery Clerk

____ 3. Corporation President

____ 4. Garbage Collector

____ 5. Movie Star

- The numbers mean:

Disagree 0 1 2 3 4 5 6 7 8 9 **Agree**

	Job A	Job B	Job C	Job D	Job E
TO DO THIS JOB BEST, IT IS DESIRABLE THAT I ...					
... feel that people are significant.	5	4	6	3	5
... feel that people are competent.	3	5	3	2	4
...like people.	4	3	6	1	4
TO DO THIS JOB BEST, IT IS DESIRABLE THAT PEOPLE ...					
... feel that I am significant.	9	9	2	7	1
... feel that I am competent.	4	9	2	8	2
... like me.	6	3	5	1	5

Answers: dcb ea

ACTIVITY 9. Job Examples

1. Do you agree with the answers to the questions on pages 73 and 76?
2. In what sense are you responsible for how people behave toward you and feel about you? Discuss with relation to the concept of choice.

RESPONSES: Activity 9. Job Examples

JOB FORM: Procedure

On page 79 is a Job Form, on which I may describe my present job in terms of behavior and feelings. This form provides data for me to explore how well I fit my present job, how satisfied I am with my work, and what to look for in planning my career. Here is the procedure for completing this form:

1. *Job definers.* For this exercise, *I* shall determine what traits are most desirable for success on my job. (I may want to check this with my boss or with someone else who has the position of describing jobs in my organization.)

2. *Interactors.* The Job Form asks me to describe the desirable traits for my relations with four groups of people. These groups are defined as follows:

    a. *Supervisor* — the person I report to. The supervisor typically (but not always) makes more money than I do; has the power to fire or strongly influence my firing; writes my performance appraisal; and has the job I would be promoted to.

    b. *Peers* — The people I work with who are at the same level in the organization as I am. Typically (but not always) they make about the same salary as I do, and we cannot fire each other. We may be doing the same or similar work if we are in the same unit; or, if we are in different units, we may work together doing different jobs and be on the same organizatioal level.

    c. *Subordinates* — Those who report to me. These people typically (but not always) make less money than I; may be fired by me, or their firing may be strongly influenced by me; have their performance appraisal filled out by me; and will have my job when they are promoted.

    d. *Clients, or end users* — The people who buy and/or use my product or services. They may be within the organization or outside it. For some jobs there are no clients.

3. *Dimensions.* The key words — inclusion, control, and openness, and significance, competence, and likeability, are those I have used earlier. They are used as defined on pages 28 and 29 and 51 to 53.

4. *Completion.* I shall now complete the Job Form on page 79 for my current job. I shall fill it out from the standpoint of a representative of the organization who is describing the characteristics of the kind of person who would perform best on my present job.

JOB FORM

JOB TITLE _____ DATE _____

- "I" on the form means the ideal job holder.

- Complete the form by placing a number from 0 to 9 in each box on the form.

- The numbers refer to your degree of agreement with the statement on the form. "In order to perform best on the job, it is desirable that I [the ideal job holder]. . . ."

- Blanks (_____) refer to each interactor listed on top.

Disagree 0 1 2 3 4 5 6 7 8 9 **Agree**

IN ORDER TO PERFORM BEST ON THE JOB, IT IS DESIRABLE THAT...	MY SUPERVISORS	MY PEERS	MY SUBORDINATES	MY CLIENTS
... I include ...	NB	NP	ND	NT
... I control ...	CB	CP	CD	CT
... I am open with ...	OB	OP	OD	OT
... I feel that ____ are significant.	SB	SP	SD	ST
... I feel that ____ are competent.	MB	MP	MD	MT
... I like ____ .	LB	LP	LD	LT
IN ORDER TO PERFORM BEST IT IS DESIRABLE THAT ____ ...				
... include me.	BN	PN	DN	TN
... control me.	BC	PC	DC	TC
... are open with me.	BO	PO	DO	TO
... feel that I am significant.	BS	PS	DS	TS
... feel that I am competent.	BC	PC	DC	TC
... like me.	BL	PL	DL	TL

ACTIVITY 10. Job Form

Shut your eyes for a minute or two.
Did anything surprise you in filling out
the Job Form? Did you clarify
something about your job that you
were not so clear about before?

RESPONSES: Activity 10. Job Form

JOB FIT

Now that I know the profile desired for successful performance on my job, I am in a position to find out whether I fit.[19] To simplify this process I may use the Job Fit Form (pages 82 to 85.)

I use this form to determine the fit between me and a job. Before I fill it out, I first complete Element B, Element F, and the Job Form for the job.

By transferring the score form these three instruments onto the Job Fit Form, I may discover how well I fit my job.

This fit is not a permanent condition. I am quite capable of changing the way I am, and job requirements are also changeable. The result shown on this form indicates how things are *at this time*.[20]

JOB-FIT FORM

Procedure

1. I enter my Element B and Element F scores in the left-hand column four times on pages 82, 83, 84, and 85, following the scale code numbers.

2. I enter my Job Form scores on the right-hand column on pages 82, 83, 84, and 85 under the letter J, following the scale code numbers.

3. I make subtractions as indicated for every pair of scores — (B–J) or (F–J)—and place the result in either the + box or the − box.

4. I add numbers for the first six subtractions, ingoring the sign, and place the result in the "Behavior Fit" box. I repeat this for the next six subtractions, and place the result in the "Feelings Fit" box. I repeat this procedure for all four coworkers.

5. I add the "Feelings Fit" and "Behavior Fit" boxes to obtain "Fit with. . . ."

6. I circle the largest scores, + or −, and corresponding descriptions in each column. These indicate points of least fit between me and my job. (Scores of zero indicate best fit.)

7. I make a written summary on page 86.

JOB FIT FORM

SUPERVISOR

ELEMENT

B	J	Δ	
		+	I will include the supervisor too much.
	− =	−	I will not include the supervisor enough.
11	NB		
		+	I will control the supervisor too much.
	− =	−	I will not control the supervisor enough.
21	CB		
		+	I will be too open with the supervisor.
	− =	−	I will not be open enough with the supervisor.
31	OB		
		+	The supervisor will include me too much.
	− =	−	The supervisor will not include me enough.
13	BN		
		+	The supervisor will control me too much.
	− =	−	The supervisor will not control me enough.
23	BC		
		+	The supervisor will be too open with me.
	− =	−	The supervisor will not be open enough with me.
33	BO		

TOTAL Δ = ☐ **Behavior Fit**

ELEMENT

F	J	Δ	
		+	I will feel that the supervisor is too significant.
	− =	−	I will feel that the supervisor is too insignificant.
15	SB		
		+	I will feel that the supervisor is too competent.
	− =	−	I will feel that the supervisor is too incompetent.
25	MB		
		+	I will like the supervisor too much.
	− =	−	I will not like the supervisor enough.
35	LB		
		+	The supervisor will feel that I am too significant.
	− =	−	The supervisor will feel that I am too insignificant.
17	BS		
		+	The supervisor will feel that I am too competent.
	− =	−	The supervisor will feel that I am too incompetent.
27	BM		
		+	The supervisor will like me too much.
	− =	−	The supervisor will not like me enough.
37	BL		

TOTAL Δ = ☐ **Feelings Fit**
(Ignore sign)

☐ **Fit with Supervisors**
(Behavior + Feelings)

JOB FIT FORM

PEERS

ELEMENT

B	J		Δ	
			+	I will include peers too much.
—	—	=	—	I will not include peers enough.
11	NP			
			+	I will control peers too much.
—	—	=	—	I will not control peers enough.
21	CP			
			+	I will be too open with peers.
—	—	=	—	I will not be open enough with peers.
31	OP			
			+	Peers will include me too much.
—	—	=	—	Peers will not include me enough.
13	PN			
			+	Peers will control me too much.
—	—	=	—	Peers will not control me enough.
23	PC			
			+	Peers will be too open with me.
—	—	=	—	Peers will not be open enough with me.
33	PO			

TOTAL Δ = [ ]   **Behavior Fit**

ELEMENT

F	J		Δ	
			+	I will feel that peers are too significant.
—	—	=	—	I will feel that peers are too insignificant.
15	SP			
			+	I will feel that peers are too competent.
—	—	=	—	I will feel that peers are too incompetent.
25	MP			
			+	I will like peers too much.
—	—	=	—	I will not like peers enough.
35	LP			
			+	Peers will feel that I am too significant.
—	—	=	—	Peers will feel that I am too insignificant.
17	PS			
			+	Peers will feel that I am too competent.
—	—	=	—	Peers will feel that I am too incompetent.
27	PM			
			+	Peers will like me too much.
—	—	=	—	Peers will not like me enough.
37	PL			

TOTAL Δ = [ ]   **Feelings Fit**
(Ignore sign)

[ ]   **Fit with Peers**
(Behavior + Feelings)

JOB AND CAREER FIT   83

JOB FIT FORM (Continued)   SUBORDINATES

ELEMENT

B	J		Δ	
			+	I will include subordinates too much.
— —	=		—	I will not include subordinates enough.
11	ND			
			+	I will control subordinates too much.
— —	=		—	I will not control subordinates enough.
21	CD			
			+	I will be too open with subordinates.
— —	=		—	I will not be open enough with subordinates.
31	OD			
			+	Subordinates will include me too much.
— —	=		—	Subordinates will not include me enough.
13	DN			
			+	Subordinates will control me too much.
— —	=		—	Subordinates will not control me enough.
23	DC			
			+	Subordinates will be too open with me.
— —	=		—	Subordinates will not be open enough with me.
33	DO			

TOTAL Δ = ☐   **Behavior Fit**

ELEMENT

F	J		Δ	
			+	I will feel that subordinates are too significant.
— —	=		—	I will feel that subordinates are too insignificant.
15	SD			
			+	I will feel that subordinates are too competent.
— —	=		—	I will feel that subordinates are too incompetent.
25	MD			
			+	I will like subordinates too much.
— —	=		—	I will not like subordinates enough.
35	LD			
			+	Subordinates will feel that I am too significant.
— —	=		—	Subordinates will feel that I am too insignificant.
17	DS			
			+	Subordinates will feel that I am too competent.
— —	=		—	Subordinates will feel that I am too incompetent.
27	DM			
			+	Subordinates will like me too much.
— —	=		—	Subordinates will not like me enough.
37	DL			

TOTAL Δ = ☐   **Feelings Fit**
(Ignore sign)

☐   **Fit with Subordinates**
(Behavior + Feelings)

84

JOB-FIT FORM (Continued) CLIENTS

ELEMENT

B	J		Δ	
			+	I will include clients too much.
—— 11	—— NT	=	−	I will not include clients enough.
			+	I will control clients too much.
—— 21	—— CT	=	−	I will not control clients enough.
			+	I will be too open with clients.
—— 31	—— OT	=	−	I will not be open enough with clients.
			+	Clients will include me too much.
—— 13	—— TN	=	−	Clients will not include me enough.
			+	Clients will control me too much.
—— 23	—— TC	=	−	Clients will not control me enough.
			+	Clients will be too open with me.
—— 33	—— TO	=	−	Clients will not be open enough with me.

TOTAL Δ = [   ] **Behavior Fit**

ELEMENT

F	J		Δ	
			+	I will feel that clients are too significant.
—— 15	—— ST	=	−	I will feel that clients are too insignificant.
			+	I will feel that clients are too competent.
—— 25	—— MT	=	−	I will feel that clients are too incompetent.
			+	I will like clients too much.
—— 35	—— LT	=	−	I will not like clients enough.
			+	Clients will feel that I am too significant.
—— 17	—— TS	=	−	Clients will feel that I am too insignificant.
			+	Clients will feel that I am too competent.
—— 27	—— TM	=	−	Clients will feel that I am too incompetent.
			+	Clients will like me too much.
—— 37	—— TL	=	−	Clients will not like me enough.

TOTAL Δ = [   ] **Feelings Fit**
(Ignore sign)

[   ] **Fit with Clients**
(Behavior + Feelings)

JOB TITLE _____   DATE _____

JOB-FIT SUMMARY

	Supervisors	Peers	Subordinates	Clients	TOTAL
Behavioral Fit					
Feelings Fit					
TOTAL FIT					

Areas of Largest Difference

Difference	Area

ACTIVITY 11. JOB FIT

1. Reflect on your differences and your reaction to the data. Do the data make sense? Are the areas where there are smallest discrepancies the areas of greatest job satisfaction? Are the areas of greatest discrepancy points of difficulty in your job?

2. Are these differences that occur because your general behavior and feelings, as reflected in Element B and Element F, are not the same as on the job? If so, think about it carefully. Is that really true?

3. What would you like to do about the discrepancies uncovered? Are there attitudes that would improve the situation? Are there environmental factors that could make a difference? Would a transfer to another job help?

4. Are these discrepancies the same as those that have occurred to you on other jobs?

JOB SATISFACTION

I have now discovered how I fit on my job — that is, how the way I relate to people in general matches the desired traits for a successful job-holder in my job. The job description form that I filled out describes what I thought the job required. This description does not necessarily describe what I want a job to be.

I will now describe:
- what I feel is actually happening on the job;
- what, ideally, I *want* from a job.

These descriptions, combined with the Job Form, allow me to measure three types of satisfaction:
- how satisfied I am with my present job (present job);
- how I feel my performance is evaluated on the job (job performance);
- how close my present job comes to my ideal job (career choice).

I then combine my scores on the Job Form with my feelings about (a) how I am now on my job and (b) how I want to be in my ideal job. I thus generate scores that will allow me to find out how satisfied I am with my work situation, and to become aware of the type of careers with which I would be most content. The Job Satisfaction Form provides the necessary data.

JOB SATISFACTION FORM

● I transfer my scores from the Job Form (page 100) to the third column (J) below, following the scale code numbers.

● I rate my Is and Want behavior and feelings on my present job from 0 to 9, and place them in the columns labeled Is (I) and Want (W). The numbers mean: **Disagree** 0 1 2 3 4 5 6 7 8 9 **Agree**

	I (IS) In my job . . .	W (WANT) In my ideal job . . .	J (JOB) In my present job THEY want me to . . .	SATISFACTION — Retain sign (+ or −) Present Job (I−W)	Job Performance (I−J)	Career Choice (W−J)
● SUPERVISOR						
. . . I include my supervisor.	71*	72*	NB	⅃71**	as**	os
. . . I control my supervisor.	81	82	CB	⅃81	bs	ps
. . . I am open with my supervisor.	91	92	OB	⅃91	cs	qs
. . . My supervisor includes me.	73	74	BN	⅃73	ds	rs
. . . My supervisor controls me.	83	84	BC	⅃83	es	ss
. . . My supervisor is open with me.	93	94	BO	⅃93	fs	ts
. . . I feel that my supervisor is significant.	75	76	SB	⅃75	gs	us
. . . I feel that my supervisor is competent.	85	86	MB	⅃85	hs	vs
. . . I like my supervisor.	95	96	LB	⅃95	is	ws
. . . My supervisor feels that I am significant.	77	78	BS	⅃77	js	xs
. . . My supervisor feels that I am competent.	87	88	BM	⅃87	ks	ys
. . . My supervisor likes me.	97	98	BL	⅃97	ls	zs
● PEERS						
. . . I include my peers.	71p	72p	NP	⅃71p**	ap**	op
. . . I control my peers.	81p	82p	CP	⅃81p	bp	pp
. . . I am open with my peers.	91p	92p	OP	⅃91p	cp	qp
. . . My peers include me.	73p	74p	PN	⅃73p	dp	rp
. . . My peers control me.	83p	84p	PC	⅃83p	ep	sp
. . . My peers are open with me.	93p	94p	PO	⅃93p	fp	tp
. . . I feel that my peers are significant.	75p	76p	SP	⅃75p	gp	up
. . . I feel that my peers are competent.	85p	86p	MP	⅃85p	hp	vp
. . . I like my peers.	95p	96p	LP	⅃95p	ip	wp
. . . My peers feel that I am significant.	77p	78p	PS	⅃77p	jp	xp
. . . My peers feel that I am competent.	87p	88p	PM	⅃87p	kp	yp
. . . My peers like me.	97p	98p	PL	⅃97p	lp	zp

	I (IS) In my job . . .	W (WANT) In my ideal job . . .	J (JOB) In my present job THEY want me to . . .	SATISFACTION Retain sign (+ or −) Present Job (I−W)	Job Performance (I−J)	Career Choice (W−J)
● SUBORDINATES						
. . . I include my subordinates.	71*d	72*d	ND	⅃71d⁻	ad#	od!
. . . I control my subordinates.	81d	82d	CD	⅃81d	bd	pd
. . . I am open with my subordinates.	91d	92d	OD	⅃91d	cd	qd
. . . My subordinates include me.	73d	74d	DN	⅃73d	dd	rd
. . . My subordinates control me.	83d	84d	DE	⅃83d	ed	sd
. . . My subordinates are open with me.	93d	94d	DO	⅃93d	fd	td
. . . I feel that my subordinates are significant.	75d	76d	SD	⅃75d	gd	ud
. . . I feel that my subordinates are competent.	85d	86d	MD	⅃85d	hd	vd
. . . I like my subordinates.	95d	96d	LD	⅃95d	id	wd
. . . My subordinates feel that I am significant.	77d	78d	DS	⅃77d	jd	xd
. . . My subordinates feel that I am competent.	87d	88d	DM	⅃87d	kd	yd
. . . My subordinates like me.	97d	98d	DL	⅃97d	ld	zd
● CLIENTS						
. . . I include my clients.	71*t	72*t	NT	⅃71t**	at**	ot**
. . . I control my clients.	81t	82t	CT	⅃81t	bt	pt
. . . I am open with my clients.	91t	92t	OT	⅃91t	ct	qt
. . . My clients include me.	73t	74t	TN	⅃73t	dt	rt
. . . My clients control me.	83t	84t	TC	⅃83t	et	st
. . . My clients are open with me.	93t	94t	TO	⅃93t	ft	tt
. . . I feel that my clients are significant.	75t	76t	ST	⅃75t	gt	ut
. . . I feel that my clients are competent.	85t	86t	MT	⅃85t	ht	vt
. . . I like my clients.	95t	96t	LT	⅃95t	it	wt
. . . My clients feel that I am significant.	77t	78t	TS	⅃77t	jt	xt
. . . My clients feel that I am competent.	87t	88t	TM	⅃87t	kt	yt
. . . My clients like me.	97t	98t	TL	⅃97t	lt	zt

+   Transfer these numbers to pages 112 and 113.

\#   Transfer these numbers to pages 116 and 117.

!   Transfer these numbers to pages 120 and 121.

*   Transfer these numbers to Scoring Summary in spaces marked "J."
        Scoring Summary.)

SATISFACTION: PRESENT JOB

- Insert scores from "Present Job" column, pages 90 and 91, in boxes below. Retain signs (+ or −).
- The Present Job score (1−W) is obtained by subtracting the behavior or feelings *I Want* in my ideal job, from the behavior and feelings that are true of my present job.
- Circle all statements of 2 or more.

SUPERVISOR

Negative Score		Positive Score
I want to include my supervisor more.	☐ 71*	I include my supervisor more than I want to.
I want to control my supervisor more.	☐ 81	I control my supervisor more than I want to.
I want to be more open with my supervisor.	☐ 91	I am more open with my supervisor than I want to be.
I want my supervisor to include me more.	☐ 73	My supervisor includes me more than I want him/her to.
I want my supervisor to control me more.	☐ 83	My supervisor controls me more than I want him/her to.
I want my supervisor to be more open with me.	☐ 93	My supervisor is more open with me than I want him/her to be.
I want to feel that my supervisor is more significant.	☐ 75	I feel that my supervisor is more significant than I want him/her to be.
I want to feel that my supervisor is more competent.	☐ 85	I feel that my supervisor is more competent than I want him/her to be.
I want to like my supervisor more.	☐ 95	I like my supervisor more than I want to.
I want my supervisor to feel that I am more significant.	☐ 77	My supervisor feels that I am more significant than I want him/her to.
I want my supervisor to feel that I am more competent.	☐ 87	My supervisor feels that I am more competent than I want him/her to.
I want my supervisor to like me more.	☐ 97	My supervisor likes me more than I want him/her to.

PEERS

Negative Score		Positive Score
I want to include my peers more.	☐ 71p	I include my peers more than I want to.
I want to control my peers more.	☐ 81p	I control my peers more than I want to.
I want to be more open with my peers.	☐ 91p	I am more open with my peers than I want to be.
I want my peers to include me more.	☐ 73p	My peers include me more than I want them to.

I want my peers to control me more.	□ 83p	My peers control me more than I want them to.
I want my peers to be more open with me.	□ 93p	My peers are more open with me than I want them to be.
I want to feel that my peers are more significant.	□ 75p	I feel that my peers are more significant than I want them to be.
I want to feel that my peers are more competent.	□ 85p	I feel that my peers are more competent than I want them to be.
I want to like my peers more.	□ 95p	I like my peers more than I want to.
I want my peers to feel that I am more significant.	□ 77p	My peers feel that I am more significant than I want them to.
I want my peers to feel that I am more competent.	□ 87p	My peers feel that I am more competent than I want them to.
I want my peers to like me more.	□ 97p	My peers like me more than I want them to.

SUBORDINATES

Negative Score		**Positive Score**
I want to include my subordinates more.	□ 71d°	I include my subordinates more than I want to.
I want to control my subordinates more.	□ 81d	I control my subordinates more than I want to.
I want to be more open with my subordinates.	□ 91d	I am more open with my subordinates than I want to be.
I want my subordinates to include me more.	□ 73d	My subordinates include me more than I want them to.
I want my subordinates to control me more.	□ 83d	My subordinates control me more than I want them to.
I want my subordinates to be more open with me.	□ 93d	My subordinates are more open with me than I want them to be.
I want to feel that my subordinates are more significant.	□ 75d	I feel that my subordinates are more significant than I want them to be.
I want to feel that my subordinates are more competent.	□ 85d	I feel that my subordinates are more competent than I want them to be.
I want to like my subordinates more.	□ 95d	I like my subordinates more than I want to.
I want my subordinates to feel that I am more significant.	□ 77d	My subordinates feel that I am more significant than I want them to.
I want my subordinates to feel that I am more competent.	□ 87d	My subordinates feel that I am more competent than I want them to.
I want my subordinates to like me more.	□ 97d	My subordinates like me more than I want them to.

SATISFACTION: PRESENT JOB, continued

CLIENTS

Negative Score		Positive Score
I want to include my clients more.	71t	I include my clients more than I want to.
I want to control my clients more.	81t	I control my clients more than I want to.
I want to be more open with my clients.	91t	I am more open with my clients than I want to be.
I want my clients to include me more.	73t	My clients include me more than I want them to.
I want my clients to control me more.	83t	My clients control me more than I want them to.
I want my clients to be more open with me.	93t	My clients are more open with me than I want them to be.
I want to feel that my clients are more significant.	75t	I feel that my clients are more significant than I want them to be.
I want to feel that my clients are more competent.	85t	I feel that my clients are more competent than I want them to be.
I want to like my clients more.	95t	I like my clients more than I want to.
I want my clients to feel that I am more significant.	77t	My clients feel that I am more significant than I want them to.
I want my clients to feel that I am more competent.	87t	My clients feel that I am more competent than I want them to.
I want my clients to like me more.	97t	My clients like me more than I want them to.

* The larger the score, that is, the difference, the more likely it is that I feel dissatisfied in my present job.

SATISFACTION:
Present Job

The difference between how I perform on my present job and how I would like to perform on my ideal job reveals areas that I can explore to discover how I am enjoying my present work.

ACTIVITY 12: Satisfaction: Present Job

1. Look over results for all four charts. Pay particular attention to those statements that are circled (score of 2 or more), especially those with high numbers. They represent the greatest difference between what you do on the job and what you want to be doing.

2. Does this information make sense to you? Is it consistent with your experience?

3. Does it fit your perception of your satisfaction with your supervisor? your peers? your subordinates? your clients?

4. Is there something you would like to change?

5. How would you change it?

6. Following the choice principle, how have you chosen to create the unsatisfactory parts of your job? (Remember, this is not blame: It is an attempt to understand.)

7. How do you collude with the others in your organization to create the situation?

8. How would you change the situation?

9. Did the answer to Question 8 differ from the answer to Question 5?

SATISFACTION: JOB PERFORMANCE

- Insert scores from the "Job Performance" column on pages 90 and 91 in box below. Retain signs (+ or −).
- The Job Performance score (I minus J) is obtained by subtracting how I think my organization (called *they*) *wants* me to behave and feel on the job, from how I act and feel on the job.
- Circle all statements of 2 or more.

SUPERVISOR

Negative Score		Positive Score
My supervisor wants me to include people more.	a*	I include people more than my supervisor wants me to.
My supervisor wants me to control people more.	b	I control people more than my supervisor wants me to.
My supervisor wants me to be more open with people.	c	I am more open with people than my supervisor wants me to be.
My supervisor wants people to include me more.	d	I want people to include me more than my supervisor wants them to.
My supervisor wants people to control me more.	e	I want people to control me more than my supervisor wants them to.
My supervisor wants people to be more open with me.	f	I want people to be more open with me than my supervisor wants them to be.
My supervisor wants me to feel that people are more significant.	g	I feel that people are more significant than my supervisor wants me to feel.
My supervisor wants me to feel that people are more competent.	h	I feel that people are more competent than my supervisor wants me to feel.
My supervisor wants me to like people more.	i	I like people more than my supervisor wants me to.
My supervisor wants people to feel that I am more significant.	j	People feel that I am more significant than my supervisor wants them to.
My supervisor wants people to feel that I am more competent.	k	People feel that I am more competent than my supervisor wants them to.
My supervisor wants people to like me more.	l	People like me more than my supervisor wants them to.

* The larger the score, that is, the difference, the more likely it is that I feel dissatisfied in my present job.

SATISFACTION: JOB PERFORMANCE, continued

PEERS

Negative Score		**Positive Score**
My peers want me to include people more.	ap	I include people more than my peers want me to.
My peers want me to control people more.	bp	I control people more than my peers want me to.
My peers want me to be more open with people.	cp	I am more open with people than my peers want me to be.
My peers want people to include me more.	dp	My peers want people to include me less.
My peers want people to control me more.	ep	My peers want people to control me less.
My peers want people to be more open with me.	fp	My peers want people to be less open with me.
My peers want me to feel that people are more significant.	gp	My peers want me to feel that people are less significant.
My peers want me to feel that people are more competent.	hp	My peers want me to feel that people are less competent.
My peers want me to like people more.	ip	I like people more than my peers want me to.
My peers want people to feel that I am more significant.	jp	People feel that I am more significant than my peers want them to.
My peers want people to feel that I am more competent.	kp	People feel that I am more competent than my peers want them to.
My peers want people to like me more.	lp	People like me more than my peers want them to.

SUBORDINATES

Negative Score		**Positive Score**
My subordinates want me to include people more.	ad*	I include people more than my subordinates want me to.
My subordinates want me to control people more.	bd	I control people more than my subordinates want me to.
My subordinates want me to be more open with people.	cd	I am more open with people than my subordinates want me to be.
My subordinates want people to include me more.	dd	My subordinates want people to include me less.
My subordinates want people to control me more.	ed	My subordinates want people to control me less.

My subordinates want people to be more open with me.	My subordinates want people to be less open with me.
My subordinates want me to feel that people are more significant.	My subordinates want me to feel that people are less significant.
My subordinates want me to feel that people are more competent.	My subordinates want me to feel that people are less competent.
My subordinates want me to like people more.	I like people more than my subordinates want me to.
My subordinates want people to feel that I am more significant.	People feel that I am more significant than my subordinates want them to.
My subordinates want people to feel that I am more competent.	People feel that I am more competent than my subordinates want them to.
My subordinates want people to like me more.	People like me more than my subordinates want them to.

Boxes labeled: fd, gd, hd, id, jd, kd, ld

CLIENTS

Negative Score / **Positive Score**

My clients want me to include people more.	I include people more than my clients want me to.
My clients want me to control people more.	I control people more than my clients want me to.
My clients want me to be more open with people.	I am more open with people than my clients want me to be.
My clients want people to include me more.	My clients want people to include me less.
My clients want people to control me more.	My clients want people to control me less
My clients want people to be more open with me.	My clients want people to be less open with me.
My clients want me to feel that people are more significant.	My clients want me to feel that people are less significant.
My clients want me to feel that people are more competent.	My clients want me to feel that people are less competent.
My clients want me to like people more.	I like people more than my clients want me to.
My clients want people to feel that I am more significant.	People feel that I am more significant than my clients want them to.
My clients want people to feel that I am more competent.	People feel that I am more competent than my clients want them to.
My clients want people to like me more.	People like me more than my clients want them to.

Boxes labeled: at, bt, ct, dt, et, ft, gt, ht, it, jt, kt, lt

* The larger the score, that is, the difference, the more likely it is that I feel dissatisfied in my present job.

SATISFACTION: Job Performance

By examining the difference between how I think *they* (the organization) want me to be and how I think I actually function on the job, I can obtain an estimate of how satisfactory I feel my work is. The largest differences point to the areas that are most unsatisfactory. This satisfaction may differ, depending on whether I am considering my supervisor, my peers, my subordinates, or my clients.

ACTIVITY 13. Satisfaction: Job Performance

1. Look over results for all four charts. Pay particular attention to those statements that are circled (score of 2 or more), especially those with high numbers. They represent the greatest difference between what you do on the job and what you think is wanted on this job.

2. Does this information make sense to you? Is it consistent with your experience?

3. Does it fit your perception of your satisfaction with your supervisor? your peers? your subordinates? your clients?

4. Is there something about your performance you would like to change?

5. How would you change it?

6. Following the choice principle, how have you chosen to perform well in some areas and not as well in others? (Remember: choice, not blame.)

7. How do you collude with others in your organization to create the situation?

8. How would you change the situation?

9. Did your answer to Question 8 differ from your answer to Question 5?

RESPONSES. Activity 13. Satisfaction: Job Performance

Hope you are writing
in each one of these.

SATISFACTION: CAREER CHOICE

- Insert scores from "Career Choice" column on pages 90 and 91 in boxes below.
- The score on Career Choice (W minus J) is obtained by subtracting how my organization wants me to be on my job, from how *I* want to be on my ideal job.
- Circle all statements of 2 or more.

SUPERVISOR

Negative Score		Positive Score
My supervisor wants me to include people more than I want to.	o*	I want to include people more than my supervisor wants me to.
My supervisor wants me to control people more than I want to.	p	I want to control people more than my supervisor wants me to.
My supervisor wants me to be more open with people than I want to be.	q	I want to be more open with people than my supervisor wants me to be.
My supervisor wants people to include me more than I want people to include me.	r	I want people to include me more than my supervisor wants them to.
My supervisor wants people to control me more than I want people to control me.	s	I want people to control me more than my supervisor wants them to.
My supervisor wants people to be more open with me than I want them to be.	t	I want people to be more open with me than my supervisor wants them to be.
My supervisor wants me to feel that people are more significant than I want to.	u	I want to feel that people are more significant than my supervisor wants me to.
My supervisor wants me to feel that people are more competent than I want to.	v	I want to feel that people are more competent than my supervisor wants me to.
My supervisor wants me to like people more than I want to.	w	I want to like people more than my supervisor wants me to.
My supervisor wants people to feel that I am more significant than I want people to feel that I am.	x	I want people to feel that I am more significant than my supervisor wants them to.
My supervisor wants people to feel that I am more competent than I want people to feel that I am.	y	I want people to feel that I am more competent than my supervisor wants them to.
My supervisor wants people to like me more than I want people to like me.	z	I want people to like me more than my supervisor wants them to.

PEERS

Negative Score		Positive Score
My peers want me to include people more than I want to.	op	I want to include people more than my peers want me to.
My peers want me to control people more than I want to.	pp	I want to control people more than my peers want me to.

My peers want me to be more open with people than I want to be.	I want to be more open with people than my peers want me to be.
My peers want people to include me more than I want people to include me.	I want people to include me more than my peers want them to.
My peers want people to control me more than I want people to control me.	I want people to control me more than my peers want them to.
My peers want people to be more open with me than I want people to be.	I want people to be more open with me than my peers want them to be.
My peers want me to feel that people are more significant than I want to.	I want to feel that people are more significant than my peers want me to.
My peers want me to feel that people are more competent than I want to.	I want to feel that people are more competent than my peers want me to.
My peers want me to like people more than I want to.	I want to like people more than my peers want me to.
My peers want people to feel that I am more significant than I want people to feel that I am.	I want people to feel that I am more significant than my peers want them to.
My peers want people to feel that I am more competent than I want people to feel that I am.	I want people to feel that I am more competent than my peers want them to.
My peers want people to like me more than I want people to like me.	I want people to like me more than my peers want them to.

The boxes are labeled (top to bottom): qp, rp, sp, tp, up, vp, wp, xp, yp, zp.

SUBORDINATES

Negative Score

Positive Score

My subordinates want me to include people more than I want to.	I want to include people more than my subordinates want me to.
My subordinates want me to control people more than I want to.	I want to control people more than my subordinates want me to.
My subordinates want me to be more open with people than I want to be.	I want to be more open with people than my subordinates want me to be.
My subordinates want people to include me more than I want people to include me.	I want people to include me more than my subordinates want them to.
My subordinates want people to control me more than I want people to control me.	I want people to control me more than my subordinates want them to.
My subordinates want people to be more open with me than I want people to be.	I want people to be more open with me than my subordinates want them to be.
My subordinates want me to feel that people are more significant than I want to.	I want to feel that people are more significant than my subordinates want me to.
My subordinates want me to feel that people are more competent than I want to.	I want to feel that people are more competent than my subordinates want me to.

The boxes are labeled (top to bottom): od*, pd, qd, rd, sd, td, ud, vd.

My subordinates want me to like people more than I want to.	☐ wd	I want to like people more than my subordinates want me to.
My subordinates want people to feel that I am more significant than I want people to feel that I am.	☐ xd	I want people to feel that I am more significant than my subordinates want them to.
My subordinates want people to feel that I am more competent than I want people to feel that I am.	☐ yd	I want people to feel that I am more competent than my subordinates want them to.
My subordinates want people to like me more than I want people to like me.	☐ zd	I want people to like me more than my subordinates want them to.

CLIENTS

Negative Score		Positive Score
My clients want me to include people more than I want to.	☐ ot	I want to include people more than my clients want me to.
My clients want me to control people more than I want to.	☐ pt	I want to control people more than me clients want me to.
My clients want me to be more open with people than I want to be.	☐ qt	I want to be more open with people than my clients want me to be.
My clients want people to include me more than I want people to include me.	☐ rt	I want people to include me more than my clients want them to.
My clients want people to control me more than I want people to control me.	☐ st	I want people to control me more than my clients want them to.
My clients want people to be more open with me than I want people to be.	☐ tt	I want people to be more open with me than my clients want them to.
My clients want me to feel that people are more significant than I want to.	☐ ut	I want to feel that people are more significant than my clients want me to.
My clients want me to feel that people are more competent than I want to.	☐ vt	I want to feel that people are more competent than my clients want me to.
My clients want me to like people more than I want to.	☐ wt	I want to like people more than my clients want me to.
My clients want people to feel that I am more significant than I want people to feel that I am.	☐ xt	I want people to feel that I am more significant than my clients want them to.
My clients want people to feel that I am more competent than I want people to feel that I am.	☐ yt	I want people to feel that I am more competent than my clients want them to.
My clients want people to like me more than I want people to like me.	☐ zt	I want people to like me more than my clients want them to.

* The larger the score, that is, the difference, the more likely it is that I feel dissatisfied in my present job.

SATISFACTION: Career Choice

Comparing the requirements for my job with what I would like in my work life provides an approach to career planning. If I were to be exactly like my organization wants me to be but this is not the way I want to be, there is not much point in remaining in my job.

The process I use to determine career-choice satisfaction may be used for any job. I compare what it takes to perform optimally in a specific job with the way I would ideally like to perform. In this way I can test myself against many job possibilities and narrow down the types of job I would enjoy having.

This is a way of planning my career in terms of interpersonal gratification. When supplemented with career considerations in the areas of skills, competencies, security, long-range benefits, opportunities for growth, and the other usual factors, this method should provide me with the tools I need to select a career path.

ACTIVITY 14. Career Choice

1. Look over results for all four charts. Pay particular attention to those statements that are circled (score of 2 or more), especially those with high numbers. They represent the greatest difference between what you would like to do on a job and what you think is wanted on this job.

2. Does this information make sense to you? Is it consistent with your experience?

3. Does it fit your perception of your satisfaction with your supervisor? your peers? your subordinates? your clients?

4. Does this indicate that you are in the proper job? If not, what are your options?

5. How can you choose to be on the career path you wish? What, if anything, is there about you that has prevented you from pursuing a path that you fully desire?

6. Shut your eyes and reflect on this chapter. Review your feelings about job description; job fit; and satisfaction with your present job, present job performance, and career choice. Open your eyes. Write your most significant answers on the next page.

PERSONAL MEANING OF JOB AND CAREER FIT

SEGUE

I have now looked carefully at the personal and relational aspects of my job, and of jobs in general. I understand that aside from the abilities needed on the job, there is a definite personal environment to each type of position. By comparing my behavior and feelings with those required for any particular job, I gain a good understanding of how I would fit and of where the problems might arise.

This information allows me to assess my satisfaction with my present employment and to develop an idea about the types of careers I may pursue that are most likely to satisfy my human desires.

I begin to wonder how I can understand why I behave and feel as I do, and whether I can find out how to change if I want to. In that way I could perhaps fit into more job situations. I also get the feeling that my behavior at work is similar to that in my personal life and toward myself.

I would like now to learn more about my feelings toward myself.

chapter five

Now we're ready to take a real look inside. The journey to the center of the self is getting more exciting.

THE KEY:
Self-Concept

One factor underlies success in all human endeavors: How I feel about *myself*— my self-concept.

The major block to my full effectiveness is my lack of confidence, or lack of a feeling of self-worth. This is also the major block concerning two of the most important problems in modern organizational life: *motivation* and *productivity*.

My relationship with you also depends largely on how I feel about myself. *Many of my troubles with you arise because you create conditions within which my doubts about myself arise.*

- If you present me with a situation that I do not feel capable of handling, I may become very angry at you and resist doing what you want me to do. If I do feel competent, I welcome the challenge and appreciate you.

- If I feel that you do not like me, I may try to get even with you or try to get you. If I feel likeable, any negative feelings you do have about me do not bother me so much.

- If I do not feel significant and you ignore me, I may feel "Why should I try hard?" and work only hard enough to keep my job. If I feel important I may tell you what I would like from you.

To the extent that I do not feel good about myself, my individual effectiveness suffers; my relationships are always troubled; and my choice of career does not matter, since I will run into the same kinds of problems in almost any job. On the other hand:

If a couple or a family or an organization is made up of people who feel good about themselves, then group and individual effectiveness are assured.

In this chapter I want to answer these questions:

- What are the elements of self-concept?

- How do my feelings of personal inadequacy affect my personal relations and my relations on the job?

- How do they affect my effectiveness and job?

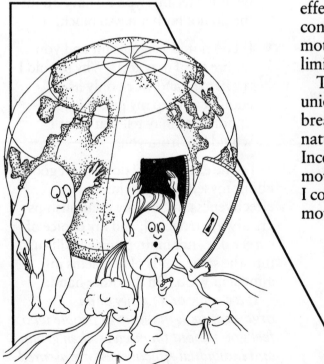

MOTIVATION

The self-concept is the key to motivation.

If I feel good about myself, I feel motivated to develop my potential, to enjoy my relationships with family and friends, and to work effectively.

For many years, organizations have been exploring methods for motivating employees. Most of these methods have used external rewards or "incentives" — increased wages, shorter hours, health plans, retirement programs, longer vacations, profit-sharing, larger offices, more assistants, even keys to the executive washroom.

These incentives are often very effective, and clearly they should be continued and expanded. As motivators, however, they have serious limitations.

The frequency of strikes and of union–management negotiation breakdowns illustrates the fragile nature of incentives in organizations. Incentives— in most cases, money — motivate me from outside myself. When I consider the incentives inadequate, my motivation often disappears.

However, if I am motivated by an internal feeling, I am less influenced by a change in outside conditions. Internal motivations are those that come from the desire to work because I feel that work is *personally gratifying and fulfilling.*

This is not to say that if I am internally motivated, I do not care about my salary or the other benefits of my job. Unless my self-concept includes being deprived, those benefits are of great importance. But the basic push toward doing a good job, being a reliable employee, remaining on the job, and enjoying the work comes from my feeling about myself.

This principle applies to all areas of my life.

Here's a pivotal event in my life.

During the loyalty-oath controversy at the University of California during the McCarthy era, I took the position that I would not sign the oath for reasons of principle. My father flew out from the Midwest and spent three days with me discussing it. "Of course you are right in principle," he said, "but you will jeopardize your future. You are just a teaching assistant. No one knows you, and others will be hired first." His argument persuaded me, and I had lunch with fellow nonsigners and told them I had decided to sign and "fight from within." When I left the restaurant and walked into the sunlight I felt as if I weighed three tons; my muscles were stiff and heavy, and I felt enveloped in darkness. A little voice whispered in my ear, "That's not the kind of person I want to be." Immediately I realized that signing or not signing was not just a problem of logic, as it was easy to summon good arguments for both sides. Rather, the issue was: What kind of person do I want to be? I decided not to sign, and my body lightened, the darkness was replaced by sunlight, and I felt wonderful. My body was telling me what I really wanted to do.

Internal sources of motivation relate to my self-concept. I work because *this is the kind of person I want to be.* This self-concept is my basic motivation.

DESCRIPTION

The specific areas of the self that make up the self-concept are the aspects that I have already examined in the area of human relations:

- Behavior — inclusion, control, and openness; and

- Feelings — significance, competence, and likeability.

Instead of exploring how I feel about you, as I did in Element B and Element F, in order to explore the self-concept I shall see how I perceive myself: How do I behave toward myself? How do I feel about myself?

The behavioral aspects of the self-concept are: "I am present (include myself)," "I am self-controlled (control myself)," and "I am aware (open with myself)."

The feeling level of the self-concept consists of: "I feel significant," "I feel competent," and "I like myself."

How I feel about and behave toward myself is the basic determinant of most of my behavior. If I improve my self-regard, I will find that dozens of behaviors change automatically. If, for example, I increase my feelings of self-competence, I will probably be less defensive, less angered by criticism, less devastated if I do not get a raise, less anxious when I come to work, better able to make decisions, less afraid of making decisions, and more able to appreciate and praise other people.

BEHAVIOR

Presence (Self-Inclusion)

To *include* myself refers to being "present" — to doing whatever I am doing with all of myself.

When I am *low* on presence, parts of me are scattered or detached or I am thinking of other things.

When I am *high* on presence, I am identified with what I am doing and I may lose the sense of myself as different from what I am observing. In the theater, a concept called "psychic distance" is very close to the concept of "presence." In order to best experience a play, I must not be too detached (or I will be unmoved by the play), nor too involved (or I will lose perspective and leave depressed after a tragedy or frightened after a horror play).

When I am *present*, I experience what is happening, but I do not become so caught up in the emotions of the moment that I lose perspective about who and where I am. I am capable of intense presence, intense detachment, or anywhere in between, depending on what is appropriate.

Spontaneity (Self-Control)

To "control" myself refers to spontaneous expression.

When I am *low* on self-control, I become out of control and I sometimes behave in ways that I later am sorry for. In the extreme, this is wild and antisocial behavior. Alcohol and drugs such as "uppers" and "downers" are often used in this context. "Uppers" release some of the users' controls so that they will be more expressive; "downers" increase their controls so that they will be calmer.

When I am *high* on self-control, I feel inhibited and hold myself back. I do not express myself fully, and I become rigid and unspontaneous. I am reluctant to take chances or to take a risk for fear of what might happen.

When I am *spontaneous*, I do everything I wish to do and stop whenever I choose to. I am able to be totally free, totally controlled, or anything in between, depending on what is appropriate.

Awareness (Self-Openness)

To be *open* with myself refers to knowing myself or to not keeping secrets from myself; in other words, self-awareness.

When I am *low* on awareness, I do not know myself well. It is difficult to be open with myself if I do not know who I am. If I am not self-aware I often behave in ways I do not understand. I am a stranger to myself, and I often do not understand why I do the things I do.

When I am *high* on awareness I begin to wallow in myself, and I begin to lose contact with the world. I am so self-occupied and introspective that I do not pay attention to anything outside myself. In the process of becoming aware, people often go through a period like this; but they do not stay stuck in it.

When I am *aware,* I know myself well and I am comfortable with myself. I am not dark and unknown, nor am I blindingly bright. I am simply clear and open. I may be totally aware, totally unaware, or anything in between, depending on what is appropriate.

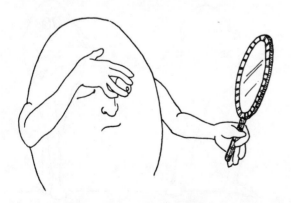

Dimensions

I sometimes go through the extremes of these dimensions and then come out of them. I will be very blind to myself, for example, and all of a sudden I will discover myself and how I function. I may then go on a binge of self-discovery and self-exploration and revel in myself. After a time, I become saturated, and I gradually make my way to a more moderate position.

In summary, *presence* is the term for the optimal including of myself. *Spontaneity* is the term for the optimal controlling of myself. *Awareness* is the term for the optimal openness to myself.[21]

One way I can visualize these dimensions is to imagine that I am playing a video game or handball.

The first requirement for success is that I see the outside situation clearly. When I am the video-game player, I must see the screen, the figures on the screen, their position, and their speed. When I am the handball player, I must see the shape of the whole court, the location of the walls, the position of my opponent, and the location, speed, and spin of the ball.

That is *presence.* If I am present I experience the environment fully. I concentrate; I focus; my attention does not wander.

Next, my muscles and brain must be prepared to act. If my muscles are chronically tense or my brain is inflexible, I will be rigid and have difficulty moving rapidly and with precision. If my muscles are flaccid and toneless and my brain is not alert, I also cannot move quickly or effectively.

My muscles must be toned but not tense, neither contracted nor extended, but capable of moving into either state quickly, as requested. My brain must be alert and open.

This is *spontaneity*. I am alert and prepared to respond appropriately to any circumstance.

The final requirement for success is to know what is going on inside of me. I must be aware of where my arms and legs are, where my hands and fingers are, where my eyes are focused, whether I am listening, whether my pelvis is anchored.

This is *awareness*. If I am aware, I know what is happening inside of me, I am aware of my own experience.

If I am present, spontaneous, and aware, I am ready to act effectively.

Finally, I must bring these three together. At the video screen I am able to intercept the figures. On the handball court I can move my legs, my arms, and the rest of my body at just the right time to hit the ball where I aim it.

In all the discussions involving a new plan for governing the company division, there were two sides: (1) those who wanted it hierarchical, with clear lines of authority, and (2) those who wanted governance to be more lateral and democratic. Phil always took the extreme position, for authority and strict lines of reporting and accountability. Although his position was usually well reasoned, his fervor seemed to be excessive even to those who agreed with his position. His Element S (see page 124) helped him to gain insight into why he felt so strongly, even at times angry, about the issue. His score was the lowest of all on self-control. This startled him, and he began to speak about his fear of getting out of control. Phil related stories of where he had done things for which he was later sorry because he had not controlled himself sufficiently. Regardless of the merits of his governance argument, Phil saw that his fervor was actually a plea for the environment— in this case, the organizational structure — to control him so that he would not once again get out of control. This insight helped him and those he worked with to develop a situation that could deal with this issue.

ACTIVITY 15.
Self-Concept: Behavior Imagery

Presence

1. Find a comfortable place to lie or sit. Shut your eyes. Relax. (Pause 10 seconds.) Imagine that something unknown appears in front of you that you cannot quite make out. Concentrate on it for a moment. Notice: Are you thinking about it? Are you looking at it? hearing it? tasting it? talking to it? smelling it? touching it? Is your heart feeling it? Are your stomach and guts reacting to it? Do you feel sexual about it? Are your legs responding to it?

   (Pause 60 seconds.) Which parts of you seem to be fully concentrating on it? Which parts find it difficult to experience focusing on it? Which parts are focused on something else? What do you see?

2. Open your eyes and reflect on what happened.

3. How does this imagery increase your understanding of the concept of presence?

You can take even more time if you wish. This activity usually repays the extra time.

Spontaneity

4. Shut your eyes. Relax. (Pause 10 seconds.) Imagine yourself as you are now. See yourself entering your body and observing all the thoughts and all the feelings that you have never let other people know. (Pause 20 seconds.) Now imagine expressing all those suppressed feelings and thoughts to their fullest. (Pause 20 seconds.) Now imagine allowing yourself to see all the things you have been blind to. (Pause 20 seconds.) Imagine hearing all the things you have been blocking out. (Pause 20 seconds.) Imagine tasting and smelling all the things you have not allowed yourself to taste or smell. (Pause 20 seconds.) Imagine expressing the things you have stopped yourself from saying, screaming, or yelling. (Pause 20 seconds.) Imagine yourself feeling all the love you have suppressed. (Pause 20 seconds.) Imagine feeling all the anger and vengeance you have suppressed. (Pause 20 seconds.) Imagine expressing all the lust and sexuality you have suppressed. (Pause 20 seconds.) Imagine experiencing all the leaving or going toward people you have blocked yourself from doing.

5. (Pause 20 seconds.) Open your eyes and reflect on what happened.

6. How does this imagery increase your understanding of the concept of control?

Awareness

7. Shut your eyes. Relax. (Pause 10 seconds.) Imagine yourself naked. Not only naked, but with transparent skin. Everything about yourself is available to you. See yourself approaching your transparent self. (Pause 60 seconds.) Do you want to look and see everything? Or do you want to look at certain parts and not others? Do you feel frightened by some parts? excited? embarrassed? Do you feel guilty? proud? ashamed? What do you want to know about yourself and what do you not want to know?

8. (Pause 60 seconds.) Open your eyes and reflect on what happened.

9. How does this imagery increase your understanding of the concept of awareness?

Make notes here, and on the next page too— you may even want to find extra paper.

RESPONSES: Activity 15. Self-Concept: Behavior Imagery

FEELINGS

The feelings of significance, competence, and likeability have been described extensively on pages 51 to 53. I shall go back and reread that page to refresh my memory. As applied to myself:

Self-significance refers to my feelings of being significant, important, worthwhile, and meaningful *as opposed to* feeling unimportant, meaningless, and of no value.

Self-competence refers to my feelings of competence, intelligence, ability, and strength *as opposed to* weakness, incompetence, and the inability to cope.

Self-like refers to my feelings of enjoying being in my own company, and of feeling good about who I am *as opposed to* not feeling good in my own company and being embarrassed or ashamed of who I am.

QUESTIONS. Self-Concept

I place the letter of my answer on the line at the left. The letters refer to these behaviors and feelings toward the self:

(P) Presence
(T) Competence
(N) Significance
(A) Awareness
(S) Spontaneity
(L) Likeability

_____ 1. When I say, "Sorry, would you repeat that? I was thinking of something else," I am low on ?

_____ 2. People who feel that they are phony and not as capable as they appear to be are low on ?

_____ 3. When I get drunk and insult the boss's wife, I am high on ?

_____ 4. People who act polite and pleasant so that people will not see how nasty and critical they are are low on ?

_____ 5. When I think that twisting my right ankle five times in a year is just "bad luck," I am low on ?

_____ 6. People who never speak because they feel that they are boring and have nothing to say are low on ?

_____ 7. When I plan everything out very carefully ahead of time before risking anything new, I am probably low on ?

_____ 8. People who are willing to risk losing their job for a principle because they know they are capable of getting another job are high on ?

_____ 9. When I find myself examining my motives for examining my motives, I am high on ?

_____ 10. People who feel that anyone who gets to know them well will despise them are low on ?

_____ 11. When I cannot watch a TV movie with a sad ending because I am depressed for the next day, I am high on ?

_____ 12. People who are not afraid to speak up to strangers because they are sure they will be paid attention to are high on ?

Answers: PTS LAN STA LPN

ACTIVITY 16.
Self-Concept: Feelings Experience

Significance

1. Relax and walk around the room.

2. Imagine that you feel totally insignificant and unimportant. Perhaps you can remember a time in your life when you felt this way. Experience the feeling. (Pause 60 seconds.) Now gradually change your image to a situation where you feel extremely significant and important. Experience that feeling.

3. (Pause 60 seconds.) Reflect on how you feel about what you experienced.

Competence

4. Walk around again. Imagine that you feel totally incompetent. Perhaps you can remember a time in your life when you felt this way. Experience this feeling. (Pause 60 seconds.) Now gradually change your image to a situation where you feel extremely competent. Experience that feeling.

5. (Pause 60 seconds.) Reflect on what you saw and how you feel about what you experienced.

These feelings you experience may relate back to earlier events in your life.

Likeability

6. Walk around again. Imagine that you feel totally unlikeable. Perhaps you can remember a time in your life when you felt this way. Experience the feeling. (Pause 60 seconds.) Now gradually change your image to a situation where you feel extremely likeable. Experience that feeling.

7. (Pause 60 seconds.) Reflect on what you saw and how you feel about what you experienced.

8. How do these experiences help you to understand the concepts of self-significance, self-competence, and self-like? Write your responses on the next page.

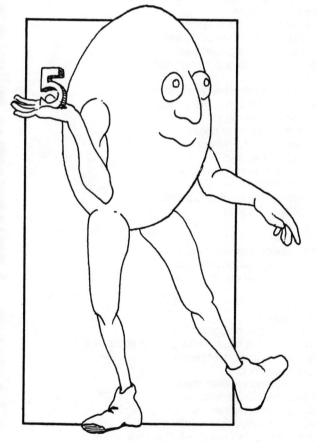

Measurement

Element S measures my behavior and feelings toward myself.

Prediction

Before I fill out Element S, I will record how I perceive myself. Turning to pages 126 and 127, in the twelve circles marked "P", I will put a score from 0 to 9, indicating how much I agree with each of the twelve statements. Nine means "most agreement"; zero means "least agreement."

Disagree 0 1 2 3 4 5 6 7 8 9 **Agree**

After the predictions are recorded, I fill out and score Element S.

ELEMENT S

There are no "right" answers. The more honest I am, the more accurate will be the information I receive from Element S.

First, I complete the column "The way it IS" for all items.

For each statement, I place a number from 1 to 6 on the line to the left of the item, in the appropriate column. The numbers indicate how much I agree with the statement.

Disagree 1 2 3 4 5 6 **Agree**

When I have finished, I return to the top of the column and respond to the same items for "The way I WANT it to be."

The Way It IS	The Way I WANT It to Be	
1		I frequently stop listening and drift off.
2		I feel that I cannot rely on my own judgment.
3		I have no secrets from myself.
4		I feel that I am important.
5		I am too controlled.
6		I feel warmth toward myself.
7		I sometimes forget what is happening.
8		I trust my own abilities.
9		There are things about myself that I would rather not know.
10		I feel insignificant.
11		I measure everything carefully before I do it.
12		I feel affectionate toward myself.
13		I sometimes feel dead.
14		I am suspicious of my own competence.
15		I do not know myself well.
16		I feel like an important person.
17		I control myself.
18		I like myself.
19		I give my full attention to what is happening.
20		I admire my abilities.
21		I am aware of all of my feelings.
22		I feel that I am an interesting person.
23		I am always in charge of myself.
24		I feel personally distant from myself.
25		I drift off.
26		I have confidence in my own abilities.
27		I sometimes hide things from myself.
28		I feel worthy of attention.
29		I sometimes get out of control.
30		I feel that I am not a nice person.
31		I am easily distracted.
32		I can depend on my own judgment.
33		I know myself well.
34		I feel that I am a stimulating person.
35		I do not take chances.
36		I hate myself.
37		I feel fully alive.
38		I am skeptical of my abilities.
39		I figure out my hidden motives.
40		I feel like a significant individual.
41		I take no risks.
42		I do not like myself.
43		I am scattered.
44		I do not trust my competence.
45		I am aware of the negative things I feel about myself.
46		I feel like an unimportant person.
47		I am undisciplined.
48		I feel very friendly toward myself.
49		I have trouble concentrating.
50		I trust my own competence.
51		I keep some things hidden from myself.
52		I feel that it does not matter whether I live or die.
53		I keep myself under tight control.
54		I feel like a nice person.

ELEMENT S: Scoring

I *compare* my response to each item of Element S with the Scored Responses printed beside the item number.

If my response is the *same as* any one of the Scored Responses, I place a check mark (✔) on the line under IS or WANT or both.

I *add* the checks in each column and record the total (0 to 9) in the box at the bottom of the column.

I *transfer* scores to pages 126 and 127.

Item	Scored Responses	Column IS	WANT
1	1,2,3		
7	1		
13	1,2,3,4		
19	5,6		
25	1,2		
31	1,2		
37	5,6		
43	1,2,3		
49	1,2,3		

I am present. ☐ 10

I want to be present. ☐ 19

Item	Scored Responses	Column IS	WANT
4	6		
10	1		
16	5,6		
22	5,6		
28	4,5,6		
34	5,6		
40	6		
46	1,2		
52	1		

I feel significant. ☐ 40

I want to feel significant. ☐ 49

Item	Scored Responses	Column IS	WANT
5	3,4,5,6		
11	4,5,6		
17	4,5,6		
23	4,5,6		
29	1,2,3		
35	4,5,6		
41	4,5,6		
47	1,2		
53	5,6		

I control myself. ☐ 20

I want to control myself. ☐ 29

Item	Scored Responses	Column IS	WANT
2	1,2		
8	4,5,6		
14	1		
20	5,6		
26	4,5,6		
32	6		
38	1,2		
44	1		
50	5,6		

I feel competent. ☐ 50

I want to feel competent. ☐ 59

Item	Scored Responses	Column IS	WANT
3	4,5,6		
9	1		
15	1,2,3		
21	5,6		
27	1,2,3		
33	4,5,6		
39	5,6		
45	5,6		
51	1,2		

I am aware. ☐ 30

I want to be aware. ☐ 39

Item	Scored Responses	Column IS	WANT
6	5,6		
12	4,5,6		
18	4,5,6		
24	1		
30	1		
36	1		
42	1		
48	5,6		
54	6		

I like myself. ☐ 60

I want to like myself. ☐ 69

ELEMENT S: Interpretation

I transfer scores from page 125 to the appropriate boxes below.

For each pair of scales I enter the Difference score.

I am present ☐ ◯
10   P10

High Score
In my opinion, all my energies are concentrated on what I am doing right here and now. I give my full attention to the moment.

Low Score
I am scattered. I have difficulty concentrating. I drift off and start thinking about other matters. I have trouble paying full attention. I am detached and feel distant from what is happening.

Positive Score
I feel more present than I want to feel. I would like to feel more detached.

I want to be present ☐ ◯
19   P19

High Score
I want to concentrate my energies on what I am doing at the moment. I want to give my full attention to what is happening.

Low Score
I want to drift off and not be so concentrated on what I am doing. I want to feel detached from what is happening.

Difference (10 minus 19) ☐
△10

Negative Score
I want to feel more present than I do. I want to be more focused on what I am doing.

I control myself ☐ ◯
20   P20

High Score
In my opinion, I am very controlled. I plan things carefully, and I rarely take chances. I make sure I stay in charge of myself and do not lose my head.

Low Score
I do not have self-control. I take risks and do not plan carefully before acting. I am not disciplined.

Positive Score
I control myself more than I want to. I want to be more spontaneous.

I want to control myself ☐ ◯
29   P29

High Score
I want to control myself. I want to be organized, to plan things out before I do them, and to not take chances.

Low Score
I want to take risks and to do things without planning. I do not want to be self-controlled.

Difference (20 minus 29) ☐
△ 20

Negative Score
I want to be more in control of myself than I am. I want to be more organized.

I am aware ☐ ◯
30   P30

High Score
In my opinion, I know myself well. I do not hide things from myself. I do not deceive myself about what I am like. I am able to acknowledge my good points and to see my deficiencies clearly.

Low Score
I do not know myself well. I often do things that surprise me. There are parts of myself that I do not know much about. I hide things from myself.

Positive Score
I am more aware of myself than I want to be. I would rather not know myself so well.

I want to be aware ☐ ◯
39   P39

High Score
I want to be aware of myself, to know myself well. I do not want to hide things from myself or deceive myself.

Low Score
I do not want to know myself well. There are things about myself that I do not want to know. I would rather they stayed hidden.

Difference (30 minus 39) ☐
△30

Negative Score
I want to know myself better than I do. I do not want to deceive myself so much.

I transfer the eighteen scores on these pages to Scoring Summary (using scale code numbers).

I feel significant ☐ ○
                  40   P40

High Score
I feel significant and important. I feel that I am as important as anyone else. People care about me. I feel that I deserve my share of benefits in the world.

Low Score
I feel that I am not significant or important. I do not mean anything. If I were to disappear, few people would be affected. I feel that I should not take up other people's time.

I want to feel significant ☐ ○
                  49   P49

High Score
I want to feel significant. I want to feel that I am an important person and that my life is meaningful.

Low Score
I want to feel insignificant and unimportant. It does not matter to me whether I feel significant or not.

Difference (40 minus 49) ☐
                        △40

Positive Score
I feel more significant than I want to feel.

Negative Score
I want to feel more significant than I do.

I feel competent ☐ ○
              50   P50

High Score
I feel that I am competent and capable of dealing effectively with life. I feel capable of earning a living, holding a job, raising a family, creating and maintaining a home, and doing anything that I decide to do.

Low Score
I feel weak and incompetent. I feel that I am not smart, strong, or attractive enough. I am fearful that I am not capable of holding a job, making a living, supporting my children, or preparing for old age.

I want to feel competent ☐ ○
              59   P59

High Score
I want to feel competent and capable of dealing effectively with my life. I want to have confidence in my abilities and capacities.

Low Score
I do not want to feel competent. I do not want to feel that I can handle my own life effectively.

Difference (50 minus 59) ☐
                        △50

Positive Score
I feel more competent than I want to feel. I would rather not feel so capable.

Negative Score
I want to feel more competent than I do. I do not feel as capable as I would like to.

I like myself ☐ ○
         60   P60

High Score
I like myself. I feel that I am a nice person whom people will like when they know me well. I feel warm toward myself.

I want to like myself ☐ ○
            69   P69

High Score
I want to like myself. I want to feel that I am a nice person and to feel warm and comfortable with myself.

Difference (60 minus 69) ☐
                        △60

Positive Score
I like myself more than I want to. I do not want to like myself so much.

Negative Score
I want to like myself more than I do. I want more to feel that I am a nice person.

ACTIVITY 17.
Self-Concept Measures

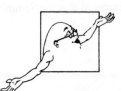

Now we're ready to bring it all together.

PART A

1. Compare your scores with your predictions. For those that are less accurate, how would you explain the difference?

2. Among the explanations you give yourself, include this possibility: "There is a part of me that I am not entirely aware of. That is the part that filled out Element S." See if you can find any truth in that possibility.

3. Do your Difference (Δ) scores fit with how you see yourself? Do the differences indicate (a) that you are dissatisfied with yourself, or (b) simply that you recognize the difference but are not dissatisfied?

4. Do your scores help you to understand anything about yourself or your relationships?

PART B

1. Compare each of your scores with the corresponding imagery on page 116 and the experience on page 121.

2. Keeping in mind the comments on self-understanding (page 46), do you have a deeper sense of your behavior and feelings toward yourself?

3. Shut your eyes, reflect on your self-concept, your Element S, and the imagery. Write down your most significant reactions.

CHANGING THE SELF-CONCEPT

I would like to feel better about myself. It is not that I necessarily feel bad, but I am sure that my life would be more enjoyable if I increased my self-esteem.

When I am not feeling good about myself, I notice a curious thing. Compliments and support from other people are pleasant to hear but these comments are not able to make me feel better for very long.

I dismiss their compliments because I believe that these people do not know me as well as I know myself. They like what they see but they do not know all the thoughts I have, all the feelings I have, all the things I have done. If they did know I am not sure that they would feel the same way about me.

Sometimes having people praise or like me is a threat. If I do something to disappoint them, they may withdraw their liking so it is risky for me to feel too good what they say good things about me.

There are payoffs for choosing to not like myself more:

- It is "stuck-up" or "arrogant" to like myself, so I will appear modest to others and they will like me better.

- I should love God. As an individual, I am relatively unimportant.

- People will not expect much of me if I appear unsure of myself.

- I will not be impertinent enough to think I am better than my parents or my siblings.

- I would be a fool if I like myself and no one else does.

I can make use of these insights to understand why I feel as I do about myself and I may choose to increase my self-esteem. Through bringing some of my unconscious feelings about myself to my awareness I may find that some negative ideas I have about myself are no longer true. I may also have not fully appreciated some positive things I feel about myself.

Returning to the idea that my primary motivation comes from being "the kind of person I want to be." I shall explore some possible sources of self-dissatisfaction with the aim of increasing my self-esteem.

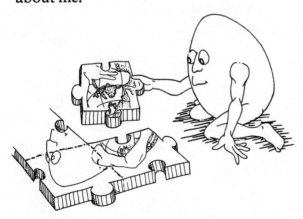

ACTIVITY 18. Ideal Self

PART A

1. How do you feel about yourself (circle one)?

   Awful 0 1 2 3 4 5 6 7 8 9 **Great**

2. Shut your eyes and picture the kind of person you want to be. See how she or he looks, moves, thinks, feels and senses. See what he or she does, has done, and has.

3. (Pause 60 seconds.) Keeping this picture in mind answer the following: Describe the kind of person you want to be: (Ignore the short lines)

____ a. _____   ____ f. _____
____ b. _____   ____ g. _____
____ c. _____   ____ h. _____
____ d. _____   ____ i. _____
____ e. _____   ____ j. _____

Describe how this person
Looks:

____ a. _____
____ b. _____
____ c. _____

Moves:

____ a. _____
____ b. _____
____ c. _____

Thinks:

____ a. _____
____ b. _____
____ c. _____

Feels:

____ a. _____
____ b. _____
____ c. _____

Describe:
This person's principles and beliefs.

_____ a. _____

_____ b. _____

_____ c. _____

What this person has done.

_____ a. _____

_____ b. _____

_____ c. _____

What this person does.

_____ a. _____

_____ b. _____

_____ c. _____

What this person has.

_____ a. _____

_____ b. _____

_____ c. _____

Describe any other important traits of this person.

_____ a. _____

_____ b. _____

_____ c. _____

4. Now take a deep breath, erase this picture from your mind and shut your eyes. (Pause 10 seconds.) Get a picture now of the kind of person you do *not* want to be. See how he or she looks, moves, thinks, feels and senses. See what she or he does, has done, and has.

5. (Pause 60 seconds.) Keeping this picture in mind answer the following:

Describe the kind of person you do *not* want to be. (Ignore the short lines)

___ a. _____   ___ f. _____

___ b. _____   ___ g. _____

___ c. _____   ___ h. _____

___ d. _____   ___ i. _____

___ e. _____   ___ j. _____

Describe how this person
Looks:

___ a. _____

___ b. _____

___ c. _____

Moves:

___ a. _____

___ b. _____

___ c. _____

Thinks:

___ a. _____

___ b. _____

___ c. _____

Feels:

___ a. _____

___ b. _____

___ c. _____

Describe:
This person's principles and beliefs.

___ a. _____

___ b. _____

___ c. _____

What this person has done.

___ a. _____

___ b. _____

___ c. _____

What this person does.

___ a. _____

___ b. _____

___ c. _____

What this person has.

___ a. _____

___ b. _____

___ c. _____

Describe any other important traits of this person.

___ a. _____

___ b. _____

___ c. _____

PART B

How do you feel about yourself now (circle one)?

Awful 0 1 2 3 4 5 6 7 8 9 **Great**

1. Go back to item 3 above. For items 3 and 5 on the line to the left of each answer you filled in, place a number from zero to nine. The numbers will indicate the degree to which *you yourself* fit the descriptions:

   I am not at all this way. 0 1 2 3 4 5 6 7 8 9 **I am exactly this way.**

2. When you have finished, circle your highest numbers for item 3 and your lowest numbers for item 5.

3. Look over these circled items. Are you stopping yourself from feeling better about yourself because of these items? Do your scores reflect the way you actually feel now? Can you recall when you began feeling this way?

PART C

1. Looking over your list of circled items and assuming the choice principle for a moment, list below the reasons — the pay-offs — you are getting for believing these items.

   a. _____

   b. _____

   c. _____

   d. _____

   e. _____

   f. _____

   g. _____

   h. _____

   i. _____

   j. _____

4. Perhaps your self-esteem will increase if you place yourself in situations where you have an opportunity to function nearer your ideal and to not function the way you do not like to be. Does this make sense to you? If so, how would you go about it?

5. Write your primary responses to this activity on the next page.

RESPONSE. Activity 18. Ideal Self

PERSONAL MEANING OF THE KEY

SEGUE

What underlies my understanding the human condition is how I behave toward and feel about myself. Behavior includes presence — how much I experience my environment; spontaneity — how free I am to act; and awareness — how acquainted I am with my inner experience. My feelings about myself include significance, competence, and likeability. By using imagery, a questionnaire (Element S), and a nonverbal experience, I once again have a multilevel knowledge of how I regard myself. I can use these three sources of information to see whether I am deceiving myself about my self-concept.

I realize that knowing how I feel about myself, even if this feeling is negative, is very valuable. To know what is true is to have the tools to change it. I notice that often simply being aware of a negative feeling I have about myself begins the process of feeling better.

If I do not feel good about myself, to that degree I will not see the world clearly. I use many mechanisms to distort the world so that I do not have to face my true feelings. I no longer need to distort my lens when I accept myself as I am.

Using these mechanisms — which often are called defenses — or even illnesses, can be very damaging to achieving what I want. To overcome these mechanisms and render them unnecessary, I must first understand them and discover how I use them.

chapter six

We all have our own ways of coping. It's not bad. It's usually better to know how we do it.

THE LENS:
How I Create My Own World

It is for good reason that the self-concept is called "The Key." I see the world through myself. I am not an objective observer. I view you, jobs, and events through what I am. If I feel a deficiency in myself it affects how I perceive everything. Just as a flaw in a lens distorts what is seen, so unresolved issues in my life distort the way I view the world. The only way I can see without any distortion is to be aware of every aspect of my life — a condition that approaches sainthood.

All the issues that I am exploring may be better understood through reference to the self-concept. How I behave and feel toward myself affects how I see you, what I want from you, what dissatisfactions I have with close friends, and what problems I have on the job.

The fact that I have problem areas in my life is not good or bad. It just is. The fact that I distort what is happening is not evil or immoral. It just is. By stressing the truth, as opposed to trying to "look good," I have an opportunity to discover how I really operate. The more I know, the better basis I have for determining my own life, relationships, and organizations, and for making them work the way I would like them to.

In this chapter I deal with these questions:

- How do I see you as a reflection of the way I see myself?

- How do I see my job as a reflection of the way I see myself?

- How do I attempt to use you to compensate for my deficiencies?

- How does my self-concept explain many work-related problems?

BLAME

Differences of opinion about what is wrong in work situations or personal situations usually evolve into blaming. The boss blames the worker for doing a sloppy job. Marketing blames the mail room for inefficiency. Middle management blames the president for poor organization. Stockholders blame the board for lack of long-range planning. Wife and husband blame each other for everything.

"I keep asking you to do it over and over again," she said, "and you never do it. Either you are irresponsible or you don't care about me."

"If you would only stop nagging I would do it. I get so tired of hearing you nag, nag, nag. I'm a big boy. I know I should do it."

"You give me no choice. Maybe if I tell you often enough it will get done."

"All right," I agree, "I'll make you a deal. Don't nag me for a month and see what happens."

"It's a deal."

A month passed. She did not nag, and I did not do it. I had to look at the fact that I did not want to do it, and that blaming her was a convenient excuse for my own guilt-laden wish to not do it.

"Accountability"—making sure that there is someone to blame if anything goes wrong—is a very popular organizational concept.

Energy spent on assigning blame is usually very unproductive. I am motivated to defend my own behavior and to find as much fault as possible with your actions. This defensive behavior is so commonplace that it has been given a name—the "CYA," or "Cover Your Ass," syndrome.

By expending energy to ensure that I am not open to blame, I make that energy unavailable for more creative or productive behavior. Furthermore, the effort I put into finding fault with your actions is very time-consuming and not at all conducive to being supportive to you.

A more valuable way to look at situations of "accountability" is to assume that:

- All people involved in any situation are totally responsible for whatever happens.

- There is something *each person* could have done that would have led to a more positive outcome.

- There is something in *each relationship* that could have been changed to lead to a more favorable outcome for the situation.

RESPONSIBILITY

The self-concept provides a basis for understanding both your contributions and my contributions to the outcome of a given situation. If I can see how my feelings about myself affect our situation, I can see my contribution to our difficulties more clearly.

This does not mean that I am to blame. A difficulty is a *problem to be solved,* not a situation in which to expose the culprit. If each of us and each relationship involved in the situation have all colluded to bring about what has happened, then everybody involved is working on the same side. Everyone is trying to figure out how we can modify our fixed positions in order to improve the situation, rather than attacking others and defending themselves. All of us are lined up against our common enemy — the problem.

Everyone is responsible and no one is to blame.

When this realignment is achieved, the resources of each of us are being used in an integrated fashion for the benefit of all of us. When factions fight each other then resources neutralize one another, and efficiency is minimal.

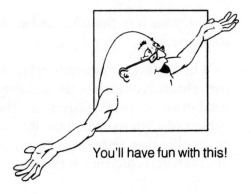

You'll have fun with this!

ACTIVITY 19. The Blame Game

1. Think of all the things about reading and experiencing this book that you have not liked. Think about how other people associated with this book could have made things better if only they had done something else. Blame the publisher, or the typeface, or the tradition from which this book arises, or anything you can think of to blame — even the author. Blame vociferously. Exaggerate.

2. (Pause 2 minutes.) Now shut your eyes and reflect. How easy was this to do? Were you convincing? Did you convince yourself? Was your behavior typical of you?

3. What is the implication of truth and choice for what you have just done?

RESPONSES: Activity 19. The Blame Game

A lending company rewarded its employees with individual bonuses, based on management's judgment of how each person performed. The result was fierce competition and undercutting. When a loan fell through, the Marketing Department blamed the Credit Department for being too conservative. The Credit Department accused the Accounting Department of taking too long to provide the needed data. Accounting accused Marketing of cutting corners to make the loan. Accusations filled the air.

Someone then suggested the bonuses be assigned equally to all personnel, depending on the productivity of the company *as a whole*. Immediately the atmosphere changed. After considerable discussion, some people in Marketing acknowledged that they did sometimes go ahead a bit recklessly in order to please the customers and to perform well. Credit personnel admitted that they sometimes were overcautious because they were afraid of being fired. Several people in Accounting conceded that they often felt ignored, and therefore dragged their feet as a way of getting even.

Some of the problems were individual — Marketing's desire to please, Credit's fear of firing; and some were relational — Accounting's feeling of being ignored by Marketing, Credit's feeling of being held back by Accounting.

As soon as these acknoweldgments were made, an air of enthusiasm took over, and new procedures were evolved. Marketing would keep Credit and Accounting informed as to what they were doing, and as to what information they needed. Marketing and Credit would get together regularly to balance risk-taking with caution. Procedures were developed based on the assumption that it was to everyone's advantage to make the entire operation work. Cooperation replaced competition. An integrated organization replaced an internally competitive one.

COPING

When I have a feeling that I do not want to have, I set about trying to cope with the conflict between my feeling and my thought. If, for example, I feel dislike for my father (or my boss), and I think that children (or employees) should not have such feelings, I set about trying to reconcile this dilemma.[22]

If I am *aware* of the conflict between my feeling and my thought, I proceed toward a rational solution. I talk to friends, read books, occupy myself elsewhere, go to sleep.

Ultimately, all my conflicts are about how I feel about myself. It is not so much my dislike for my father that bothers me; it is my dislike of myself for disliking him. If I choose to repress or deny the conflict, then I begin to distort the way I see the world. My lens becomes aberrated. I start to misinterpret what people say, get angry for no particular reason, see people as hostile.

Mechanisms

If I push the conflict into my unconscious, one way I cope with it is to use what are popularly known as defense, or coping, mechanisms. These arise when I distort the unacceptable part of the conflict.

If, for example, my unconscious feeling is "I don't like myself," then I may distort this feeling by changing the subject of the sentence ("I"). For example, I may change "I" to "you," and say, "You don't like me." This is called *projection*. Activity 12 will illustrate this mechanism.

I may also distort the object of the sentence ("myself") and change it to "you," as in "I don't like you." This is called *displacement*.

Periodically, I became critical of my wife. Everything she did was wrong. No matter how trivial, she botched it up. We started to explore what was happening. She was very irritated and could not understand why I became so critical so suddenly. As we reviewed her failings, an insight struck me. I was feeling very bad about myself. By criticizing her I could avoid knowing my self-critical feeling; I could also reduce the difference between us, since if she was flawed then my flaws were not so glaring. I saw that whenever I became excessively critical of her, I was *displacing* my own negative feelings toward myself onto her.

Or I may change both subject and object, as in, "I think that you don't like yourself." This is called *identification*.

Differences in foreign policy may be seen as the result of the identification mechanism. If I feel that if I am more powerful than you are, then I will dominate you and you will do what I tell you to do, I may become a "hawk" in foreign policy. That is, I assume that the enemy feels as I do — if Russia became stronger, they would dominate the United States. On the other hand, if I feel that when I meet someone stronger my fear motivates me to become stronger myself, or to fight him, then I may become a "dove." I assume that Russia — like me — would not become submissive if it were weaker, but would be pugnacious as I would be, thus increasing the likelihood of war.[23]

Neither of these positions is necessarily wrong. It is simply that nobody really knows what Russia will do; so in part I use my own personal experience to try to understand that situation.

All these mechanisms have the same function: to keep me from having to deal with an unwanted feeling about myself.

Table 4 summarizes these ideas.

TABLE 4. Forms of Distortion

		Subject	
		I	*You*
Object	*Me*	I don't like myself. (Actual unaware feeling)	*You* don't like me. (Projection)
	You	I don't like *you*. (Displacement)	I think that *you* don't like *yourself*. (Identification)

NOTE: The italicized words are distortions.

Compensation is another method I may use to cope with my unconscious conflicts. This is the process through which I try to get other people to make up for deficiencies that I feel I have. If I do not feel competent, for example, I seek out people who feel that I am competent, and I demand that they keep telling me. Compensation is expressed as: "I want other people to behave and feel toward me as I do *not* behave and feel toward myself."

"I married my husband because he is stable. I am flighty and volatile and express my feelings all the time, while he never expresses anything. It often makes me angry, and sometimes I scream at him, 'Show me a feeling, any feeling. Don't just sit there.'"

"I married my wife because she has no trouble expressing feelings, and I don't even recognize mine when they're there. Maybe if I'm around her long enough I'll feel more. But Christ, sometimes I wish she'd calm down. Like 'Enry 'Iggins, I often wonder, 'Why can't a woman be more like a man?'"

This frequent marital pattern — *the raw nerve* and *the dead weight* — is a good example of compensation. She wants him to settle her down, and he wants her to make him feel. After they marry, they try to change each other. The paradox is that if they succeed, they will not get what they married each other for.

Illness is another way that I may attempt to cope with my unwanted feeling. Since I choose everything, I also choose to be ill. I literally "embody" my conflict. I shall consider the ways I do this in the next chapter.

Of course, all these coping mechanisms can offer no more than temporary relief, since they do not deal with the conflict consciously. The first step, however, in dealing effectively with the conflict is to become aware of the coping mechanisms, and through them to make the unconscious conflict conscious.

Distortion

In order for me to use any coping mechanisms, I must be unaware that I attribute my feelings to you.

It is this unawareness that may get me in trouble. For instance, I may get very angry at my boss for not recognizing what a good worker I am, and I may express anger with great hostility. However, the truth may be that he *does* think highly of my work (although he may not say it), but that *I* do not (projection). Since I may not like to face this feeling, I keep myself from knowing about my own low opinion of my competence, and I attribute my feeling to the boss.

Awareness of my feelings about myself contributes to the accuracy of my perceptions. If I am unaware of my self-concept, through the mechanism of projection I may tend to distort how others see me. If I am totally aware of my own self-concept, I will see other people as they really are.

Even if I do project, I am usually somewhat accurate because I am particularly sensitive to the action or feeling that I am interpreting. For example, if I project my lack of self-liking onto you, it is probable that there is some truth to my distorted perception; that is, even if you generally like me, you probably also have some dislike for me.

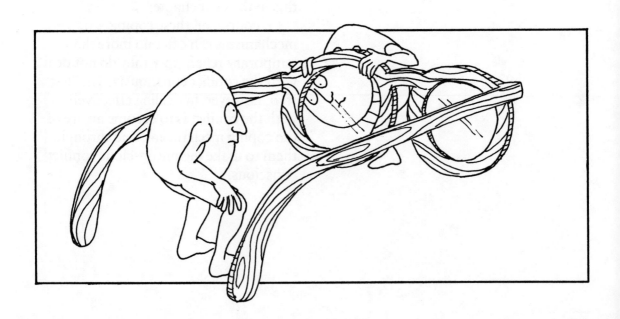

Depending on how aware I am of my own feelings toward myself, to some degree I see you as you are, and to some degree I project onto you the way I feel about myself. To put it diagramatically:

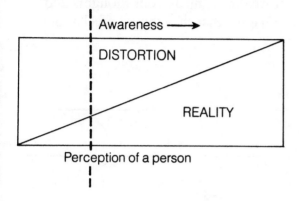

In words: Every time I have a feeling about you, my feeling is partly what you are "really" like and partly my distortion of how you act and feel. The more aware I am of how I see myself, the more my perceptions are toward the right of the diagram — that is, most of my perception is realistic. The more unaware I am of my own self-concept, the more my perceptions will be toward the left side of the diagram — that is, most of my perception is a distortion, an expression of what is inside of me that I am not letting myself know about.

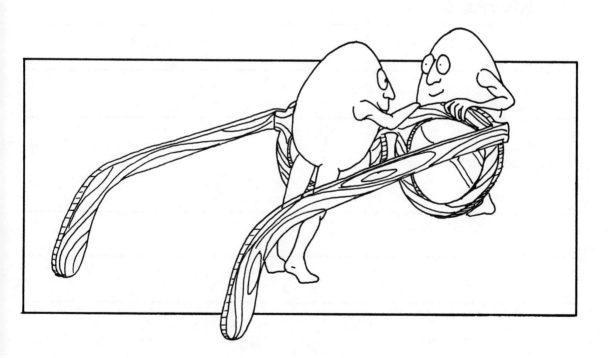

ACTIVITY 20. Projection

PART A

Better to just write down the first thing that pops into your head.

1. Think of three categories of people — your boss, your spouse or closest friend, and people in general — observing your every move, knowing all your thoughts and movements of the past week. What do you imagine that they think or feel about you?

Your boss:

_____ 1. _____

_____ 2. _____

_____ 3. _____

Your spouse or closest friend:

_____ 1. _____

_____ 2. _____

_____ 3. _____

People in general:

_____ 1. _____

_____ 2. _____

_____ 3. _____

PART B

Now think of how *you* feel about yourself, knowing all your own thoughts and movements. To the left of each of the nine statements above that you imagined other people would think about you, put a number from 1 to 6 indicating the degree to which you agree with each statement. The numbers mean:

Disagree 1 2 3 4 5 6 **Agree**

For example, if you feel that your boss would think or feel that you are confused, you wrote:

Your boss:

_____ 1. *You are very confused.* _____

And if *you* feel strongly that you are very confused, then place a 6 to the left of the item:

__6__ 1. *You are very confused.* _____

Do this with each statement.

PART C

1. The items with the higher numbers represent possible projections. It may be that you are attributing to other people the way you feel about yourself.

2. Does this exercise help to clarify the use of projection? How does it help you understand your relationships better?

RESPONSES: Activity 20. Projection

QUESTIONS. Mechanisms

_____ 1. A boss who surrounds herself only with yes-men or yes-women who admire her decisions may be compensating for lack of feeling (a) significant, (b) competent, (c) likeable.

_____ 2. If I think that everyone feels like a phony, I may be (a) identifying, (b) compensating.

_____ 3. If I feel that no one pays any attention to me or cares about me, and I do not feel important, I may be (a) projecting, (b) displacing.

_____ 4. One reason I may feel that people are too rigid is that I am (a) identifying, (b) displacing.

_____ 5. A wife who marries a man who declares his love for her often, and who demands that he keep telling her that she is loved, may be compensating for the lack of feeling (a) significant, (b) competent, (c) likeable.

_____ 6. A person who goes to a psychotherapist may be attempting to compensate for (a) lack of presence, (b) lack of self-control, (c) lack of self-awareness.

Answers: baa bcc

Compensation

Compensation is the process through which I try to get you to make up for the deficiencies I feel I have. *I do this without realizing that I am doing it.* For example, if I do not feel significant, I seek out people who feel that I am an important person and who pay attention to me. In this way, I hope to avoid the discomfort of facing my feelings of insignificance.

I use the mechanism of compensation to the degree that I am not self-aware. If I am self-aware, then I know when I am attempting to get others to compensate for my own lack of good feelings toward myself. It is when I am not self-aware that I may use compensation. Every relationship is partly realistic and partly a compensation.

As soon as the Element S scores were posted, the group focused on Harry and Alice, because their use of projection and compensation provided a deeper insight into their relationship. Alice, who did not feel respected by Harry, felt herself to be incompetent. Harry, who felt that Alice did not like him, did not like himself and projected that Alice also did not like him. He became angry and sad over it. Actually, Alice did like Harry. After the situation was clarified, Harry felt much more relaxed around Alice and more open to seeing that she liked him. She was involved in the same distortion over being seen as competent. Both Harry and Alice started to realize how they repeated the same pattern with their families and friends.

There are two difficulties that limit the use of the mechanism of compensation. (1) If I look to you to make up for my deficiency, I demand that you continue to feel that I am, for example, competent. I may become threatened and angry if you ever stop; because if you do, I may have to face my feeling of incompetence once again. (2) Compensation can never offer more than temporary relief. It is not a permanent solution. No matter how many awards and promotions I get, they will not make me happier for long if I still feel incompetent. the permanent solution is to deal with the cause of my problem, my own personal feelings about myself, rather than to try to control how you feel about me.

If I see a distorted picture of the stars through the lens on my telescope, it does not help to try to adjust the stars.

Measures of compensation are derived from comparing how I behave or feel toward myself with how I want *you* to behave or feel toward me. "You" includes people in general, my partner, and my ideal job. That measure means: "I don't feel good about myself in certain ways. To compensate, I want people (or you, or my job) to behave and feel toward me the way that I do not behave and feel toward myself."

I was training some prison guards on how to deal with inmates. There were two types of guards: the "old bulls," who were tough and experienced, who went into the cells and took knives away from tough cons; and the social workers from the local university. Unexpectedly, the "old bulls" were the more effective group therapy leaders for the inmates, although their knowledge of group principles was considerably inferior to that of the social workers. Interviews revealed the reason: Most inmates were in prison because they did not control their violent impulses. They saw the old bulls as capable of compensating for their uncontrolled aggressive impulses by containing them. They could therefore relax and attend to the group sessions. The same compensation was not provided by the social workers. The inmates saw them as too permissive and not willing or capable of being the external enforcer. Their resulting anxiety prevented them from focusing on the group therapy.

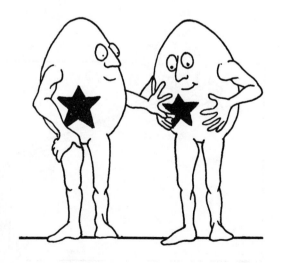

ACTIVITY 21. Compensation

PART A

Complete the following statement for ten of your friends or acquaintances. "Things would be better between us if only you would...."

Friend

_____ _____	1.	_____
_____ _____	2.	_____
_____ _____	3.	_____
_____ _____	4.	_____
_____ _____	5.	_____
_____ _____	6.	_____
_____ _____	7.	_____
_____ _____	8.	_____
_____ _____	9.	_____
_____ _____	10.	_____

Now look over your sentence completions and decide how true they would be if they completed this sentence:

"Things would be much better between us if only *I* would. . . ." For each of the ten responses, write down a number on the line in front of the response. The numbers mean:

Disagree 1 2 3 4 5 6 **Agree**

For example, if you put down:

"Things would be much better between us if only you would:

_____ 1. *Have more respect for my ability."*

Then use that response this way:

"Things would be much better between us if only I would have more respect for my ability."

If you feel that the statement is essentially accurate, place a 5 or 6 in front of this response. For example,

" __*5*__ 1. *Have more respect for my ability."*

Do this for all ten responses.

PART C

1. The completed sentences with the higher numbers represent possible areas of compensation. You want other people to relate to you in ways you are not relating to yourself.

2. Does this exercise help you to clarify the use of compensation? How does it help you understand your relationships better?

PART D

1. Explore the relationship between truth and choice on the one hand, and the mechanisms of projection, displacement, identification, and compensation on the other.

2. Shut your eyes. Reflect on the concepts of coping mechanisms—projection, displacement, identification, and compensation. Write down your most significant reactions.

PERSONAL MEANING OF THE LENS

SEGUE

My attempt to deal with the parts of my self-concept that I do not like leads me to distort the world in various ways. I may project my feelings into you or displace them onto you or see you having the same feelings toward yourself as I have toward myself (reflection), or I may try to get you to compensate for what I do not give to myself. I do all these acts without awareness so that I do not have to deal with my unacceptable feelings.

I can become aware of which mechanisms I use by observing that I rigidify my perceptions and fail to see others as individuals. I may see everyone as not liking me, for example, when it is probably true that individuals vary considerably in their feelings toward me. My feelings keep me from seeing other people clearly.

Once I identify which mechanisms I use for what types of issues, I have a good opportunity to deal directly with my feelings, drop the need to distort, and see people more accurately.

I have another way of dealing with an internal difficulty that I am not aware of, do not want to deal with, and therefore deny or repress: I may *embody* it — that is, convert it into a physical symptom.

Having this understanding about behavior, feelings, and my self-concept, I am in a position to understand much more about health and illness.

Let's take a look at how we can take charge of our own health.

chapter seven

HEALTH AND ILLNESS:
How I Choose Specific Illnesses

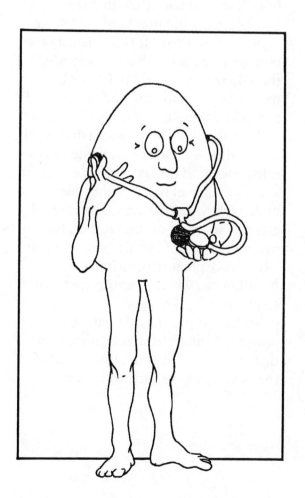

Understanding illness offers a huge potential payoff. The amount of discomfort and the money and time lost due to illness and injury can be staggering, and any improvement in the situation promises a handsome reward.

One major way to reduce sickness is to enlist my creative capacities to prevent and treat my own illnesses. If I am able to detect when I am becoming ill, and if I know why I am giving myself the illness, then I may be able to prevent it. Beyond prevention, when I learn to express my full potential I experience the joy that motivates me to be robust and healthy.[24]

EMBODIMENT

In addition to the coping mechanisms described in Chapter Six that I use to deal with unconscious conflicts or unacceptable feelings, I also use my body to cope. If I do not want to face a particular conflict, I may "embody" it. Since I am exploring the implications of the choice principle, I assume that I choose to be ill, I choose which kind of illness I will give myself, and I have the ability to heal myself once I am sick. This choice, I recall, may be either conscious or unconscious.

I realize that this is not a widely accepted idea in the medical profession, but I shall explore it to see whether I find it useful. If it does not prove of value I can always drop it and return to the more popular belief that assumes much less responsibility for both contracting a disease and for effecting a cure.

Because this is not a typical way of seeing things, I must keep in mind constantly that saying "I choose to be ill" is not an accusation. It does not mean that I am bad or careless or evil or immoral. It does not mean that I should feel guilty or ashamed, or that no one should help me. It simply states what happened, and it allows me to better pursue the possibility of understanding what happens.

Seeing illness as a choice allows me to view it as a learning opportunity. This lens allows me to see illness as my body's way of telling me that there is a conflict in my life that I am not letting myself be aware of. If I can identify the conflict and deal with it consciously, then there is no necessity for my body to embody it, and I may be on the road to healing myself.

As with all the phenomena discussed so far, illness at bottom is related to the self-concept. If I do not feel adequate in some area, I feel that I cannot deal effectively with that area. Therefore, I attempt to avoid or distort it. If, for instance, I do not feel significant, I may experience great frustration and humiliation, which I repress (put "out of my mind"). This may lead to some physical symptoms. If I come to terms with my feelings of significance, I may deal with them directly, thus avoiding the need to repress and to become ill.

BODY AWARENESS

Essential to any ability to control my health is an awareness of my own body. My body constantly sends me unlimited numbers of messages, and most of them pass me by. By and large, I have little awareness of how my body moves; of how it is situated in the field of gravity; of what muscles function when I make certain movements; of which muscles I use to move me; how my organs are crowded, or free, as I stand in certain ways; or of the uneven distribution of weight as I stand or move.

Injury and Body Image

If I am not aware of my body, then I am not aware of me. If I am not conscious of the position of a certain body part, then that part of me, and probably some of its functions, is not integrated with my being. This is the key to injuries, especially in sports. If I am not aware of the location of my ankle while I am running, my ankle is available to outside agents for injury.

Jim Brown, the famous football running back, reported that before each game he imagined all the possibilities. In his fantasy, he would see what would happen if, for example, he ran off tackle and the middle linebacker broke through the blocker and tackled him. He also would see all the other possibilities. By the time the game started, he had already essentially played it. In 119 professional games, during most of which he carried the ball at least twenty times, he missed only one game because of injury.[25]

If I know where all the parts of my body are all the time, then I can position them to fit the situation. If I do not know where they are, then these parts are vulnerable. This is probably why I tend to injure the same part repeatedly.

One important reason why I might withdraw my awareness from a particular body part is fear. Perhaps I injured that part, and I lost confidence in it even after it was healed. Perhaps I feel ashamed of some part, or I feel it looks ugly and undesirable in some way, and I detach myself from it. Perhaps I contracted part of my body to protect myself from a blow and kept it contracted, so that there is little feeling there. A simple exercise will help me construct a map showing which parts of my body I am most aware of and which parts I am least aware of.[26]

ACTIVITY 22. Body Position

1. Lie on your back, relax, and take a deep breath. Feel your body on the floor. Does the left side touch the floor in the same way as the right side, or is one side higher, or lighter, or broader?

2. Imagine a straight line starting on top of your head, going between your eyes down to your feet. Does it land halfway between your feet or does it go off to one side? Can you sense where it goes off center? Is your head on straight—that is, directly over your spinal column?

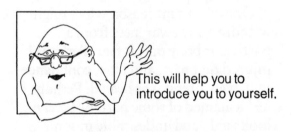

This will help you to introduce you to yourself.

3. Sense where your body is raised off the floor—for example, the small of the back. See if you can let it go and lie straighter. Note your shoulders and pelvis. Are they straight or tilted?

4. Slowly rise. Now exaggerate all the aberrations you felt on the floor. If your head was tilted, tilt it more. If one arm stuck out to the side, stick it out further.

5. When you are in this position, see whether any feelings or old memories arise. The characteristic position of your body usually is the result of spending a great deal of time in that position. Often, for example, people with raised shoulders feel fear and sometimes recall being startled by someone who caught them in a forbidden act.

6. Resume normal posture and reflect on all the information in your body that you rarely use. Write your primary responses on the next page.

RESPONSES: Activity 22. Body Position

Trauma

Often, as the result of early physical or emotional trauma, I remove awareness or consciousness from a certain part of my body. If I broke a leg when I was young, I may have shifted my weight to the other leg and then compensated by readjusting my upper body to balance the lower body. When the leg was healed I may have continued not to trust it and to make the imbalances permanent.

The parts of my body that I feel unaware of are the parts most likely to be injured. Because I am not aware of their location, I am not as able to protect them.

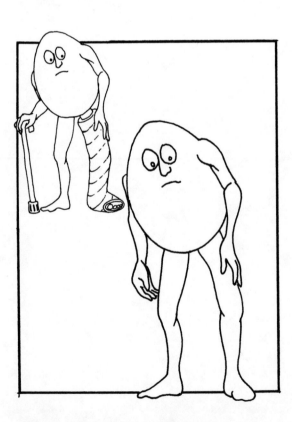

You may be surprised.

ACTIVITY 23. Body Awareness

1. Lie on your back. Relax, breathe. Feel your body into the floor and see if it feels different after your internal meditation of the last activity.

2. Picture a paint brush. Select any substance you wish for doing an imaginary painting of your body.

3. Imagine painting your body starting at the top of your head and going from side to side. Do this until you have gone all the way to the bottom of your feet. Then roll over and imagine painting your back side.

4. When you have finished, sit up.

5. Which parts could you feel clearly and which parts were difficult to sense? Are the difficult parts associated with any specific events in your life?

6. Did you miss painting any part of your body? Your ears? Your genitals? The soles of your feet?

7. Reflect on how conscious you are of yourself. How might your lack of awareness of certain parts be affecting your life?

RESPONSES: Activity 23. Body Awareness

BODYMIND

What I think affects how I feel. Although there has been a great deal of research on this point, I can believe it much more if I can experience it myself.

ACTIVITY 24. Bodymind

1. Relax and shut your eyes.

2. Imagine a fresh lemon on a cutting board. Watch a sharp knife slice through the lemon, and see the juice squirt out from the lemon. Experience this as clearly as you can.

3. Notice what is happening in your mouth. Are you salivating? Can you feel any physical or physiological changes?

4. Notice what happened to you. Reflect on the fact that there was no lemon, no cutting board, no knife. Whatever physical changes occurred happened as a result of your thoughts. Can you think of other examples of how your thinking affects your physical or physiological functions?

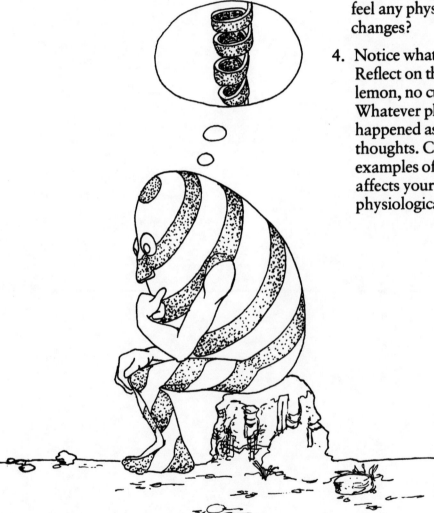

RESPONSES: Activity 24. Bodymind

Typically I experience each feeling in a different part of my body. Some Eastern disciplines feel that there are certain universal locations: love is felt in the chest and heart area; anger is felt in the stomach; and so on. This may or may not be true. This is what mine looks like.

ACTIVITY 25. Feelings Map

1. Lie or sit in a comfortable position. Relax and take three deep breaths.

2. Imagine a time when you were very hurt. Experience it as strongly as you can. Feel all the feelings you felt then.

3. (Pause 60 seconds.) Notice where in your body you feel it most. Put your hand on that part of the body.

4. (Pause 60 seconds.) Remove your hand and take a deep breath.

5. Repeat this procedure for anger, loving, jealousy, fear, being loved, lying, withholding, and being sexually attracted.

6. Notice where each emotion is located in the body. Are any emotions felt in the same place? Are some feelings located in more specific areas and some more general, or located in more places?

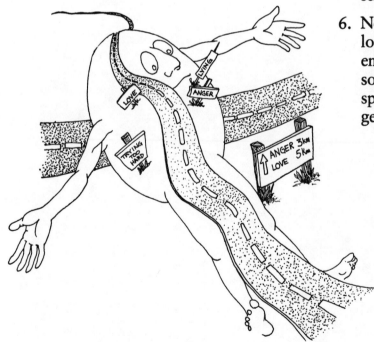

RESPONSES: Activity 25. Feelings Map

Self-Prevention

The practical advantage of discovering the body locations of my emotions comes when I reverse the process. If, for example, I find that my stomach tightens when I am withholding, then whenever I feel my stomach tighten, possibly this is because I am withholding something and am not aware of it. If I become aware of it, then my stomach can relax.

From this experience it is a short leap to seeing that if I have complex or important feelings that I am not dealing with and if these feelings persist over time, my body may develop tensions. Furthermore, these tensions could become chronic and could cause more serious symptoms and, ultimately, illness.

Specificity

An illness is my attempt to resolve a conflict, a life problem. Giving myself an illness has a payoff. It may allow me to quit work, to take a rest, to avoid responsibility, to postpone deadlines, to be waited on, to get attention, or to be given sympathy, flowers, and bon-bons.

Specific diseases have specific payoffs. Headaches give me a reason not to think; arthritis prevents me from moving or striking out, a heart attack results in my being taken care of.

ACTIVITY 26. Illness

Let's see if all of this fits your experience.

1. Think of all the illnesses you have had and the payoff you received for each. What are the differences in payoffs for each illness?

2. Do you recall what events, or perhaps unconscious conflicts, you were having in your life just prior to the onset of the illness? (Remember: This is not an exercise in blaming, simply an attempt to understand.)

3. Does it make sense of say that each conflict was primarily one of either inclusion, control, or openness? Consider this possibility.

4. Write down your immediate reactions on the next page. If any other thoughts come to you later, jot them down at the bottom of the page.

RESPONSES: Activity 26. Illness

WHICH ILLNESS?

Organ systems each have specific functions. Children's anatomy books often refer to the nervous system as the communications system of the body; to the circulation system as the body's transportation system; to the skin as the body's city limits, its boundary; to the excretory system as the garbage disposal; and so on. This is more than just a metaphor.

The key to understanding which illness I will choose is realizing that within my body is a physical parallel to all my personal issues. My struggles to control my world, for example, are paralleled by the muscular and nervous systems that control my body. Lining up which organ systems correspond to which life issues is the key to understanding why I choose certain illnesses. The issues may be classified by using inclusion, control, and openness.

If I look at my relation to my body in the same way I look at my relation to you, I have a basis for specifying what illness I choose. If I use my body to express an unconscious conflict about inclusion, for instance, I will express it through an illness of one or more of the organ systems that deal with including my body in the world.[27]

Inclusion Illness

On the physical level, inclusion refers to the boundaries between myself and the rest of the world. Therefore, it deals primarily with:

- *the periphery of my body*
  the skin
  the sense organs (eyes, ears, nose, and mouth);

- *the systems of the body that exchange with the environment*
  the respiratory system, which takes in oxygen and gives out carbon dioxide
  the digestive-excretory system, which exchanges food and feces with the environment.

My attitudes about these organs are related to my attitudes about being included by others.

Illnesses of the skin, senses, respiration, or digestion-excretion are expressions of out-of-awareness conflicts about inclusion. If I am unconsciously conflicted about inclusion, I may develop hives or acne or shinges or rashes. This keeps people away from me.

If I am uncomfortable being in proximity to people, I may not see them clearly until they are ten feet away — that is, I become farsighted. Or if I am comfortable with close friends but afraid of strangers, I may see things clearly up to a few feet away and then see only a blur — that is, I become nearsighted.

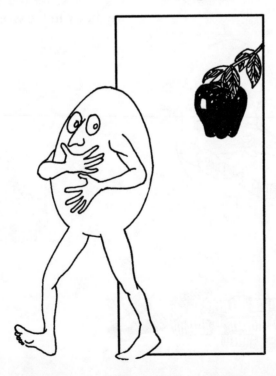

Even Eyesight!?

If I do not want to hear what people have to say, I may make myself deaf. Many deaf people did not listen before they became deaf.

If I do not feel significant (inclusion) as a child, I may fail to inhale the normal amount of air. My chest becomes too narrow, my rib cage is small, and I am more susceptible to respiratory illnesses because I do not breathe fully. If I am anxious that if I exhale I may never get another breath, my rib cage becomes too deep. I am barrel-chested. I believe that if I breathe normally I will be forgotten.

Eating has an inclusion element to it. Too little or too much food carries an implication of caring and being paid attention. In addition, there is a control element present in digestion, especially with regard to the power struggle around "eating everything on your plate," and especially when excretion and toilet training become involved. Diseases of digestion and excretion represent a transition between problems of inclusion and problems of control.

Cancer is primarily an inclusion disease, although the location of the cancer also is significant. Cancer patients are often extremely low on wanting to be included in activities with other people. They have little desire to be in a group but rely on their own resources.

The general sense of the traditional cancer patients is of those who have given up, who have opted out of this life. Sometimes it appears that they have a strong will to live, but there is probably a strong unconscious part of them that wishes to die. Inferences could be made about public figures who contracted cancer and died quickly after an event that could be interpreted as existentially terminal. For example, Senator Joe McCarthy died of cancer shortly after being censured by his Senate colleagues and losing his power. Hubert Humphrey died of cancer after he lost his final bid to become president.

Because all my childhood training was opposite this view, I must remember that *saying that I choose an illness is not an accusation*. It is not saying that I should be ashamed, or guilty, or anything negative. It is simply an attempt to understand what is happening. I must remind myself of this constantly; otherwise the idea remains so foreign to me that I will not even consider exploring the possibility that I chose my illness.

ACTIVITY 27. Inclusion Illness

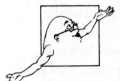

Let's take a closer look.

1. Have you had any "inclusion illnesses"? Do you recall the circumstances preceding the illness?

2. Have you had more than one inclusion illness?

3. Are inclusion illnesses the ones you are most likely to get if you become ill? Are inclusion illnesses prominent in your life? (Check your Element B, Element F, and Element S.)

4. Did you have acne during your adolescent years? If so, do you recall any inclusion concerns at that time, such as getting accepted by the "right" group or wearing the "right" clothes?

Control Illness

The organ systems that I use to control my body are the muscles and skeleton, the nervous system, and the endocrine glands. These are the systems that I use to cope with the world, to protect myself, and to assert myself.

When I embody an out-of-awareness conflict about control, I give myself a disease of these systems. It is more difficult for me to move when I have arthritis—especially arthritis of the joints of the legs. Arthritis of the hands is a way to physically prevent myself from striking out.

Headaches are a milder form of nervous disorder. I have headaches when I feel incompetent. They often occur when I am about to go to a meeting unprepared, or when there is so much going on that I do not understand what is happening.

The tragic control illnesses are spinal disease and "accidents" that result in spinal damage. Spinal accidents frequently result from macho activities, which often reflect conflict about competence. These activities mainly involve riding motorcycles, driving automobiles, or diving, and mainly it is young men who are injured.

Here's a personal experience.

Tucker called from a hospital in Los Angeles. "I am paralyzed from the neck down. I have Guillain-Barre syndrome and I have no idea why." This was a startling revelation. Tucker was an extraordinarily strong, vigorous, active man.

"I would like to work with you," said Tucker.

"I would suggest that you do imagery in which you imagine going into your body, go down your spinal cord and see if you can fix what is wrong.[28] Do it two or three times a day. And think about the possibility that you have an unconscious conflict about control."

"Can't think of anything," he said.

"You might start with this. You are one of the few people I've met in a group whom I was afraid of."

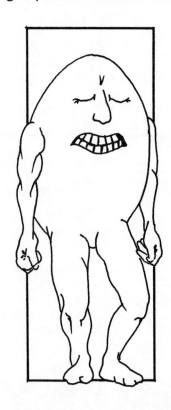

"I'm astonished," he replied. Then he began to work on his feelings about strength. He prided himself on having a strong body. By being good at "fighting, fucking, and football," he felt he could get people to like him. Apparently his conflict about that belief was something he did not allow in his awareness. These realizations led him to do important therapeutic work in order to deal with these feelings.

He proceeded with both the imagery and the investigation of his feelings about control. In two weeks he had a relapse and got worse.

Three weeks after the relapse, I received a call from him. "I can walk again. I'm in Seattle. The doctors said it's the fastest recovery they had seen. I just kept doing the imagery and the work on control, even though I had a bad time at first. It worked."

Openness Illness

Openness and likeability are expressed in the body through love (the heart) and sex (the genitals). My circulatory system expresses my state of affection. I often use such phrases as "broken-hearted," "I open my heart to you," "sweetheart," "heartthrob." The relation of the heart and circulatory system to affection explains why when love is good, all the world is right, and why when love is bad or absent, nothing seems to work. My blood circulation nourishes my whole body. If it is constricted, my entire organism has difficulty in getting sufficient nourishment. If blood flows freely through a relaxed and open heart, my whole self is well fed.

Genital ailments such as vaginitis and herpes, as well as syphilis and gonorrhea, often occur at embarrassing moments. They occur when I am not aware of a conflict over love, particularly the sexual aspect of love. If I feel sexual guilt, or if religious or social mores are being violated, and I am not letting myself be aware of my conflict, then I am most likely to have genital illnesses.

The tragic diseases of openness are heart disease and heart failure. Heart attacks often occur when I am conflicted over my love relations.

This insight does not preclude your compassion for me if I become a heart patient. The fact that I have unconsciously chosen this difficulty means that the disease can be turned into an important learning experience. My body is telling me that I have some conflict in the area of openness and likeability or lovability that I am not letting myself be aware of. Awareness may lead to greater self-knowledge and control of my life.

Here's another experience I had with a very close friend.

Murray had a massive heart attack in Europe. There was extensive damage and he narrowly missed death. I wrote to him and invited him to entertain the possibility that his condition was related to an unconscious conflict about openness and affection. Several weeks later I received his reply.

"I received your letter and as usual it was very irritating. As I thought of it, I realized that I probably was feeling guilty about the affair I'd been having for two years. I asked my wife to fly over, and we talked for several days. She revealed that she had been hating me for two years. As we talked, it became clear that we no longer wanted to be together. It was an amicable parting, but a definite separation nonetheless.

"Two months later I returned to the doctor for an examination and he refused to believe the evidence. The damage was almost totally repaired. I am now playing racquetball twice a week and feeling great."

At this point, let me remind you that you are simply entertaining these ideas about illness. If they do not make sense to you, if you do not find them of value, ignore them. If you do find them a useful way to look at illness or if you find them of partial value, you are, of course, free to use them to that degree.

ACTIVITY 28.
Control and Openness Illness

1. Have you ever had a "control or openness illness"? Do you recall the circumstances preceding the illness?

2. Have you had more than one control illness? more than one openness illness?

3. Are control illnesses the ones you are most likely to get if you get sick? openness illnesses? Are these areas prominent in your life? (Check Element B, Element F, and Element S.)

4. Think of examples from your experience that either support or question the idea of classifying diseases into the areas of inclusion, control, and openness.

RESPONSES: Activity 28. Control and Openness Illness

SEX

Although not an illness, sexual intercourse is also an area where the body expresses unconscious conflicts. Sexual expression is primarily an openness function, although various aspects of the sexual act parallel inclusion and control.

Inclusion problems refer to the initial phases of intercourse—feelings about penetration. If I am a male with problems of inclusion of which I am unaware, I probably would have difficulties with *potency*. My conflict over whether to penetrate would be reflected in the enervation of my penis and its unwillingness to enter. If I am a woman with inclusion problems, my tight, dry vagina would express my unwillingness to receive a penis.

The control aspect of the sexual act centers around *orgasm*. Orgasm timing expresses control and willingness to surrender fully. I may withhold orgasm in an attempt to make it easy for you to feel unsatisfactory as a sexual satisfier. I may come quickly and create conditions within which you will find it more difficult to have an orgasm. I may try to direct your physical movement or let you do the moving as an expression of our power relations with each other. When my relationship is in its control phase, orgasm usually is the area of sexual difficulty. When the control problem is clarified, the orgasm problem is alleviated.

The openness aspect of the sexual act is the *feeling* that follows completion of intercourse. This feeling may be anything from a flood of warm, affectionate, loving feelings to revulsion and thoughts such as "What am I doing here?" or "No, I won't take you to breakfast." The feeling depends, in part, on how well my heart and genitals are connected. Openness is the aspect of sex that is much better when there is a deep love between us.

SUMMARY

Table 5 summarizes the characteristics of inclusion, control, and openness.

TABLE 5. Manifestations of Inclusion, Control, Openness

	Inclusion	*Control*	*Openness*
Issue	In or Out	Top or Bottom	Open or Closed
Self-Concept	Significance	Competence	Likeability
Sexual Response	Potency	Orgasm	Feeling
Organ System	Skin Senses Respiratory Digestive-Excretory	Nervous Muscular-Skeletal Endocrine	Reproductive Circulatory
Extreme Illness	Cancer	Spinal Disease	Heart Trouble

THE POSITIVE

Knowing the basis of disease may certainly reduce my illness, absenteeism, and lack of energy on the job. The ability for early detection of the symptoms of disease, along with a knowlege of techniques for discovering the motivation for illness, may reduce drastically the frequency of my illnesses.

A more basic application of this information is to train myself to be aware of what I am feeling at all times so that I deal with conflicts as they arise and do not have to embody them. This, of course, requires a strengthening of my self-concept so that I do not fear facing any thought or feeling I may have.

Following the principle of choice, I stay healthy because I choose to. I choose to because I feel joyful and want to be healthy, and I feel joy whenever I am developing and using my creativity and potential human abilities and traits. This is my path to ultimate health.

ACTIVITY 29. Self-Health Imagery[29]

Here is a method for beginning to control your own health.

1. Find a comfortable spot, relax, shut your eyes, and take several breaths.

2. Locate a place in your body that does not feel good. It may be a present ache or pain or it may be a chronic area of difficulty.

3. Picture yourself getting very small and entering your body at any point you wish. See yourself go to the trouble spot and simply look around and see what is there.

4. Notice whether there is anything that is not the way you want it to be. If it is, set about to change it, if you want to.

5. If you can change it by yourself to the way you want it, that is best. If not, picture whatever you need—another person, a flashlight, dynamite, a magic wand, a wise person to give advice, Jesus, God, or whomever or whatever you feel will be helpful.

6. Continue this until everything in your body is the way you want it. Then gradually open your eyes and come back to the present.

7. Notice whether there is any change in the troubled part of your body. There is often considerable lessening of the pain if the imagery ended successfully. If it was not completed, the pain usually remains.[30]

8. How do the concepts of truth and choice relate to this concept of illness?

9. How does this concept help you to understand your behavior and the behavior of your coworkers in your job?

10. Shut your eyes and reflect on the ideas in this chapter—the notion that illness derives from unconscious conflicts, and the notion of inclusion, control, and openness illnesses. Did any of them seem useful to you? Open your eyes. On the next page, write down your most important reactions to this chapter.

RESPONSES: Activity 29. Self-Health Imagery

PERSONAL MEANING OF HEALTH AND ILLNESS

SEGUE

In addition to using coping mechanisms, I may also convert my unconscious conflicts into body symptoms and illness. The organ systems of my body that perform the functions that I am not dealing with consciously are the ones that become ill. If I am unconsciously conflicted about being in or out of a relationship or a job, for example, a part of my body concerned with boundaries (the skin, perhaps) will be the part that becomes diseased.

As I gain this insight, I have a better opportunity to control my own health. By regarding an illness symptom as my body's signal that there is some conflict that I am not aware of, I gain more understanding of myself as a whole, integrated person. I may use my ability to choose to discover the underlying causes of the conflict and therefore to deal more effectively with my health.

I now have more insight about behavior and feelings in general, and about how I feel about myself. I also have some good ideas about how I distort my perceptions and my relationships and how I use my body to defend myself against unwanted feelings. Along the way I have acquired several tools to strip away some of my unawareness and make some decisions to put myself more in charge of my life. I have learned the value of truth, especially self-truth, in this quest. I now see lying as a huge block to personal development, as an energy drain, and as a contributor to a mundane, boring life.

I shall now bring all this insight to understand my personal relationships. Earlier I became clearer about how I felt on the job. Now I would like to take a deeper look at what is really happening in my relationships.

chapter eight

RELATIONS:
Expression

 Now let's apply the qualities you need to achieve the first three truth levels— expressing how you feel, being aware of your reactions, and seeing what events led to your feelings, to better understand your relationships.

Relations are the basis of our existence. This is true in couples, friendships, and families. It is even true in organizations: No matter how much I speak of management structures, tables of organization, lines of authority, corporate policy, and patterns of communication, all organizational activity ultimately is carried out by one person relating to one or more other persons.

In this chapter, I examine one relationship in detail. I can use this exploration not only to learn about relationships but also to understand better how coping mechanisms function. I shall investigate a relationship with one person, perhaps a spouse, a supervisor, a friend, or an employee.

My orientation is this:

I am not a wife or a vice president or a secretary or a son. I am a person playing the role of wife or vice president or secretary or son.

Therefore, when I understand a relationship, I am actually understanding how people interact, not how roles interact.[31]

If I understand one relationship thoroughly, I understand all relationships.

The basic ingredients of all relations are the same. These ingredients are the same ones that were used before— behavior (inclusion, control, and openness) and feelings (significance, competence, and likeability). If I combine these factors in some new ways, I have a basis for understanding human relationships.

The questions I want to answer in this chapter are:

- How can you and I communicate better?

- What are the causes of incompatibility between us?

- How can I identify the causes of incompatibility?

- What types of dissatisfaction are there, and how can they be measured?

- What is the importance of seeing you accurately?

PARTNER

You may complete this chapter alone or with a partner. If you want to explore your relation with a partner — your spouse, close friend, boss, or work colleague — this chapter provides that opportunity.

If you choose to do it with a partner, it is of some help if he or she completes Element B; however, this is not necessary. The chapter is constructed so that you can complete it (1) alone, (2) with a partner who has filled out Element B, or (3) with a partner who has not.

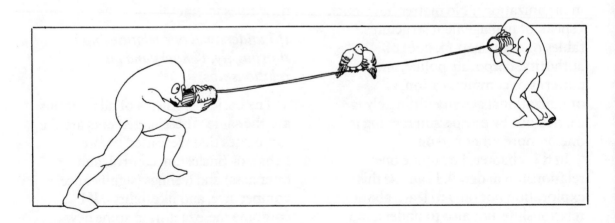

LEVELS OF TRUTH

In this chapter I will pursue an application of the levels of truth described on page 12. By examining one relation progressively through all levels, I may begin to understand what the concept of truth implies in a relationship and whether I find it to be a useful concept.

In this chapter I shall express how I see you (Level 1: "You are . . .") and how I feel toward you (Level 2: "About you I feel . . ."). Our discussion of these feelings will involve locating the events that led us to these feelings (Level 3: "Because . . .").

In Chapter Nine I shall investigate my defense or coping mechanisms (Level 4: "Which means . . .") and my self-concept (Level 5: "About me I fear . . .") in order to take me to the deepest level of understanding of a relationship.

Success at Levels 1 and 2 requires our willingness to communicate how we feel toward each other and an awareness of what those feelings really are.

COMMUNICATION "PROBLEMS"

Investigations of personal and organizational difficulties often conclude with the "discovery" that those difficulties are the result of the breakdown of communications. "If our messages were clearer, if we had the same meaning for our words, if we kept everyone informed, if we spoke of incipient difficulties before they became serious — then our problems would be alleviated."

This is a very appealing conclusion because it contains the seeds of truth. If all those troubles in communication were solved, certainly life would be much improved. However, this diagnosis has two shortcomings:

1. *The problem of communications is that we communicate too well, not that we do not communicate well enough. What is communicated is the feeling, not necessarily the words. If I am dissatisfied with you and I do not tell you of my dissatisfaction, you usually pick it up anyway and feel a vague uneasiness around me.*

Being a college professor, I reported to my new job at the university and made my proper call on the dean of the school. We exchanged pleasantries, described our research to each other, and parted cordially.

The next day a colleague confronted me. "What in the world did you tell the dean?" he asked. "He told me that after his talk with you, he had the impression that you thought his research was worthless."

"Nonsense," I protested, "I said nothing of the kind. I told him that I thought it was interesting. If we had a transcript of the talk, I am sure I could convince you that I am innocent."

All of a sudden, an insight hit me. I realized that I truly felt that the dean's research was worthless. In a court of law I would be acquitted because I did not *say* that the dean's research was worthless. But the dean had perceived correctly. I actually felt that way. What I communicated to the dean was my feeling more than my words.

2. Furthermore, communications difficulties are symptoms of problems, not the problems themselves. The problem is that, in some sense, I do not want to communicate. The reason lies in the interpersonal relationship. When that is resolved, it usually is not difficult to devise a way to communicate accurately.

To solve communications problems I must explore why we *do not want* to communicate. For that explanation I turn to the types of satisfaction and dissatisfaction that we have with each other and to the ways in which I distort messages — in other words, to an exploration of our compatibility.

ATMOSPHERE COMPATIBILITY

One popular theory of compatibility is reflected in the phrase, "Birds of a feather flock together." Birds of a feather do flock together — when "feather" refers to the atmosphere within which relationships occur. When you and I prefer the same atmosphere (or "climate," or "context") we have a common basis on which to resolve differences.[32]

Atmosphere incompatibility results from disagreement about the basis for resolving differences, not from the differences themselves.

Inclusion Atmosphere

High. An atmosphere of high inclusion occurs when we have a great deal of contact. High-inclusion atmosphere describes a situation in which we communicate, meet, and interact with each other a great deal. Work teams or people who must work closely together and reach decisions jointly are examples of a high-inclusion atmosphere.

Low. An atmosphere of low inclusion describes a situation in which our contact is very low. Meeting, communicating, even seeing each other is minimal. Jobs in which we each have our own task and work at it alone in a private office are examples of a low-inclusion atmosphere.

Use how your body feels to fill in the number.

ACTIVITY 30.
Inclusion-Atmosphere Preference

In the box below, place a number between 0 and 9 indicating your preferred inclusion atmosphere. Nine means the highest inclusion atmosphere; zero means the lowest.

Inclusion atmosphere incompatibility occurs when I like a high-inclusion atmosphere and you prefer a low-inclusion atmosphere. I want to get together and interact, while you want to be left alone. Our difference is similar to that between extroverts and introverts. In marriage, this difference is seen when the wife wants to go out at night with friends (high inclusion) while the husband wants to stay home and watch television (low inclusion).

The difficulty in this kind of incompatibility becomes evident when we have conflicts. I want to solve the conflicts through interaction; you want to solve them through isolated individual action. Our methods for resolving conflicts are so different that we have little basis for coming to agreement.

Control Atmosphere

High. An atmosphere of high control exists where there is a strict hierarchy, a structure, clear lines of authority, and an expectation of giving and taking orders. Plans typically are made far ahead of time. The military is an excellent example of a high-control atmosphere. The lines of control are quite explicit. Wearing bars or stripes keeps the hierarchy unmistakable.

Low. A low-control atmosphere exists where there is a minimal hierarchy, where we each have approximately equal decision-making power, or where that power shifts from me to you, depending on the situation. Plans are made at the last minute; preference is given to "going with the flow." Truly democratic or laissez-faire organizations have an atmosphere of low control.

ACTIVITY 31.
Control-Atmosphere Preference

In the box below, place a number between 0 and 9 indicating your preferred control atmosphere. Nine means the highest inclusion atmosphere; zero means the lowest.

You might want to read over the descriptions again, then use body feeling to arrive at a number.

Control-atmosphere incompatibility occurs when I want a clear power structure with everything planned out ahead of time, and you want an equalitarian structure with decisions made only when absolutely necessary. Disciplinarian versus permissive, and authoritarian versus democratic, are expressions of control-atmosphere incompatibility. Again, the problem of working together does not arise from disagreement.

Jimmy and Martha went on vacation. Martha wanted to plan out the trip in detail. She wanted to decide where they would spend each day, get reservations ahead of time, and call AAA for strip maps of the best roads to take. Jimmy wanted to get in the car and go anywhere they wanted to go. He wanted to look at the scenery and change his mind several times if that felt right.

The most he would compromise was to make plans only on the condition that they could be changed at any time. That was not satisfactory for Martha. She wanted the certainty that the plans would prevail. For her the plans became the authority. For Jimmy the authority remained with him and Martha.

Naturally, their vacations were rarely pleasurable—not because of what they did but because of their disagreement on the process of how it should be done.

The difficulty arises because I do not agree with you on *how conflicts are to be resolved.* I want the conflict resolved by a decision from the person with the most power. You want the conflict negotiated by everyone equally.

Openness Atmosphere

High. An atmosphere of high openness occurs when we relate to each other in an open way. Examples: cottage industries where people work and live together in a community; a team of social workers who examine their own relations as they work with other people; a family where members share their intimate feelings.

Low. Low-openness atmosphere exists in a corporation where there is little openness, or where personal relations on or off the job are discouraged. This is often expressed as a "businesslike" atmosphere in which our personalities are not considered.

ACTIVITY 32.
Openness-Atmosphere Preference

In the box below, place a number between 0 and 9 indicating your preferred openness atmosphere. Nine means the highest inclusion atmosphere; zero means the lowest.

More use of intuitive body feel is best.

Openness atmosphere incompatibility happens when I want a personal atmosphere and you want it impersonal. The problem, as in other areas, arises through our disagreement over how to resolve the differences. I want to consider the feelings of the people involved, while you want resolution on the basis of the "facts."

Simon, the department head, was aware of serious problems in the department and scheduled a meeting to "lay everything on the table." He knew people distrusted him, and he was critical of the way certain men were doing their jobs. He wanted to air all these grievances and clear things up. However, once at the meeting, Simon ran into strong opposition. Fred, a key section leader, did not want to discuss these matters; he simply would not express his opinions. The meeting failed. Later, Fred told the consultant that he did not feel it was safe to say what he was really feeling for fear of being fired.

The problem was openness atmosphere incompatibility. Regardless of the content of the differences between Simon and Fred, they could not resolve these differences. Simon wanted to be open; Fred did not. Their problems may have been easily solvable, but the two men were stuck on the rules for solution. During a workshop this fundamental difference became clear, and Simon and Fred saw that they did not necessarily disagree on the issue. They arranged to meet with a third person to work on the issue.

Failure to be aware of atmosphere differences leads to disagreement about each specific issue. Unless we recognize the existence of our atmosphere incompatibility and deal with it directly, we will have difficulty agreeing on the details of any project.

TABLE 6. Atmospheres

	High Atmosphere	Low Atmosphere
Inclusion	"Talk it through."	"Work it out individually."
Control	"Plan it and use structure."	"Go with the flow."
Openness	"Put cards on the table."	"Be discreet and judicious."

EXAMPLE: Atmosphere Compatibility

Assume atmosphere preference scores (from Activities 30–32) below for two partners, George and Laura, who are starting a new company.

	Atmosphere Preference Scores	
	George	Laura
Inclusion Atmosphere Preferred	9	2
INCLUSION ATMOSPHERE COMPATIBILITY (Difference) 7		
Control Atmosphere Preferred	1	9
CONTROL ATMOSPHERE COMPATIBILITY (Difference) 8		
Openness Atmosphere Preferred	6	2
OPENNESS ATMOSPHERE COMPATIBILITY (Difference) 4		

(The greater the difference, the greater the atmosphere incompatibility.)

When George and Laura get together to develop a management philosophy for their new company, they are going to have problems.

The inclusion-atmosphere compatibility score of 7 (out of a possible 9) is very large. George would probably like many meetings and much contact and interaction among company members, while Laura probably believes that people should work with as little contact among themselves as possible.

Their control-atmosphere compatibility score (8) also indicates a serious problem. Whereas George wants very low structure and few power differences, Laura believes that hierarchy and structure should be very clear and central in the organization. The control difference indicates a very high atmosphere incompatibility. George leans toward laissez-faire, while Laura prefers a more authoritarian structure.

In openness, Laura's score (2) is somewhat less than George's (6). George prefers an open atmosphere, while Laura prefers a more impersonal, businesslike setting. Their atmosphere compatibility score on openness (4) signifies that Laura and George have different conceptions of the atmosphere in which they want their business to function. George leans toward a personal, democratic interacting atmosphere, while Laura inclines toward a discreet, doors-closed, impersonal atmosphere. However, their difference here is considerably less marked than in the other two areas.

QUESTIONS. Atmosphere Compatibility

1. For each item: If you think George would be more likely to support it, put a check (✔) in George's column. If you think Laura would be more likely to support it, put a check (✔) in Laura's column.

George   Laura

Disagreements between boss and employee should be resolved by:
_____ _____ a. Boss's decisions.
_____ _____ b. Discussion with employees affected by decision.
_____ _____ c. Whoever feels more strongly about it.
_____ _____ d. Written directive from boss.

When office space is designed, it should have:
_____ _____ a. Separate offices with doors.
_____ _____ b. "Nests" of spaces with easy access to each other.
_____ _____ c. A room where employees can socialize on breaks.
_____ _____ d. Large meeting rooms where everyone can fit.

Bosses should have:
_____ _____ a. An "open door" policy.
_____ _____ b. A secretary to make appointments.
_____ _____ c. An assistant to screen people who want appointments.
_____ _____ d. Time to spend in work space of employees.

Off the job, fellow workers should:
_____ _____ a. Confide in each other if they wish.
_____ _____ b. Not have emotional involvements.
_____ _____ c. Avoid seeing each other socially; keep their business and social lives separate.
_____ _____ d. Discuss their feelings about the organization.

Bosses should make decisions:
_____ _____ a. Firmly and finally.
_____ _____ b. Definitely, but change them if it seems appropriate.
_____ _____ c. In consultation with others.
_____ _____ d. Strongly, and not admit errors or else their credibility is weakened.

Answers: George: bc   bcd   ad   ad   bc
          Laura: ad   a   bc   bc   ad

2. Later Laura and George were married and had several children. Indicate below what you think their attitudes toward children would be if they remained consistent with their atmosphere preference scores. Again, for each item, if you think Laura would be more likely to support it, put a check (✔) in Laura's column. If you think George would be more likely to support it, put a check (✔) in George's column.

George Laura

Children should:

____ ____ 1. Each have their own room with a lock.
____ ____ 2. Be told what to do.
____ ____ 3. Participate in family decisions.
____ ____ 4. Be allowed to witness affection between parents.
____ ____ 5. Be told everything they want to know.
____ ____ 6. Be given values.
____ ____ 7. Be encouraged to develop their own values.
____ ____ 8. Sit with adults at large meals.
____ ____ 9. Be told about sex by their parents.
____ ____ 10. Not discuss sex with their parents.
____ ____ 11. Share a large room together.
____ ____ 12. Be encouraged to have friends over.
____ ____ 13. Be satisfied with the reason, "because I say so."
____ ____ 14. Not be allowed to witness arguments between parents.
____ ____ 15. Be told what they should know for their age.
____ ____ 16. Have their own separate seating at large meals.
____ ____ 17. Be encouraged to stay overnight with friends.
____ ____ 18. Not know how parents feel about each other.

If children want something:

____ ____ 19. They should be asked "Why?"
____ ____ 20. Parents should grant it unless parents have a good answer to "Why not?"

Answers: George 3, 4, 5, 7, 8, 9, 11, 12, 17, 20
             Laura 1, 2, 6, 10, 13, 14, 15, 16, 18, 19,

ACTIVITY 33.
Atmosphere Compatibility

1. Define the concept of atmosphere compatibility until you are sure that you understand it.

2. Read each question on pages 200 and 201. Do you agree with the answers given? How would you *personally* react to the items in the questions? Discuss.

The examples bring these concepts to life.

3. Explain the statement, "Unrecognized atmosphere incompatibility leads to endless disagreement about specifics." Think of one example from your personal life and one example from your work experience for each kind of atmosphere incompatibility — inclusion, control, or openness.

4. Think of some suggestions for resolving situations of atmosphere incompatibility.

5. Does the concept of compatibility help you to understand your own personal life better? How? Does it help you to understand your work situation? How?

MEASUREMENT

Table 7 aids in computing the atmosphere compatibility between you and your partner. You may enter your scores as measured by the preference rating. By completing the tables, you can compute your atmosphere compatibility scores for inclusion, control, openness, and overall.

TABLE 7. Atmosphere Compatibility

PROCEDURE
1. Enter your Atmosphere Preference scores (pages 195 to 197) and those of your partner.
2. Subtract Atmosphere Preference scores to obtain Compatibility scores.
3. Add all three Compatibility scores to obtain Total Atmosphere Compatibility score.

	SELF	PARTNER
Inclusion Atmosphere Preference (from page 195)		
INCLUSION ATMOSPHERE COMPATIBILITY (DIFFERENCE)		
Control Atmosphere Preference (from page 196)		
CONTROL ATMOSPHERE COMPATIBILITY (DIFFERENCE)		
Openness Atmosphere Preference (from page 197)		
OPENNESS ATMOSPHERE COMPATIBILITY (DIFFERENCE)		
TOTAL ATMOSPHERE COMPATIBILITY		
Sum of INCLUSION, CONTROL and OPENNESS COMPATIBILITY)		

(A high score means high incompatibility.)

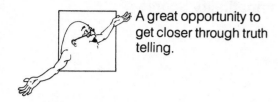
A great opportunity to get closer through truth telling.

ACTIVITY 34.
Atmosphere Compatibility Scores

1. Look at your compatibility scores.

2. Do these scores make sense from what you know of your relationship? Discuss each score with each other. Let this discussion go wherever it wants to — including old unfinished events and unsaid feelings. Use the scores as a springboard for an honest discussion of your relationship.

ROLE COMPATIBILITY

A second popular theory of compatibility is expressed in the phrase, "opposites attract." While this seems contradictory to "birds of a feather flock together," in fact it is quite complementary. Opposites attract when we are talking about the specific roles I take with respect to you. If you want to control people, for example, we will get along well if I want to be controlled. However, if I also want to control people, we may have some competitive difficulties. However, if we are concerned with the atmosphere within which we relate to each other, as described in atmosphere compatibility, then "birds of a feather" is more accurate.

Atmosphere compatibility refers to the context in which the interaction takes place. Role compatibility refers to the roles we take with respect to each other within that context.

Role incompatibility results from lack of complementarity of the role I take with respect to you.

In the example of Jimmy and Martha on vacation, atmosphere compatibility refers to *whether* plans are made or not—that is, whether the trip will be well planned or spontaneous. Role incompatibility may arise over *who* will make the plans.

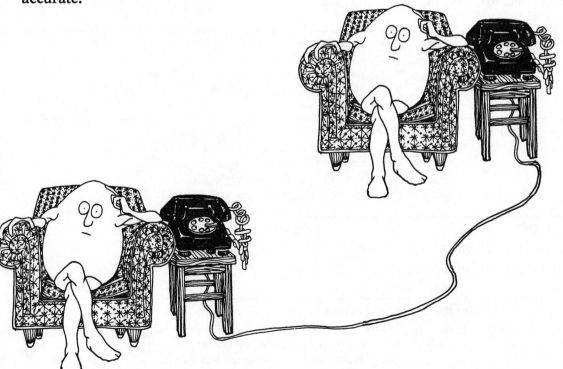

QUESTIONS. Role Situations

Below are some examples of hypothetical scores on Element B. In each case, a beginning statement is given for verbal interaction between two people. Complete the interactions by supplying a response that follows from their Element B scores.

CASE A	WIFE	HUSBAND
I Want to Include People	6	1
I Want People to Include Me	8	1

Wife: "John, let's have a weekly meeting of the family."
_____ 1. HUSBAND: a. Wonderful idea, dear.
                                 b. If you want to.
                                 c. I don't think it would be helpful.

Husband: "Harriet, I think it's better if we all work by ourselves."
_____ 2. WIFE: a. No, I think it's better if we get together.
                               b. Whatever you think is best.
                               c. I'm glad you feel that way.

CASE B	EMPLOYER 1	EMPLOYER 2	EMPLOYEE
I Want to Control People	8	3	2
I Want People to Control Me	1	9	7

Employer 1: "Bill, get that machine fixed right now."
_____ 3. EMPLOYEE: a. Yes, sir, right away.
                                   b. It doesn't need fixing.
                                 c. Are you sure that's what you want?

Employee: "Sir, what should I do next?" (Give one answer for each employer.)
_____ 4. EMPLOYER 1:   _____ 5. EMPLOYER 2:
                                   a. Finish this project by tomorrow.
                                   b. Whatever you think is most important.
                                 c. I'll ask my boss and get back to you.

CASE C	FATHER	SON
I Want to Control People	1	1
I Want People to Control Me	3	7

Father: "You've done this sort of thing before, so you just go ahead."
_____ 6. SON: a. Thank you.
                                 b. I'm not sure what you want done.
                                 c. Don't worry, Dad, you'll like the way I do it.

Son: "Father, I've got to get my report in by tomorrow. What should I do?"
—— 7. FATHER: a. I'll show you how to do it.
                              b. Don't bother me with it. Do it some way.
                              c. Has this happened before?

CASE D

	EMPLOYER	EMPLOYEE 1	EMPLOYEE 2
I Want to Be Open With People	6	9	2
I Want People to Be Open With Me	7	8	0

Employer: "Dan, I feel I can be open with you." (Give one answer for each employee.)
—— 8. EMPLOYEE 1   —— 9. EMPLOYEE 2:
                          a. I'm delighted. I feel the same about you.
                          b. All I want is for you to feel I'm doing a good job.
                          c. I hope my buddies don't care.

Employee 1: "Boss, my wife and I would like to talk to you about what is happening between us. Would you come to dinner at my house this Saturday night?"
—— 10. EMPLOYER: a. Delighted to come.
                          b. Sorry, Dan, I don't socialize after hours.
                          c. Have to check with my wife.

—— 11. EMPLOYEE 2 (hearing of this invitation):
                          a. They are asking for trouble.
                          b. Why didn't he invite me?
                          c. I would never do that.

CASE E

	HUSBAND	WIFE
I Want to Control People	7	9
I Want People to Control Me	2	1

Husband: "This is an important project. I want to be involved at every stage."
—— 12. WIFE: a. It will be easier if I finish it before consulting you.
                          b. I'll tell you what I'm doing every day.
                          c. Tell me how you want me to do it.

Wife: "Let me do it my way and it will be done right."
—— 13. Husband: a. I want to approve it before you begin.
                          b. I like your spirit. Go ahead.
                          c. Anything you want is OK.

Answers: ca   aac   bb   abac

Two Measures

I may measure my role compatibility with you by using our Element B scores. My "I control people" score (scale code 21), for example, should equal your "I want people to control me" score (scale code 24) for maximum compatibility.

This method is very useful if we do not know each other well. If we both complete Element B, we can estimate our role compatibilities in this way. This method is valuable if I want to build teams that will work well together, or if I want to predict how we would get along if we were to have a relationship.[32]

If we know each other, we can measure our role compatibility more precisely by completing an instrument with ourselves in mind. Rather than talking about people in general, as in Element B and Element F, I will answer for you specifically. You may do exactly the same thing for me. In this book I shall explore this method.

The instrument that accomplishes these ends is Element R: Relations.

There are two sources of dissatisfaction in a relationship:

Get (you to me): I do not like how you relate to me.

Do (me to you): I do not like myself when I relate to you.

Relations: Get

My feeling about you depends in part on what, in my opinion, I Get from you.

I may feel, for example, that you do not include me enough or that you control me too much or that you do not initiate enough openness. I also may feel that you do not think I am significant or competent, or that you do not like me.

Obviously, any of these feelings may have a severe impact on how we get along together and on how well we work together. These feelings may lead to hostility, anger, competition, or behind-the-back maneuvering; or they may lead to coldness, distance, sarcasm, mockery, or undermining. Such dissatisfactions are often the reason behind many cases of bad communication, lack of cooperation, and personal stress and anxiety.

I sometimes express personal dissatisfactions subtly, through such activities as going over your head, passive obstructionism, loss of motivation, unreliability, lack of loyalty, or leaving you.

In short, my dissatisfactions with relationships are a prominent source of problems, and it is not always obvious that these dissatisfactions affect the way we are together. But they do. When I grasp this fact, I can see all the problems listed above for what they are: symptoms, not problems. The problem lies in the relation between you and me. When this relation is negative, it is expressed in a rash of destructive ways.

It is therefore essential that in this chapter you and I explore the state of our relation — that is, behavior and feelings — to each other in detail, and with candor and openness. If we can resolve these issues, dozens of problems fade away without requiring effort.

By comparing how you relate to me with how I want you to relate to me, I derive a measure of how satisfied I am with your behavior toward me and with your feelings about me.

Melvin had worked for Helen for many years. There was always a bittersweet quality to their relationship. In many ways, Melvin and Helen were more like each other than like anyone else in the organization; yet they had never felt comfortable with each other. When they completed Element R for each other, they found that neither felt good in the other's presence. The underlying reasons seemed to be that Melvin did not feel respected by Helen, and that Helen did not feel liked by Melvin. When they compared their individual descriptions, they discovered their distortions. Both perceptions were denied. Helen felt that Melvin's work was of a very high caliber, perhaps sometimes even better than her own (which may have been a reason she did not express her admiration). Melvin had always liked Helen and had always felt sad that they had not gotten closer, but he was afraid of being rejected. With great relief, they began talking more openly. Several months later they report that they are working together far more effectively and feeling very good about their personal relationship.

My dissatisfaction occurs when you act either too much or too little in the areas of inclusion, control, and openness, and feel too much or too little in the areas of significance, competence, and likeability. Therefore, there are twelve sources of dissatisfaction I may have with you. Each of these becomes the name of a dimension. These dimensions are measured by Element R: Get.

TABLE 8. Dissatisfactions with What I GET from You

	...Include	...Control	...Are (Be) Open With
You___ me too much.	"Leave me alone."	"Don't order me around."	"Don't tell me your troubles."
I want you to___ me.	"Include me more."	"Tell me what you want me to do."	"Tell me what you feel."

	...Significant	...Competent	...Likeable
I am more___ to you than I want to be.	"Don't notice me so much."	"Don't expect me to know everything."	"Don't like me so much."
I want you to feel that I am more___ .	"Pay more attention to me."	"Have more respect for my abilities."	"Like me more."

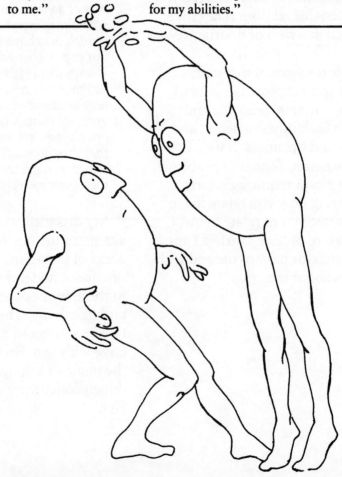

QUESTIONS. GET

I place the letter of my answer on the line at the left. The letters represent these attitudes:

(a) You include me too much.
(b) You control me too much.
(c) You are open with me too much.
(d) I want you to include me more.
(e) I want you to control me more.
(f) I want you to be open with me more.
(g) You feel that I am too significant.
(h) You feel that I am too competent.
(i) You like me too much.
(j) I want you to feel that I am more significant.
(k) I want you to feel that I am more competent.
(l) I want you to like me more.

Which of these attitudes is expressed by the following statements?

_____ 1. I wish you would leave me alone. I want more privacy. When the door is closed, stay out.

_____ 2. I want you to give me more direction. Tell me what to do and I'll do it. I don't like you to leave things up to me.

_____ 3. We talk sometimes but you want to keep things businesslike. I'd like you to want to know me better.

_____ 4. You never notice me. I get the feeling that I am of no importance to you.

_____ 5. You think I know much more than I do. I wish you didn't expect me to be able to answer all your questions.

_____ 6. It makes me uncomfortable that you like me so much when you hardly know me. I feel I can hurt your feelings too easily.

On the next few pages are a set of questions (Element R: Get). If you are doing this chapter with a partner both of you complete Element R: Get. If not, select a person you know well, either someone you work with (boss, colleague, employee, client) or someone you are personally close to (spouse, friend, parent, child). Place that person's name on page 214 in the lower left-hand corner on the line after "You _____."

ELEMENT R: Get

There are no "right" answers. The more honest I am, the more accurate will be the information I receive from Element R: Get.

First, I complete the column "The way it IS" for all items.

For each statement, I place a number from 1 to 6 on the line to the left of the item, in the appropriate column. The numbers indicate how much I agree with the statement.

Disagree 1 2 3 4 5 6 **Agree**

When I have finished, I return to the top of the column and respond to the same items for "The way I WANT it to be."

You _____

The Way It IS	The Way I WANT It to Be	
1		You spend time with me.
2		You are the dominant person when you are with me.
3		You are totally honest with me.
4		You join my group.
5		You have me do things you want done.
6		You confide in me.
7		You include me in your informal social activities.
8		You influence my actions.
9		You keep from getting too close to me.
10		You include me in your plans.
11		You take charge of things when I am with you.
12		You keep your private feelings to yourself.
13		You have me around you.
14		You have me do things the way you want them done.
15		You keep some things hidden from me.
16		You join me when I am doing things with other people.
17		You make the decisions when we are together.
18		You keep from me some things about yourself.
19		You are with me.
20		You tell me what to do.
21		You tell me everything important about you.
22		You include me in the things you do.
23		You let me do whatever I want to do.
24		You keep some things private.
25		You participate in my activities.
26		You order me around.
27		You have a close, open relationship with me.
28		You feel that I am important.
29		You feel that you cannot rely on my judgment.
30		You feel that I am important.
31		You feel that I am a significant individual.
32		You feel skeptical of my abilities.
33		You feel affectionate toward me.
34		You feel that I do not mean anything to you.
35		You admire my competence.
36		You feel personally close to me.
37		You feel neutral toward me.
38		You admire my abilities.
39		You feel personally distant from me.
40		You feel unconcerned about me.
41		You trust my abilities.
42		You feel bitter toward me.
43		You feel indifferent to me.
44		You feel suspicious of my competence.
45		You feel cordial toward me.
46		You are interested in me.
47		You trust my competence.
48		You are very friendly toward me.
49		You are intrigued by me.
50		You feel confidence in my abilities.
51		You feel cool toward me.
52		You are stimulated by me.
53		You feel that you can depend on my judgment.
54		You hate me.

ELEMENT R: GET Scoring

I *compare* my response to each item of Element R with the Scored Responses printed beside the item number.

If my response is the *same as* any one of the Scored Responses, I place a check mark (✔) on the line under IS or WANT or both.

I *add* the checks in each column and record the total (0 to 9) in the box at the bottom of the column.

I *transfer* scores to pages 216 and 217.

Item	Scored Responses	Column IS	WANT
1	5,6		
4	4,5,6		
7	5,6		
10	6		
13	6		
16	4,5,6		
19	3,4,5,6		
22	5,6		
25	5,6		

You include me. ☐ 43

I want you to include me. ☐ 44

Item	Scored Responses	Column IS	WANT
2	4,5,6		
5	3,4,5,6		
8	3,4,5,6		
11	3,4,5,6		
14	4,5,6		
17	3,4,5,6		
20	2,3,4,5,6		
23	1,2,3,4		
26	4,5,6		

You control me. ☐ 53

I want you to control me. ☐ 54

Item	Scored Responses	Column IS	WANT
3	5,6		
6	5,6		
9	1,2		
12	1		
15	1,2,3,4		
18	1		
21	5,6		
24	1,2		
27	6		

You are open with me. ☐ 63

I want you to be open with me. ☐ 64

Item	Scored Responses	Column IS	WANT
28	5,6		
31	5,6		
34	1		
37	1		
40	1		
43	1		
46	6		
49	5,6		
52	5,6		

You feel that I am significant. ☐ 47

I want you to feel that I am significant. ☐ 48

Item	Scored Responses	Column IS	WANT
29	1		
32	1		
35	5,6		
38	5,6		
41	5,6		
44	1		
47	5,6		
50	5,6		
53	6		

You feel that I am competent. ☐ 57

I want you to feel that I am competent. ☐ 58

Item	Scored Responses	Column IS	WANT
30	5,6		
33	5,6		
36	6		
39	1,2		
42	1		
45	3,4,5,6		
48	6		
51	1		
54	1		

You like me. ☐ 67

I want you to like me. ☐ 68

ELEMENT R: GET: Interpretation

I transfer scores from page 215 to the appropriate boxes below.

For each pair of scales I enter the Difference score.

You include me ☐
43

High Score
When we are together you include me in your social activities. You initiate contact and spend time with me.

Low Score
You do not initiate contact with me and you spend little time with me.

Positive Score
You include me more than I want you to.

I want you to include me ☐
44

High Score
I want you to include me in your activities and to spend time with me.

Low Score
I do not want you to include me in your life.

Difference (43 minus 44) ☐
▲43

Negative Score
I want you to include me more than I think you do.

You control me ☐
53

High Score
When we are together you tend to take charge, to give orders, to be influential, and to make decisions.

Low Score
You do not control or influence me when we are together.

Positive Score
You control me more than I want you to.

I want you to control me ☐
54

High Score
I want you to control me, to tell me what to do.

Low Score
I do not want you to make decisions when we are together.

Difference (53 minus 54) ☐
▲53

Negative Score
I want you to control me more than I think you do.

You are open with me ☐
63

High Score
You have very few secrets from me, and you initiate being open with me.

Low Score
You keep a personal distance between us and do not cultivate a friendship.

Positive Score
You are open with me more than I want you to be.

I want you to be open with me ☐
64

High Score
I want you to be open with me and not to withhold anything.

Low Score
I do not want you to be open with me. Keep your personal feelings to yourself.

Difference (63 minus 64) ☐
▲63

Negative Score
I want you to be open with me more than I think you are.

I transfer the eighteen scores on these pages to Scoring Summary (using scale code numbers).

You feel that I am significant ☐
47

High Score
You feel that I am a significant and important person and that I am of interest to you.

Low Score
You do not feel that I am an important person in your life, and you have no strong feelings, positive or negative, toward me.

I want you to feel that I am significant ☐
48

High Score
I want you to feel that I am a significant person and that I am important to you.

Low Score
I do not want you to feel that I am important to you.

Difference (47 minus 48) ☐
Δ47

Positive Score
You feel that I am more significant than I want you to feel.

Negative Score
I want you to feel that I am more significant than I think you do.

You feel that I am competent ☐
57

High Score
You feel that I am competent, that I have ability, that I am reliable, and that I can make good decisions.

Low Score
You feel that I am not very competent and that I cannot be trusted to make good decisions.

I want you to feel that I am competent ☐
58

High Score
I want you to feel that I am a competent, capable person.

Low Score
I do not want you to feel that I am competent.

Difference (57 minus 58) ☐
Δ57

Positive Score
You feel that I am more competent than I want you to feel.

Negative Score
I want you to feel more competent than I think you do.

You like me ☐
67

High Score
You like me and you feel personal warmth for me.

Low Score
You feel personally distant from me and perhaps you even dislike me.

I want you to like me ☐
68

High Score
I want you to like me and to feel warmth for me.

Low Score
I do not want you to like me.

Difference (67 minus 68) ☐
Δ67

Positive Score
You like me more than I want you to.

Negative Score
I want you to like me more than I think you do.

Another chance to take the relationship to a deeper level.

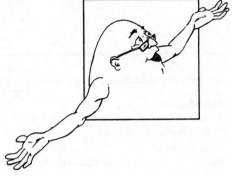

ACTIVITY 35. Get Differences

1. Have your partner fill out Element R: Get for you as partner. (If there is no partner, examine your own Element R: Get).

2. Examine your sources of difference with each other. Discuss each score. See if you can identify the reasons for the differences. Do any examples come to mind? Remember, a difference may mean either a dissatisfaction or a simple recognition that some aspect of the relation is not where you would prefer it to be.

3. Discuss your conclusions. Use these scores as a springboard to explore specific interactions and feelings in your relationship.

Relations: Do

My relationship with you also depends on how I feel about how I am and what I Do when I am with you. I like the way I am when I am with some people. I can be funny or intelligent or powerful, or friendly or generous or whatever I like to be. But other people "bring out the worst in me." I act nasty or ungenerous or phony or deceptive or hostile, or other ways that I do not like to be.

Usually, I feel better around the first kind of person. I can "be myself." I like myself better; as a result, I usually like that person more.

If I want to feel better about myself when I am with you, I must first be aware of what is happening. Then I must find exactly in what way I am not doing (acting and feeling) what I want to be doing. After that, I can discuss with you the areas of difficulty. When this happens, the possibilities of improving our relationship are very good.

By comparing how I relate to you with how I want to relate to you, I derive a measure of how satisfied I am with my behavior toward you and with my feelings about you.

My dissatisfaction derives from acting either too much or too little in the areas of inclusion, control, and openness, and feeling too much or too little in the areas of significance, competence, and likeability. There are, therefore, twelve sources of dissatisfaction I may have with myself. Each of these becomes the name of a dimension. These dimensions are measured by Element R: Do.

The following table and questions will help me understand the sources of dissatisfaction with what I Do toward you.

TABLE 9. Dissatisfactions with What I DO in Your Presence

	. . . Include	. . . Control	. . . Am (Be) Open With
I ___ you too much.	"I want to leave you out more."	"I don't want to tell you what to do."	"I tell you too much."
I want to ___ you more.	"I want to invite you more."	"I want you to do what I say."	"I want to tell you how I feel."

	. . . Significant	. . . Competent	. . . Likeable
You are too ___ to me.	"I don't want to pay so much attention to you."	"I don't want you to be so competent."	"I don't want to like you so much."
I want to feel that you are more ___	"I want you to mean more to me."	"I want to trust your abilities more."	"I want to like you more."

QUESTIONS. DO

_____ 1. It bothers Marge that she has no interest in Sam. He might do her some good some day, but he is not important to her. Marge would like to feel that Sam is (a) more significant, (b) more competent, (c) more likeable.

_____ 2. Ramona cannot get her employees to obey her orders. She feels she is doing too little (a) including, (b) controlling, (c) initiating openness.

_____ 3. Although Vivian must work with Gerald, she does not like him. She knows life would be easier if she did. Vivian wants Gerald to be more (a) significant, (b) competent, (c) likeable.

_____ 4. Frank invites Fran to many meetings, even though he does not really want to, because he is afraid of hurting her feelings. Frank feels that he is doing too much (a) including, (b) controlling, (c) initiating openness.

_____ 5. Marvin does not like the fact that Shirley is so efficient. She might get the promotion he wants. Marvin would like to feel that Shirley is less (a) significant, (b) competent, (c) likeable.

_____ 6. Because she wants to be liked by everybody, June confides her true feelings to Harold, even though she does not like him. She feels that she is doing too much (a) including, (b) controlling, (c) initiating openness.

Answers: abc   abc

ELEMENT R: Do

There are no "right" answers. The more honest I am, the more accurate will be the information I receive from Element R: Do.

First, I complete the column "The way it IS" for all items.

For each statement, I place a number from 1 to 6 on the line to the left of the item, in the appropriate column. The numbers indicate how much I agree with the statement.

Disagree 1 2 3 4 5 6 **Agree**

When I have finished, I return to the top of the column and respond to the same items for "The way I WANT it to be."

You _____

The Way It IS	The Way I WANT It to Be	
1	_____	I spend time with you.
2	_____	I make the decisions when we are together.
3	_____	I am totally honest with you.
4	_____	I join your groups.
5	_____	I am the dominant person when I am with you.
6	_____	I keep from getting too close to you.
7	_____	I include myself in your informal social activities.
8	_____	I have you do the things I want done.
9	_____	I confide in you.
10	_____	I include you in my plans.
11	_____	I influence strongly your actions.
12	_____	I keep my private feelings from you.
13	_____	I have you around me.
14	_____	I take charge of things when I am with you.
15	_____	I keep some things hidden from you.
16	_____	I join you when you are doing things with other people.
17	_____	I have you do things the way I want them done.
18	_____	I keep some things about myself from you.
19	_____	I avoid being away from you.
20	_____	I tell you what to do.
21	_____	I tell you everything important about me.
22	_____	I include you in the things I do.
23	_____	I let you do whatever you want.
24	_____	I keep some things private.
25	_____	I participate in your activities.
26	_____	I order you around.
27	_____	I have a close, open relationship with you.
28	_____	I feel that you are important.
29	_____	I feel that I cannot rely on your judgment.
30	_____	I feel warm toward you.
31	_____	I feel that you are a significant individual.
32	_____	I am skeptical of your abilities.
33	_____	I feel affectionate toward you.
34	_____	I feel that you do not mean anything to me.
35	_____	I admire your competence.
36	_____	I feel personally close to you.
37	_____	I feel neutral toward you.
38	_____	I admire your abilities.
39	_____	I hate you.
40	_____	I have no interest in you.
41	_____	I trust in your abilities.
42	_____	I feel personally distant from you.
43	_____	I feel indifferent to you.
44	_____	I am suspicious of your competence.
45	_____	I feel bitter toward you.
46	_____	I am interested in you.
47	_____	I trust in your competence.
48	_____	I feel cordial toward you.
49	_____	I feel intrigued by you.
50	_____	I have confidence in your abilities.
51	_____	I feel very friendly toward you.
52	_____	I am stimulated by you.
53	_____	I feel that I can depend on your judgment.
54	_____	I feel cool toward you.

ELEMENT R: DO Scoring

I *compare* my response to each item of Element R with the Scored Responses printed beside the item number.

If my response is the *same as* any one of the Scored Responses, I place a check mark (✔) on the line under IS or WANT or both.

I *add* the checks in each column and record the total (0 to 9) in the box at the bottom of the column.

I *transfer* scores to pages 224 to 225.

Item	Scored Responses	Column IS	WANT
1	6		
4	4,5,6		
7	5,6		
10	5,6		
13	4,5,6		
16	4,5,6		
19	4,5,6		
22	5,6		
25	4,5,6		

I include you. ☐ 41

I want to include you. ☐ 42

Item	Scored Responses	Column IS	WANT
2	4,5,6		
5	4,5,6		
8	3,4,5,6		
11	4,5,6		
14	4,5,6		
17	4,5,6		
20	4,5,6		
23	1,2,3,4,5		
26	3,4,5,6		

I control you. ☐ 51

I want to control you. ☐ 52

Item	Scored Responses	Column IS	WANT
3	5,6		
6	1,2,3		
9	4,5,6		
12	1		
15	1,2		
18	1,2		
21	6		
24	1		
27	4,5,6		

I am open with you. ☐ 61

I want to be open with you. ☐ 62

Item	Scored Responses	Column IS	WANT
28	6		
31	6		
34	1		
37	1,2		
40	1		
43	1		
46	6		
49	6		
52	6		

I feel that you are significant. ☐ 45

I want to feel that you are significant. ☐ 46

Item	Scored Responses	Column IS	WANT
29	1,2		
32	1,2		
35	6		
38	5,6		
41	6		
44	1		
47	5,6		
50	5,6		
53	5,6		

I feel that you are competent. ☐ 55

I want to feel that you are competent. ☐ 56

Item	Scored Responses	Column IS	WANT
30	6		
33	5,6		
36	5,6		
39	1		
42	1,2		
45	1		
48	6		
51	6		
54	1		

I like you. ☐ 65

I want to like you. ☐ 66

ELEMENT R: DO: Interpretation

I transfer scores from page 223 to the appropriate boxes below.
For each pair of scales I enter the Difference score.

I include you ☐
41

High Score
I include you in social activities. I initiate contact and spend time with you.

Low Score
I do not initiate contact with you, and I spend very little time in your presence.

I want to include you ☐
42

High Score
I want to include you in my activities.

Low Score
I do not want contact with you or to spend time with you.

Difference (41 minus 42) ☐
△41

Positive Score
I include you more than I want to.

Negative Score
I want to include you more than I do.

I control you ☐
51

High Score
When we are together, I tend to take charge, give orders, be influential, and make decisions.

Low Score
I do not control or influence you when we are together.

I want to control you ☐
52

High Score
When we are together, I want to control you, to make the decisions.

Low Score
I do not want to control you or to tell you what to do.

Difference (51 minus 52) ☐
△51

Positive Score
I control you more than I want to.

Negative Score
I want to control you more than I do.

I am open with you ☐
61

High Score
I have very few secrets from you. I am quite open with you.

Low Score
I am not open with you. I withhold myself from you.

I want to be open with you ☐
62

High Score
I want to be open with you and to keep no secrets from you.

Low Score
I do not want to be open with you. I do not want to tell you about myself.

Difference (61 minus 62) ☐
△61

Positive Score
I am open with you more than I want to be.

Negative Score
I want to be open with you more than I am.

I transfer the eighteen scores on these pages to Scoring Summary (using scale code numbers).

I feel that you are significant □
45

High Score
I feel that you are a significant and important person, and that you are of considerable interest to me.

Low Score
You are not a very important person in my life, and I have no strong feelings, positive or negative, toward you.

I want to feel that you are significant □
46

High Score
I want to feel that you are an important person to me.

Low Score
I do not want to feel that you are a significant person in my life.

Difference (45 minus 46) □
△45

Positive Score
I feel that you are more significant than I want you to be.

Negative Score
I want to feel that you are more important to me than I do feel.

I feel that you are competent □
55

High Score
I feel that you are competent, that you have ability, that you are reliable, and that you can make good decisions.

Low Score
I do not feel that you are competent, nor that you can be trusted to make good decisions.

I want to feel that you are competent □
56

High Score
I want to feel that you are reliable and that I can rely on your abilities.

Low Score
I do not want to feel that you can be trusted to make good decisions.

Difference (55 minus 56) □
△55

Positive Score
I feel that you are more competent than I want to feel you are.

Negative Score
I want to feel that you are more competent than you are.

I like you □
65

High Score
I like you and I feel a personal warmth for you.

Low Score
I feel personally distant from you and perhaps even dislike you.

I want to like you □
66

High Score
I want to like you and to feel warmth toward you.

Low Score
I do not want to like you. I do not want to feel close.

Difference (65 minus 66) □
△65

ACTIVITY 36. Do Differences

1. Have your partner fill out Element R: Do for you as partner. (If there is no partner, examine your own Element R: Do.)

2. Examine your sources of difference with each other. Discuss each score. See if you can identify the reasons for the differences. Do any examples come to mind? Remember, a difference may mean a dissatisfaction, or it may mean a simple recognition that some aspect of the relation is not where you would prefer it to be.

3. Discuss your conclusions. Use these scores as a springboard to explore your relationship.

4. Close your eyes and review this chapter — the concepts of atmosphere and role compatibility, and your specific relation with a partner. Record your primary reactions on the next page.

PERSONAL MEANING OF RELATIONS: EXPRESSION

SEGUE

Up to this point I have focused primarily on myself and on how to empower myself through understanding, self-awareness, and the use of several tools. In this chapter I began to explore the bases of fit between people, both in personal relations and in job settings. Application of what I have learned to a relationship or to team building begins with understanding the facets of compatibility and with my willingness to let my partner know how I feel.

Atmosphere compatibility refers to our agreement on the context, or environment, in which we prefer to function. We may compare our preferences about three types of atmosphere: inclusion atmosphere — how much I like to do things with people, and how much alone; control atmosphere — how much I like to have things structured, planned, with clear lines of control, and how much I like to let things happen and adjust to them as we go; and openness atmosphere — how much I like to reveal my feelings and how much I like to keep them to myself. Our atmosphere compatibility increases as our atmosphere preferences coincide.

Role compatibility is highest when we are complementary. If you like to be in control, for example, and I like to be controlled, we should get along well. If we both wish to control we would have a competitive incompatibility. If we both prefer to be controlled, we are in danger of being incompatible due to apathy.

Joan was the leader of a group whose work overlapped that of Chuck's group. It was clear to Joan that cooperation between the two groups would be extremely productive, but she did not feel that it was "her place" to suggest it to Chuck. Joan felt that Chuck might be offended, might think her pushy, and might not like her. Joan could even give herself several more reasons for not talking to Chuck about this issue.

During the course of a workshop, Chuck and Joan were in the same small group. Chuck thought of an example of apathetic incompatibility in the openness area: "You know, Joan, for a year now I've been thinking that we should get together and plan a work schedule that would integrate our overlapping efforts, but I've been reluctant because I thought you might think I was trying to take over your group."

For a year they had both wanted the same thing but had been reluctant to initiate, resulting in an obvious decrease in efficiency. Once their common desires were aired, they planned a meeting to work out their issue. As they reflected on the consequences of their timidity, they understood why several employees had complained of overwork. Joan and Chuck's failure to integrate meant that employees were asked to do similar jobs over again.

Element R provides an opportunity to express our feelings for each other in very specific ways, and serves as a springboard for discussions of our relationship.

chapter nine

RELATIONS:
Understanding

This last chapter has led you through the first three levels of truth: expressing feelings toward each other, about yourself, and making connections between events and feelings. You are now in a position to explore levels four and five and see how your self-concepts and defenses affect your relationships and how you can use this awareness to strengthen it.

We have now explored our atmosphere compatibilities, how I feel about your relating to me (Truth Level 1: "You are . . .") and how I feel about myself when relating to you (Truth Level 2: "About you I feel . . ."). And we have explored connections (Truth Level 3: "Because . . ."). It is now time to use what I have learned in the previous chapters about my coping mechanisms (Truth Level 4: "Which means . . .") and about my self concept (Truth Level 5: "About myself I fear . . .") to better understand our relationship, and particularly my contribution to it. In this chapter I shall also explore some of the practical applications of this exploration.

As I have discovered, the place where I tend to see through a distorted lens is the place where I *have a low opinion of myself*. In those areas, I make efforts to alter my experience so that I do not have to face the unpleasant feeling of low self-esteem.

I first examine my Element S and determine in which areas my self-concept is low. These are the areas I shall focus on to determine the coping mechanisms I use that distort our relationship.

DISTORTION

The chapter on the lens described various types of misperception. I will use that information to give myself an idea of how I might be using those mechanisms in my relationship with you. I may not be perceiving you accurately (projection, displacement, identification), and I may be trying to get you to do certain things for my benefit (compensation).

Completing Tables 10, 11, and 12 will allow you to do Activity 37.

TABLE 10. Projection

- Using the Scoring Summary or your scores on Element R: Get (page 215) and Element S (page 125), fill in your scores below. Follow scale code numbers.
- Make indicated subtractions and place the results in the box.
- If the number in any box is 2 or more, you are probably not projecting.
- If the number in any box is 0 or 1, circle the box and the perception described to the right.

ELEMENT R	ELEMENT S	IF THIS SCORE IS 0 OR 1	THEN MY PERCEPTION IS THIS:	
43 You include me.	− 10 I am present (I include myself).	= ☐ Ignore sign	You include me to the same degree that I include myself.	*And I may be projecting— that is, I may be assuming that you act or feel toward me the same way I act or feel toward myself, whether you actually do or not.*
53 You control me.	− 20 I control myself.	= ☐ Ignore sign	You control me to the same degree that I control myself.	
63 You are open with me.	− 30 I am aware (open with myself).	= ☐ Ignore sign	You are open with me to the same degree that I am open with myself.	
47 You feel that I am significant.	− 40 I feel significant.	= ☐ If 4 or more, put X in	You feel I am significant to the same degree that I feel I'm significant.	
57 You feel that I am competent.	− 50 I feel competent.	= ☐ If 4 or more, put X in	You feel that I am competent to the same degree that I feel I am competent.	
67 You like me.	− 60 I like myself.	= ☐ If 4 or more, put X in	You like me to the same degree that I like myself.	

TABLE 11. Displacement

- Using the Scoring Summary or your scores on Element R: Do (page 223) and Element S (page 125), fill in your scores below. Follow scale code numbers.

- Make indicated subtractions and place the results in the box.

- If the number in any box is 2 or more, you are probably not displacing.

- If the number in any box is 0 or 1, circle the box and the perception described to the right.

| | | IF THIS SCORE | THEN MY PERCEPTION |
ELEMENT R	ELEMENT S	IS 0 OR 1	IS THIS:

41 I include you.	10 I am present (I include myself).	= ☐ Ignore sign	I include you to the same degree that I include myself.	*And I may be displacing—that is, I may be acting or feeling toward you the way that I act or feel toward myself, regardless of who you are.*
51 I control you.	20 I control myself.	= ☐ Ignore sign	I control you to the same degree that I control myself.	
61 I am open with you.	30 I am aware (open with myself).	= ☐ Ignore sign	I am open with you to the same degree that I am open with myself.	
45 I feel that you are significant.	40 I feel significant.	= ☐ Ignore sign	I feel that you are significant to the same degree that I feel that I am significant.	
55 I feel that you are competent.	50 I feel competent.	= ☐ Ignore sign	I feel that you are competent to the same degree that I feel that I am competent.	
65 I like you.	60 I like myself.	= ☐ Ignore sign	I like you to the same degree that I like myself.	

TABLE 12. Compensation

- Using the Scoring Summary or your scores on Element R: Get (page 215) and Element S (page 125), fill in your scores below. Follow scale code numbers.

- Make indicated subtractions and place the results in the box.

- If the number in any box is 2 or less, you are probably not compensating.

- If the number in any box is 3 or more, circle the box and the perception described to the right.

ELEMENT R	ELEMENT S	IF THIS SCORE IS 3 OR MORE	THEN MY PERCEPTION IS THIS:	
44 I want you to include me.	10 I am present (I include myself).	= ☐ Ignore sign	I do not include myself the way I want to. I want you to include me that way.	*And I may be compensating— that is, I may be dissatisfied with the way I act or feel about myself and want you to act or feel about me the way I want to feel about myself.*
54 I want you to control me.	20 I control myself.	= ☐ Ignore sign	I do not control myself the way I want to. I want you to control me that way.	
64 I want you to be open with me.	30 I am aware (open with myself).	= ☐ Ignore sign	I am not open with myself the way I want to be. I want you to be open with me that way.	
48 I want you to feel that I am significant.	40 I feel significant.	= ☐ Ignore sign	I do not feel as significant as I want to feel. I want you to feel that I am significant.	
58 I want you to feel that I am competent.	50 I feel competent.	= ☐ Ignore sign	I do not feel as competent as I want to feel. I want you to feel that I am competent.	
68 I want you to like me.	60 I like myself.	= ☐ Ignore sign	I do not like myself as much as I want to. I want you to like me.	

ACTIVITY 37. Coping Mechanisms

1. Both of you examine Tables 10, 11, and 12. Talk about the circled areas — the ones where you may be using mechanisms.

2. Can you identify how you may be using them in this relationship? Think of examples.

3. Can you identify when you might be using them in the workplace or in your personal relations? Give examples.

4. Does this discussion help you to understand this relationship better? What areas or events does it clarify?

5. Does this discussion help you to understand better your relationships in general? Give examples.

It is helpful to avoid being defensive. Remember this exercise is for discovery, not blame. Enjoy.

Atmosphere Distortion

Now that I have seen how my perceptions of you and my behavior and feelings toward you may be distorted, I will take a similar look at our relationship atmosphere compatibility.

For the same reasons that I distort how I see you and how I perceive your behavior and feelings toward me, I also may prefer an atmosphere because it is less threatening to me. This preference allows me to avoid experiencing something I do not want to look at.

Because of a weakness in my self-concept, I have certain fears about myself (for example, that I am insignificant) that I am unaware of. My excessive zeal for a particular atmosphere may be because I anticipate that the atmosphere itself will alleviate my fear. In terms of coping mechanisms, this anticipation may be called a *compensation coming from the atmosphere*. If I do not feel competent, for example, I may imagine that an atmosphere of high control will provide me with instructions for what to do so that my incompetence will not be revealed. The atmosphere will provide me with the appearance of competence.

Gaining insight into why I may cling to a certain atmosphere may lead to more flexibility in entering into another atmosphere. Again, I must remember not to be defensive but to consider what is possibly true about each fear.

Table 13 lists some possible fears and hopes that could account for a beyond-rational attachment to a particular atmosphere. There are, of course, good rational arguments for the efficacy of each atmosphere for certain situations. Table 13 lists reasons that go beyond the rational.

TABLE 13. Bases of Rigid Atmosphere Preferences

Fear	Atmosphere	Hope
I can't stay present.	High Inclusion	You will keep me focused.
I can't stay present.	Low Inclusion	I can concentrate easier without people to distract me.
I don't feel significant.	High Inclusion	You will pay attention to me.
I don't feel significant.	Low Inclusion	I will ignore you before you ignore me.
I don't control myself enough.	High Control	You will control me.
I control myself too much.	Low Control	You won't control me too.
I don't feel competent.	High Control	You will take responsibility for what I do.
I don't feel competent.	Low Control	Little will be expected of me.
I am not aware.	High Openness	You will help me find myself.
I am not aware.	Low Openness	You won't find out how unaware I am.
I am not likeable.	High Openness	You will tell me if you don't like me. No unexpected rejection.
I am not likeable.	Low Openness	I won't know if you don't like me.

It is also possible that I may use an atmosphere in one area to solve a problem in a different area. For example, if I do not feel likeable, I may want to avoid being with people altogether (low-inclusion atmosphere).

Generally speaking, if I have an unsatisfactory self-concept in any area, I may deal with it in either of two ways, in terms of atmosphere:

• By withdrawing from it (very low atmosphere). This is an unconscious way of saying, "I know you are going to ignore [inclusion], humiliate [control], or reject [openness] me so I will not give you a chance."

• By diving into it (very high atmosphere) and trying to make people treat me as I don't feel toward myself (compensation). This is an unconscious way of saying, "I don't feel significant or competent or likeable but I am going to do everything I can to get you to feel that I am these ways."

These are more subtle, but you are now in a position to be more open with each other.

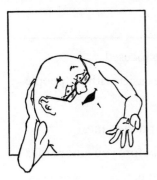

ACTIVITY 38.
Atmosphere Distortion

1. Study Table 13. Which of these statements may apply to you?

2. Think of your scores on atmosphere preference (pages 195 to 197). Do any of the possible reasons mentioned make sense to you?

3. Discuss these possibilities with each other.

4. Once you are aware of these factors, do you feel that you could be more flexible about the atmosphere you prefer?

RESPONSES: Activity 38. Atmosphere Distortion

IMPLICATIONS

I have now explored all the levels of truth about our relationship. First I looked at our atmosphere compatibility and what I was not satisfied with about you. Then I talked about what I was not satisfied with about my behavior, and in our discussions we uncovered some of the incidents and events that led us to our feelings. Finally, we explored how our own fears about ourselves, and the ways in which we defended ourselves, might have contributed to the way we were.

Next, I would like to explore some practical applications of these discoveries.

Choice, Compatibility, and Self-Concept

Since I am assuming that I choose everything, the concept of compatibility only holds if I choose to let it. If I am incompatible with you, I can choose to change and learn how to become compatible, and so can you. Our incompatibility, in other words, is a collusion we have entered into. By first becoming aware that we are now incompatible and by letting ourselves know the ways in which this state arises, we have the tools to change the situation.

If we know, for example, that you like to do things together and I like to do them separately (inclusion atmosphere incompatibility), you can choose to do some things apart and I can choose to do some things together.

Or suppose we have discovered that you feel unsure of your abilities, and that having a structure (high-control atmosphere) may help you avoid obvious errors and humiliation. For my part, I feel that I am not able to withstand the pressure that I feel when I know that people disagree with me: I fear that I will capitulate because I want people to like me, and then I will feel weak and wishy-washy. If we can simply allow ourselves to acknowledge our personal fears, it makes it easier to let go of the rigidity of our positions.

Letting go has two valuable outcomes: Our immediate task gets done more effectively, since we have broken the logjam of how to proceed in order to solve our problem. And in the long run, we each have the opportunity for personal growth. I may begin to see that I can hold my ground in a group, and you may find that your ideas are sound without having to check them with other people.

C-P Effect

The effect of compatibility on productivity (C-P effect) varies with the task. Some jobs require cooperation in order to be done well. Other jobs may be done by one person as well as (sometimes better than) a group. Many jobs may be organized either to require cooperation or to be accomplishable by individual effort.

The C-P effect is greatest for tasks where cooperation is necessary to achieve results. For tasks that do not require cooperation, this effect is minimal.

The C-P effect increases with increased pressure. Experiments have demonstrated that under time pressure, compatible groups perform even better than they do without pressure, while incompatible groups become more ineffective.

This is contrary to the popular belief that any group of people can work well together if the task is of sufficient importance. This was the belief during the Korean and Vietnam Wars; however, the frequent instances of the rearrangment of the power structure, regardless of rank, and of officers being shot in the back by their own men during battle conditions, attest to the fallacy of this notion. Compatibility is even more necessary for successful working together when there is pressure to produce.

A practical suggestion that follows from this finding is: If it is not feasible to change the composition of an incompatible team, family, or couple, and if the people or organization involved do not want to expend the time and energy to change, then the job itself may be changed.

We argued over money and we argued over vacations. They both became the source of acrimony and power struggles. We had a choice: either figure out why we argued, or simplify money and vacation problems. We decided, at least temporarily, on the latter. We agreed that she was more imaginative in choosing vacation sites and I was more accurate in keeping track of money. From then on she did the vacation plans alone and I kept the books alone. Unless there was a strong objection from the other — at which time we would discuss it — we each prevailed in our own realms, and friction was reduced.

In summary, if we are not functioning well, we may:

- go through a training that will lead us to the realization that we can choose to be different, and that will provide us with the tools for making this change;

- switch members of certain teams to maximize compatibility; or

- restructure the job so as to require less cooperation in order to achieve efficiency.

Development of Relations

Compatibility is not static. Families, teams, couples, and relationships in general are neither compatible nor incompatible for all time. relationships evolve through time, often in predictable ways.

I have had relationships that started very badly and ended up very well; or relationships that began well and deteriorated; or relationships that were good from the beginning and remained that way; or relationships that were never good. Looking at how relations develop over time will help me understand why this is so.

There is a sequence of stages through which relationships develop. The dimensions of inclusion, control, and openness occur *in that order* in the development of a relation. Inclusion issues (the decision to be in or out of the relation), arise first, followed by control issues (top or bottom), and finally followed by openness issues (open or closed). Although this order is not rigid, the nature of group life is such that we tend first to determine whether we want to be a member, then to find out what place of influence we will occupy, and finally to decide how personally open we will become.[33]

INCLUSION PHASE

The inclusion phase of the development of a relationship begins with the formation of the team. As a member of a new team, I want first to find where I fit. My initial concerns are to decide whether I want to be in or out of the team, to establish myself as a specific individual, and to see whether I am going to be paid attention to or going to be ignored. When I am anxious about these inclusion issues, I tend toward individual-centered behavior, such as overtalking, extreme withdrawal, exhibitionism, or recitation of my biography.

At the same time, I am deciding to what degree I will commit myself to this relationship—how much investment I will withdraw from my other life-commitments to invest in this new relationship. Essentially, I am asking: "How much of myself will I give to this relationship and to its activities? How important will I be in this setting? Will they appreciate who I am and what I can do, or will I be indistinguishable from many others?" This is the problem of identity. I am primarily deciding how much contact, interaction, and communication I wish to have.

CONTROL PHASE

Once the sense of being together in a team, or a couple, is somewhat established, then control issues become prominent. These include making decisions, sharing responsibility, and the distribution of power. During the control stage, characteristic behavior includes a struggle for leadership and competition. At this point my primary anxieties center on having too much or too little responsibility, and on having too much or too little influence. I try to establish myself in such a way that I will have the amount of power and dependency that is most comfortable for me.

OPENNESS PHASE

Following some resolution of the issue of control, openness issues take center stage. We have come together to form a relationship. We have differentiated ourselves with respect to responsibility and to power. Now we explore the issue of becoming emotionally integrated. At this stage, it is characteristic to see expressions of positive feeling, direct personal hostility, jealousy, pairing off (for teams), and, in general, heightened emotional feeling.

My primary anxieties focus on not being open enough, or on being too open. I am striving to obtain the most comfortable amount of openness exchange, that is, the most comfortable position with regard to the amount of initiating and receiving openness.

To illustrate this developmental sequence, here is a fantasy lifeboat scene — a composite taken from the cinema.

- First phase: Who will be in the lifeboat? Will evil Peter Lorre beat off pregnant Raquel Welch? . . . Heroic sacrifices, rescues, pullings aboard . . . with George Lazenby representing nonresolution by swimming behind the boat. (The issue: in or out.)

- Second phase: The power struggle. Who is the captain, Charles Laughton or Indiana Jones? Will Captain Kirk be satisfied to be the first mate, or will he organize a rebellion? (The issue: top or bottom.)

- Third phase: As the long journey wears on, personal stories are recounted. Hidden attractions are revealed — Jane Fonda and Tyrone Power discover each other. Lifelong secrets are told — Richard Pryor admits that he was on the Rutgers rowing team, Dolly Parton reveals that she is really Errol Flynn's daughter — while Brando and Michael Jackson choose to remain silent and aloof. (The issue: open or closed.)

QUESTIONS. Group Development

_____ 1. The army tries to solve the inclusion problems of its soldiers by (a) giving them stripes, (b) issuing uniforms, (c) preventing home leave.

_____ 2. In order for a team to come into existence, members must decide (a) who will be the leader, (b) who likes whom the best, (c) to commit themselves to the team.

_____ 3. Right after the relation is established, it is important to decide (a) how power and responsibility are distributed (control), (b) who is willing to put his or her energy into the team (inclusion), (c) how open people will be with each other (openness).

_____ 4. Being a member of a team usually is not satisfying enough to keep the team together over a long period unless there (a) are tight controls, (b) is a certain amount of openness, (c) are rewards for achievement.

_____ 5. When people just meet, they will get along well if they are compatible in the area of (a) inclusion, (b) control, (c) openness.

Answers: bca ba

Compatibility Development

It now becomes clear why relationships sometimes wax or wane. Consider the case of George and Laura on page 199. Their atmosphere compatibility scores indicated poor compatibility in inclusion (7), worse compatibility in control (8), and moderate compatibility in openness (4). The prediction for their relationship would be: troublesome when they meet (inclusion phase); worsening as they work together (control phase); but finally (if they survive) improving as the relationship enters the openness phase.

Understanding the flow of a relationship over time may help me to be more tolerant. It may help me to pinpoint or to anticipate the source of interpersonal problems.

Compatibility and relationship development, like all the phenomena described in these chapters, are always changeable. The principle of choice states that I choose everything. I choose to describe my behavior in a certain way on Element B. I choose to work well with some people and not with others. I choose to be the way I am. *And I am completely capable of changing any of these choices.*

"Choice" implies that there are natural laws—laws of physics, physiology, psychology, etc.—and that they function unless I decide to change them. The laws of nature constitute the program for the universe's computer; but I have a manual override—I can alter these laws if I decide to learn how. This principle applies to the laws of compatibility (as described above), the laws of relation development, and the laws of development compatibility. These laws function unless I decide to become aware of them and to change them.

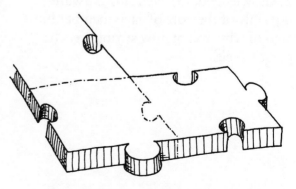

Consensus and Cooperation

The decision-making technique that is most consistent with the idea of compatibility, and the one that takes greatest advantage of compatibility, is the method of consensus. Since you and I are compatible, our ability to speak honestly to each other is enhanced. This allows each of us to participate to the maximum of our abilities so that we may make the best decisions.

Consensus as a decision-making procedure for a team differs from unanimity (which requires that we all agree on the issue), and from majority (which requires that more than half of us agree on the issue), and also from authoritarianism (which requires the vote of just one person). *In consensus, a decision is made when we all agree with it even if we disagree about the issue.*

If, for example, a small minority of board members oppose a merger, then consensus would call for the following: (1) minority members express their feelings about the merger; (2) majority members acknowledge these feelings, express their own, and have them acknowledged; (3) each side is aware not only of the vote of each member but also of why and of how strongly each person feels.

The outcome may be that minority members — recognizing that the majority wanted the merger even after hearing and understanding the minority's feelings — would then agree to the merger for the sake of making a move for the company. Or the outcome may be that the majority feels that since the minority members feel so strongly against the merger, it would be prudent to postpone a decision until later. In either case, both the thoughts *and feelings* of all members are considered.

Consensus usually leads directly to mutual understanding and cooperation. If we each take account of the feelings of the other members before making decisions, cooperation logically follows. Contention and lack of acknowledging the feelings of each member only delay decisions. *Although decisions made by this method sometimes take longer to make than do autocratic decisions, they are almost always executed more effectively. This is because we who are to carry out the decision have participated in the decision-making process, and feel motivated to carry it out.*

Consensual decisions are typically more creative. The consensual method elicits greater participation from each of us, and therefore a wider variety of potential solutions are considered. Further, hearing each other and building on each other's ideas leads to the stimulation of new and more thoughtful decisions.

Each year an organization made a decision as to which of the 12 central office members would attend and staff the annual meeting. In the past, this decision had been made in an authoritarian fashion, and was a constant source of animosity. Those who went felt overloaded, and those who remained felt ignored and left out. The group decided to use the consensual model this year to determine who would go to the conference.

After a rehash of the previous complaints and a rather lackluster discussion of which people should go, one member emerged with a new conception. "Why do we all stay stuck in the old model that never worked?" he said. "Why don't we take the money we have available for travel and expenses and divide it twelve ways? That way we can all go? We may have to put in $10 of our own or eat a little less, but then no one has to stay home and there will be plenty of us to run the conference efficiently, without becoming exhausted as we usually do."

Immediately, morale went up. Everyone resonated to the idea; details were worked out; and it ended up being the most satisfying conference that the staff had ever experienced. The consensual process had spawned a new idea that had never occurred to the director, which turned out to be much more effective for both morale and efficiency.

A good example of an informal consensual decision came when Sugar Ray Leonard, the renowned boxer, decided to make a comeback despite the misgivings of his wife, Juanita. The newspaper gave an account of the events preceding Sugar Ray's announcement:

"You're fighting, right?" she said.
"Well, sort of," Leonard said.
Juanita, who has been known to faint at ringside, is opposed to the comeback, but Sugar Ray says she'll accept it. "She gave me that look, but she went along with it."

In consensual terms, Juanita was saying, "I don't agree with the content of your decision but, given our roles and our relationship, I believe it is best for us if I support your decision."

ACTIVITY 39. Consensus

1. Select a topic of importance to you and your partner — one about which there is disagreement. If a topic does not come to mind, you might try an immediate one such as, "What is the best way to proceed with this book?" The topic should be one that requires you to decide on a definite course of action.

2. Proceed to have a consensual decision-making meeting. Note these characteristics:

   a. You are both free to participate fully.

   b. Discussion continues until you both agree to support the final decision.

   c. Use the following technique to check agreement: When the decision is ready to be made, both of you indicate whether you agree with the decision by saying the word yes or the word no. If either says *anything* other than yes, assume that they mean no, and continue the discussion. (People who feel reluctant to oppose the group often will not say no directly, but rather will indicate their resistance by not fully agreeing verbally. They may say "yeah," "sure," "OK," "go ahead." Asking if anyone is opposed simply finds out who is willing to say they are opposed. It is *not* a way to assure consensus.)

This is a very valuable tool. You can use it in every decision-making situation.

3. When the discussion is completed, shut your eyes and think of these points:

   a. Are you satisfied with the decision?

   b. Do you feel that your thoughts and your feelings about the issue have been understood and acknowledged?

   c. Do you feel that you will unconflictedly support the decision?

   d. How do you feel about the other person? Has there been any change in your feeling?

   e. Is there a way that the discussion could have been shortened? made more efficient? How would you improve it?

   f. What are the strengths and weaknesses of the consensual method?

   g. Discuss the implications of truth and choice for the consensual process, and for the concept of compatibility.

4. Open your eyes and discuss these ideas.

5. How does this decision-making method compare with those you are used to? What are the implications?

This is the ultimate goal.

The real advantage of this chapter for improving relationships lies in what happens after the chapter is digested. Element R, the interpretations and the theory, are valuable for indicating the significant area of interaction and for illuminating the reality of human relations. But they are no more than a springboard.

Relationships change only if you are willing to relate to each other honestly, if you are willing to tell the truth about how you feel about each other. Once the truth is revealed, the chances of changing and improving your relationship are very high.

If the truth is withheld, then you both must guess at what is going on in the other. Strategy replaces honesty, diplomacy replaces truth, subtle competition replaces open exchange.

The purpose of this chapter is to reveal what human relations are all about. It simply provides information and points the way to a process based on truth and choice, through which personal difficulties may be solved and human efficiency, energy, and joy may be maximized.

ACTIVITY 40. Atmosphere of Truth

1. Discuss the idea of truthful atmosphere, as described. Do you agree or disagree? Why? What is your position?

2. How does the concept of truth relate to your relationship? Discuss.

3. How does the concept of choice affect your understanding of a relationship and of how it may change?

4. Shut your eyes and reflect on this chapter. Think about: the deepest levels of truth in a relationship; atmosphere and role compatibility; results of Element R; use of defenses in your relation; the self-concept in relation to your relationships; C-P effect; development of relationships; consensus; and the atmosphere of truth. Open your eyes and write down your most significant reactions to this chapter on the next page.

PERSONAL MEANING OF RELATIONS: UNDERSTANDING

SEGUE

The ways in which I defend my fragile parts affect the way in which I relate to you. I distort my perception of you by projecting, displacing, or reflecting. I make unreasonable demands on you when I compensate. We both operate in these ways. This exploration is a mutual attempt to understand our relationship better, not to assign blame.

These same mechanisms operate in the workplace. They form the basis for strengthening team building, just as they function in a personal relationship. Combining the concepts of compatibility with a knowledge of the sequence through which groups develop — inclusion, control, openness — allows me to predict how groups and relationships will develop over time, and gives me a basis for understanding the vicissitudes of a relationship.

Compatibility has more of an effect on productivity in a relationship that requires interdependence. This is true for all close relations, and also for many work relationships that require cooperation in order to accomplish a task. It is also true that, contrary to popular belief, stress does not bring all groups closer and make them productive. Pressure on a compatible group does lead to higher performance, but pressure on a basically incompatible group leads to lower performance.

As a decision-making procedure, consensus — agreement to support a decision even if not everyone agrees on the content — is the most efficient for utilizing the resources of all people involved. It leads to greater creativity and to more effective carrying out of decisions.

This completes, for now, the applications I am making of the principles. I shall now go back and review what I have learned about myself, and consider the steps that apply after I finish this book and take what I have learned into my daily living.

chapter ten

A LOOK BACK AND A LOOK FORWARD

The self-concept is the key to unlocking the mysteries of human behavior. Now that I have explored my reactions to people in general (Element B, Element F), to my job (Job Satisfaction Form), to myself (Element S), and to one partner (Element R), I am in a position to pull all these areas together to see myself in a total way. I can see which parts of myself and my relations are now just the way I want them to be, and which parts I would like to be different.

An advantage of looking at how I feel about myself is that I increase my awareness. Therefore I enhance my ability to run my own life. It is a major step toward *empowerment*.

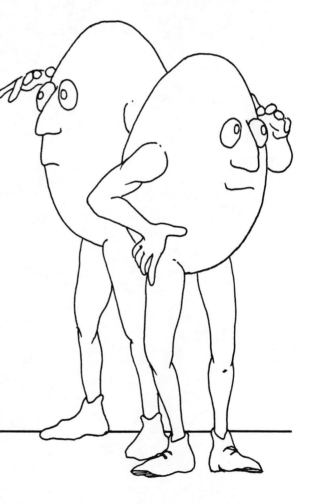

I had a recurring dream when I was a child. I was on the roof of a tall apartment building that was on fire. My children were in the courtyard on the ground and I was trying to get down to help them. But there was a brick chimney on the roof that was falling down all around me. My frustration was that as long as I had to protect myself from the falling bricks of the chimney, I was not able to be of any assistance to my children.

As long as my energy is occupied in defending myself, I am not able to be truly helpful to anyone else.

As I reduce my fears and negative self-evaluations, I am able to see myself more clearly, and to make any changes that I wish to make. I am less defensive. I am more capable of being a caring, loving person able to understand and empathize with others. As long as I am preoccupied with hiding and defending myself, I cannot afford to see you clearly. Only when my lens is clear is that possible.

I am now in a position to see more clearly what mechanisms I use to cope with my fears. The wide scope of the information I have acquired in these chapters may now be brought together to form a concise and comprehensive picture of my patterns of coping.

The next pages provide a simple method for integrating scores from all the Elements to provide an overall picture. Before beginning this process I must be sure that my Scoring Summary is complete. I will use it to fill in the numbers required.

SELF-CONGRUENCE SUMMARY

By collecting all the different scores from all of the Elements, you can derive a profile for the areas in which you are already what you want to be, and those in which you want to be different from the way you are,

To complete Table 14 with the (Difference) scores from all the Elements, use the Scoring Summary, which will greatly simplify the task.

TABLE 14. Self-Summary

- Transfer the appropriate scores from the Scoring Summary to Table 14.
- Add all scores across each row and place the total in the box at right.
- Ignore the sign (+ or −); just add values.
- Add all scores down each column and place the totals in the boxes at bottom.
- Combine the column totals, as indicated, to obtain overall score.
- The lower the Total scores, the more satisfied (difference between IS and WANT) I am with myself in that area.

Δ11	Δ13	Δ41	Δ43	Δ71	Δ73	Δ10	▶	INCLUSION
Δ21	Δ23	Δ51	Δ53	Δ81	Δ83	Δ20	▶	CONTROL
Δ31	Δ33	Δ61	Δ63	Δ91	Δ93	Δ30	▶	OPENNESS
Δ15	Δ17	Δ45	Δ47	Δ75	Δ77	Δ40	▶	SIGNIFICANCE
Δ25	Δ27	Δ55	Δ57	Δ85	Δ87	Δ50	▶	COMPETENCE
Δ35	Δ37	Δ65	Δ67	Δ95	Δ97	Δ60	▶	LIKEABILITY
								OVERALL
PEOPLE IN GENERAL		PARTNER		JOB		SELF	OVERALL	

1. Record the eleven Total scores from Table 14 onto the bottom half of Profile (pullout page), placing a horizontal line (____) on each set of three columns corresponding to Total scores. For example, if your Total score above on INCLUSION is 23, on the Profile graph draw a straight line across the top of the three (22s) above INCLUSION. (Ignore the top half of graph for now.)
2. The bottom scores (28, 48, 168) mean that number *or more* (e.g., a score of 37 for inclusion would be marked at 28).
3. With a magic marker, fill in each row from the bottom to your mark.
4. The result is your bar graph. The higher the bar, the more you are what you want to be.

Interpretation

The height of the bar indicates the degree of difference between my Is and Want scores. The higher the bar, the smaller the difference. I recall that a large difference may mean either that (1) I am dissatisfied with how I am, or (2) I simply recognize that I would like to be different than I am. However, a small difference may be interpreted as self-satisfaction (being the way I want to be).

Inclusion: including and being included by people in general (Element B and Element F), partner (Element R), job (Job-Satisfaction Form), and self (Element S).

Control: controlling and being controlled by people in general, partner, job, and self.

Openness: being open toward and having others be open with me for people in general, partner, job, and self.

Significance: feeling that others are significant and being felt significant by people in general, partner, job, and self.

Competence: feelings of competence toward and from people in general, partner, job, and self.

Likeability: feelings of liking toward and from people in general, partner, job, and self.

People in General: all behaviors (inclusion, control, openness) and all feelings (significance, competence, likeability) toward and from people in general.

Partner: all behaviors and feelings toward and from my one partner (on Element R).

Job: all behaviors and feelings toward and from persons on the job.

Self: all behaviors and feelings from me toward myself.

Overall: all behaviors and feelings toward and from people in general, partner, job, and self.

ACTIVITY 41. Self-Congruence

1. Reflect on the results on the Profile. Do they make sense? Do they fit your picture of yourself?
2. Do the low-congruence scores indicate your dissatisfaction with yourself, or simply a recognition of a difference?
3. Is there anything you would like to do to change anything? What?

RESPONSES: Activity 41. Self-Congruence

COPING MECHANISMS SUMMARY

Using all the Elements also allows me to investigate better how I use the coping mechanisms. The likelihood that I am using a coping mechanism becomes much greater if (1) I tend to view people in the same way, regardless of context (that is, if I see people in general, one partner, and people on the job as being the same), and (2) the way that I view them is related to how I experience myself.

If I am seeing the world without using a mechanism, I will make differentiations depending on the situation. I will see, for example, that my partner may like me a great deal, that people in general are moderate, and that on the job I may not be well liked. A pattern like this indicates that I am seeing each person and each situation individually. On the other hand, if I see everyone in all situations as not liking me and if I do not like myself, then there is a good possibility that I am projecting.

Tables 15, 16, and 17 provide information about your use of coping mechanisms.

TABLE 15. Projection Summary

- Enter the scores from the Scoring Summary.
- Add and subtract as indicated. Ignore the sign.
- The lower the Sum, the more likely the statement is to be true.
- Circle the largest Sums and the statement to the right of it.

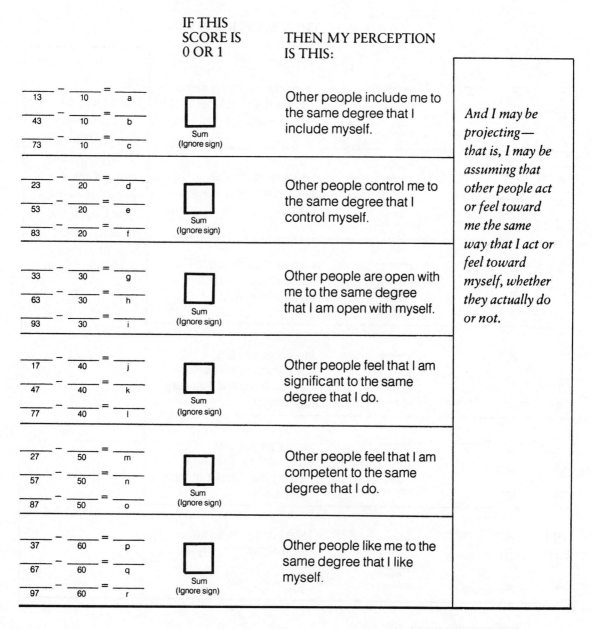

IF THIS SCORE IS 0 OR 1	THEN MY PERCEPTION IS THIS:	
Sum (Ignore sign)	Other people include me to the same degree that I include myself.	*And I may be projecting— that is, I may be assuming that other people act or feel toward me the same way that I act or feel toward myself, whether they actually do or not.*
Sum (Ignore sign)	Other people control me to the same degree that I control myself.	
Sum (Ignore sign)	Other people are open with me to the same degree that I am open with myself.	
Sum (Ignore sign)	Other people feel that I am significant to the same degree that I do.	
Sum (Ignore sign)	Other people feel that I am competent to the same degree that I do.	
Sum (Ignore sign)	Other people like me to the same degree that I like myself.	

TABLE 16. Displacement Summary

- Enter the scores from the Scoring Summary.
- Add and subtract as indicated. Ignore the sign.
- The lower the Sum, the more likely the statement is to be true.
- Circle the largest Sums and the statement to the right of it.

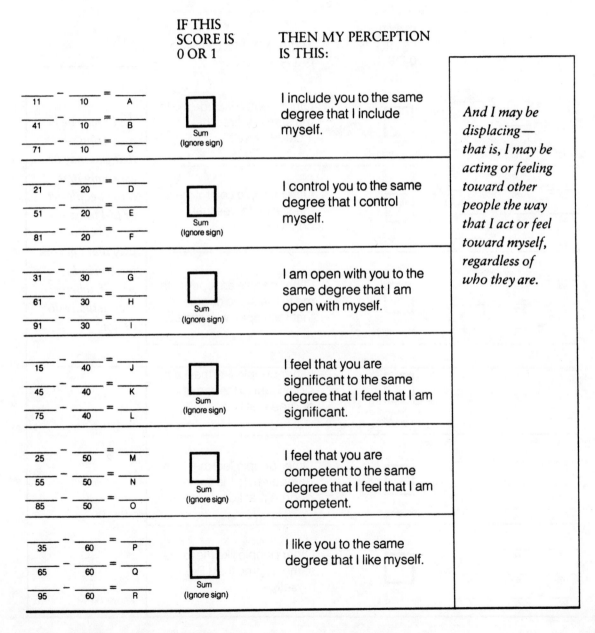

	IF THIS SCORE IS 0 OR 1	THEN MY PERCEPTION IS THIS:	
___ − ___ = ___ 11 10 A ___ − ___ = ___ 41 10 B ___ − ___ = ___ 71 10 C	□ Sum (Ignore sign)	I include you to the same degree that I include myself.	*And I may be displacing— that is, I may be acting or feeling toward other people the way that I act or feel toward myself, regardless of who they are.*
___ − ___ = ___ 21 20 D ___ − ___ = ___ 51 20 E ___ − ___ = ___ 81 20 F	□ Sum (Ignore sign)	I control you to the same degree that I control myself.	
___ − ___ = ___ 31 30 G ___ − ___ = ___ 61 30 H ___ − ___ = ___ 91 30 I	□ Sum (Ignore sign)	I am open with you to the same degree that I am open with myself.	
___ − ___ = ___ 15 40 J ___ − ___ = ___ 45 40 K ___ − ___ = ___ 75 40 L	□ Sum (Ignore sign)	I feel that you are significant to the same degree that I feel that I am significant.	
___ − ___ = ___ 25 50 M ___ − ___ = ___ 55 50 N ___ − ___ = ___ 85 50 O	□ Sum (Ignore sign)	I feel that you are competent to the same degree that I feel that I am competent.	
___ − ___ = ___ 35 60 P ___ − ___ = ___ 65 60 Q ___ − ___ = ___ 95 60 R	□ Sum (Ignore sign)	I like you to the same degree that I like myself.	

TABLE 17. Compensation Summary

- Enter the scores from the Scoring Summary.
- Add and subtract as indicated. Ignore the sign.
- The lower the Sum, the more likely the statement is to be true.
- Circle the largest Sums and the statement to the right of it.

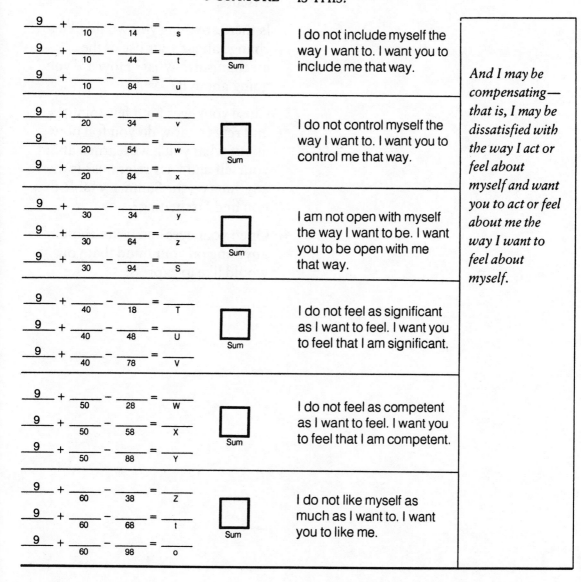

IF THIS
SCORE IS
3 OR MORE

THEN MY PERCEPTION
IS THIS:

$\dfrac{9}{} + \dfrac{}{10} - \dfrac{}{14} = \dfrac{}{s}$

$\dfrac{9}{} + \dfrac{}{10} - \dfrac{}{44} = \dfrac{}{t}$

$\dfrac{9}{} + \dfrac{}{10} - \dfrac{}{84} = \dfrac{}{u}$

Sum

I do not include myself the way I want to. I want you to include me that way.

$\dfrac{9}{} + \dfrac{}{20} - \dfrac{}{34} = \dfrac{}{v}$

$\dfrac{9}{} + \dfrac{}{20} - \dfrac{}{54} = \dfrac{}{w}$

$\dfrac{9}{} + \dfrac{}{20} - \dfrac{}{84} = \dfrac{}{x}$

Sum

I do not control myself the way I want to. I want you to control me that way.

$\dfrac{9}{} + \dfrac{}{30} - \dfrac{}{34} = \dfrac{}{y}$

$\dfrac{9}{} + \dfrac{}{30} - \dfrac{}{64} = \dfrac{}{z}$

$\dfrac{9}{} + \dfrac{}{30} - \dfrac{}{94} = \dfrac{}{S}$

Sum

I am not open with myself the way I want to be. I want you to be open with me that way.

$\dfrac{9}{} + \dfrac{}{40} - \dfrac{}{18} = \dfrac{}{T}$

$\dfrac{9}{} + \dfrac{}{40} - \dfrac{}{48} = \dfrac{}{U}$

$\dfrac{9}{} + \dfrac{}{40} - \dfrac{}{78} = \dfrac{}{V}$

Sum

I do not feel as significant as I want to feel. I want you to feel that I am significant.

$\dfrac{9}{} + \dfrac{}{50} - \dfrac{}{28} = \dfrac{}{W}$

$\dfrac{9}{} + \dfrac{}{50} - \dfrac{}{58} = \dfrac{}{X}$

$\dfrac{9}{} + \dfrac{}{50} - \dfrac{}{88} = \dfrac{}{Y}$

Sum

I do not feel as competent as I want to feel. I want you to feel that I am competent.

$\dfrac{9}{} + \dfrac{}{60} - \dfrac{}{38} = \dfrac{}{z}$

$\dfrac{9}{} + \dfrac{}{60} - \dfrac{}{68} = \dfrac{}{t}$

$\dfrac{9}{} + \dfrac{}{60} - \dfrac{}{98} = \dfrac{}{o}$

Sum

I do not like myself as much as I want to. I want you to like me.

And I may be compensating— that is, I may be dissatisfied with the way I act or feel about myself and want you to act or feel about me the way I want to feel about myself.

Hope by this time that you are not hard on yourself, but remember that you are simply exploring.

ACTIVITY 42. Copers

1. Circle the largest numbers in the Sum boxes in Tables 16, 17, and 18. Do these seem to you to be areas where you use defense mechanisms? Think of examples from your own life, professional or personal, that would confirm or deny this result. Discuss.

2. Is there anything you would like to change about your use of the mechanisms? What? How are you going about it?

3. Close your eyes for a few minutes and reflect. How do you feel now about what you have learned about yourself and your relations? Is there anything on the Summary table that you find fascinating?

4. Open your eyes and write about anything on your mind that you would like to express.

RESPONSES: Activity 42. Copers

INTEGRATION

I am now ready for a total summary picture of myself as I have chosen to be right now.

If I combine my pattern of coping mechanisms with the congruence I feel between how I am and how I want to be, I will be able to see:

(1) areas of discrepancy — places where I am not what I would like to be; and

(2) places where I project, identify, and/or compensate.

Of particular interest are those areas in which I would like to be different and in which I am very likely to be using a coping mechanism. For example, if I do not like myself and I see everyone not liking me (projection), that insight affords me an important awareness.

Table 18 provides the data you need for making this exploration.

Directions

1. Transfer scores as indicated from Tables 15, 16, and 17 to Table 18
2. Add rows and columns, as indicated, to obtain Total scores.
3. Place Total scores thus obtained on the top half of the Profile.
4. Place a horizontal line in each column and fill in the columns from the top down.

TABLE 18. Summary of Coping Mechanisms

	PROJECTION				DISPLACEMENT				COMPENSATION			
	PEOPLE (G)	PARTNER (R)	JOB (J)	PROJECT (P)	PEOPLE (G)	PARTNER (R)	JOB (J)	DISPLACE (D)	PEOPLE (G)	PARTNER (R)	JOB (J)	COMPENSATE (T)
INCLUSION (I)	a	b	c	IP	A	B	C	ID	s	t	u	IT
CONTROL (C)	d	e	f	CP	D	E	F	CD	v	w	x	CT
OPENNESS (O)	g	h	i	OP	G	H	I	OD	y	z	S	OT
SIGNIFICANCE (S)	j	k	l	SP	J	K	L	SD	T	U	V	ST
COMPETENCE (M)	m	n	o	MP	M	N	O	MD	W	X	Y	MT
LIKEABILITY (L)	p	q	r	LP	P	Q	R	LD	Z	t	o	LT
	GP	RP	JP	EP	GD	RD	JD	ED	GT	RT	JT	ET

ov

ACTIVITY 43.
Satisfaction and Reality

1. Which are the areas which (1) are most meaningful to you, (2) where you are not the way you want to be and (3) where you distort reality?

2. Think of specific occasions so that this information may help you understand better. Does it help to have another interpretation?

3. Are you keeping in mind that no judgment is involved in having this insight? If anything, there is usually an advantage in having increased awareness.

4. Are you keeping in mind that you have the capacity to change anything you want changed?

5. Is there some way you would like to change? How would you go about it?

SELF-DESCRIPTION SUMMARY

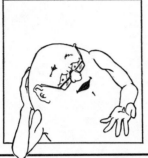

You may find it valuable to reflect on all the information that comes out of *The Truth Option*. Pulling it together in a convenient way will help you to look it over whenever you feel like it, or whenever you get an insight that you would like to check out. Table 20 provides this convenience by summarizing all the scores (in contrast to the difference scores used in the Profile) presented in these chapters, including those from Elements B, F, R, and S, and the job.

TABLE 20. Summary of Self-Descriptions

		PEOPLE		PARTNER		JOB		SELF
		DO	GET	DO	GET	DO	GET	
INCLUSION	IS	11	13	41	43	71	73	10
	WANT	12	14	42	44	72	74	19
CONTROL	IS	21	23	51	53	81	83	20
	WANT	22	24	52	54	82	84	29
OPENNESS	IS	31	33	61	63	91	93	30
	WANT	32	34	62	64	92	94	39
SIGNIFICANCE	IS	15	17	45	47	75	77	40
	WANT	16	18	46	48	76	78	49
COMPETENCE	IS	25	27	55	57	85	87	50
	WANT	26	28	56	58	86	88	59
LIKEABILITY	IS	35	37	65	67	95	97	60
	WANT	36	38	66	68	96	98	69

ACTIVITY 44.
Self-Description Summary

Here are some suggestions for analyzing these scores:

1. Add columns to get Total scores.
2. Add rows to get Total scores.
3. Compare the same dimension in different areas.
4. Observe trends.
5. Note outstandingly large or small scores.
6. Note scores that do not fit the pattern.
7. Note scores that surprise you.
8. Be totally creative!

RESPONSES: Activity 44. Self-Description Summary

FINAL SEGUE

I feel trepidation. I have gone through this book and feel quite different than I did before I read it. But what happens next?

As the author I would like to respond to some of the concerns you may be having. I would like to dialogue with you about some questions that people frequently ask themselves.

Question: It may be fine for me to tell the truth, but what if other people don't want to? Won't they have an advantage over me, or at least won't they think I'm odd?

You have a choice. If you want to be truthful and they do not, you can adopt their values or retain your own. I prefer to follow my own because I feel good about myself when I am truthful. Also, I find that truth telling is contagious. Deep down most people would love to tell the truth but they are afraid. When I tell the truth I take the step they find difficult and it frees them to follow. Following is usually easier than breaking the ice. It is also my experience that truth telling is ultimately practical. Although some people may try to use your truth against you, most people like and admire truthful people and tend to favor them for jobs and for friendship. So there are three reasons for telling the truth whether other people do or not: (1) it feels good; (2) it helps others to tell the truth; (3) it is practical.

Question: Truth telling may be OK while I'm on my own, but how can I carry it out at work when there are pressures to go back to being the way I was?

It is again a matter of choice. You can prepare yourself to not carry back any of the things you have learned — compile an impressive list of why "they" won't let you. Sure enough, you will find that you are right — you haven't retained your changes, just as you predicted! Or you can devote that same energy to figuring out your gains and deciding how to maintain and enlarge them. As with most things, the first step is to be aware of when you are backsliding, then the next step is to be in touch with the payoff you get from backsliding.

I have noticed a tendency among many people who are just beginning on this new path to return quickly to an old familiar pattern if there is some difficulty. As illustrated by Tucker (page 180) when he was dealing with his paralytic condition, it is important to be persistent. You are reorienting your life in some sense, and this requires a total *body* experience of reorganization, which often takes some time.

Granted there are aspects of the environment that must be dealt with. From your old viewpoint these may be seen as difficult. They may, however, be looked at as challenges to test your will and your ability to maintain the changes.

Question: Can't I become *too* aware, so that I spend all my time contemplating my navel?

You can overdo it if you wish. But remember: Having the capacity to be aware is not the same as having to be continually introspective. The fact that you know how to diagnose and repair a television set need not prevent you from enjoying the TV programs. Being aware simply means that if things are not going the way you want them to go, you have the tools to change them. You can be just as aware as you wish.

Question: Perhaps. But won't all this inner awareness drive people away?

Your friends may change. Those people who do not feel comfortable looking more closely at themselves quite possibly will drift away, while those who do may become closer friends. This phenomenon is reported frequently. It is important not to be evaluative about people in this regard. Everyone is choosing the amount of awareness they feel best with. It's a choice, not a matter of bad or good.

This latter point is important to keep in mind if you have a tendency to be an evangelist. Often when people find something that has made a dramatic difference in their lives, they want to tell everyone, with enthusiasm. This is fine; but then they make the mistake of assuming that everyone else would have the same reaction to the experience that they did. That is usually not the case.

Question: How can I follow up and continue in this direction?

Appendix C of this book lists some places to write to and some books to read. Start there, and follow where your interests are. You might also write to me and tell me of your experiences. I will keep you up to date on current activities, and put you on my mailing list if you wish.

I also offer training for organizations. If you feel that your organization is interested in using this approach, you can contact me.

Finally, if this way of viewing the world really appeals to you, you might want to become a trainer and offer workshops yourself. Mention that to me, too.

EPILOGUE:
THE HUMAN SPIRIT

In *The Truth Option,* we have focused on the human experience. I have presented a point of view, and an invitation to suspend judgment on that viewpoint until you had experienced all of the material in this book. Now that you are almost finished, let us reflect on this approach.

- Your life, including your personal and professional life, is in your hands. You can choose it, you can change it, you can learn to enjoy it, you can shape it any way you wish.

- You have the power, but you do not *have to* do anything. You have the ability, not the obligation.

- There is no evaluation in this approach. It is aimed at helping you to understand, not to assign blame.

- Your feelings about yourself are the basic determinants of everything else. If you do not have a good feeling about yourself, life is difficult. Attempts to understand problems that do not deal with the self-concept inevitably lead to temporary solutions. We operate from within, and it is our core that we must understand if we are to make permanent changes.

- Awareness is a key to successful human functioning. It is difficult to reach our destination if we do not know the territory. *The Truth Option* provides some tools for understanding human behavior, human feelings, human relationships, job fit, and the mechanisms we use to protect our fragile parts. The more we know of these phenomena, the more prepared we are to make wise decisions for ourselves.

- I have stressed the truth throughout. Truth—the grand simplifier. Truth—the value we learn at our parents' knee and yet, for most of us, a frightening reality. By and large we fear the truth. We fear the consequences of letting people know who we really are. We even fear knowing ourselves.

- When we are brave enough to risk being honest, especially being honest with awareness, magical things occur, as I hope you have already experienced somewhere during this exploration. Truthful relating is exhilarating, alive, exciting, freeing, tension-releasing, warmth- and closeness-producing. And it inevitably leads to immensely increased creativity and effectiveness. —even prior to 2001.

These are the simple precepts. We are limitless. Given the tools of truth, awareness, self-responsibility, and a healthy self-regard, there are no limits to where the human spirit may soar.

ACTIVITY 45. Finale

1. Stand up and shut your eyes. Feel a huge ball, warm and powerful, right under your navel inside your body. Feel it gradually grow down your legs and out your toes; up your torso, down your arms and out your fingers; up your neck, through your head, and out your crown.

2. Feel fully the warmth, the power, the slight vibration filling your whole being.

3. Keeping that sensation, feel yourself as totally significant, competent, and lovable. Concentrate on each feeling so that you feel each fully, then all of them together, and the warm, powerful, vibrating sensation.

4. Experience that for a few minutes. Then, keeping that feeling, open your eyes and walk around the room. Do whatever you feel like doing spontaneously.

5. This is your feeling. You can have it forever — if you want it.

PERSONAL MEANING OF
A LOOK BACK, A LOOK FORWARD

Appendix A
HISTORY OF THE TRUTH OPTION

Home

As anyone who is the oldest son in a Jewish family will attest, the family push is on accomplishment: "First become president, then go make something of yourself!" Accompanying that clear admonition is an evaluation of each accomplishment: "Nothing is ever quite good enough."

Accepting these guidelines, I sallied forth into the academic world, went to a respectable university (UCLA), received a Ph.D. at a young age, and proceeded to do everything my Jewish mother (I later found out that these attitudes are not confined to Jews) wanted me to do so that I would "be happy," and so that she could tell her Mah Jongg and Canasta partners about her son. I taught and did research at Harvard, Chicago, Berkeley, and several other prestigious institutions.

Scientist

Not only did I teach at the "right" places, I became a "scientist." I concentrated in psychology but studied virtually as much philosophy—in particular, scientific method, philosophy of science, logical empiricism, and research design (from no less a figure than Hans Reichenbach). I taught statistics, produced a dissertation in which I created a new statistic, did a summer workshop on mathematics for social scientists, and worked with Paul Lazarsfeld on a fellowship in social science methodology, which resulted in an article in *Psychometrika*. In short, I immersed myself in the world of science.

I found this fascinating, and I was thoroughly enjoying the respectability and elitism of knowing about numbers. All this culminated in my first book, *FIRO: A Three Dimensional Theory of Interpersonal Behavior* (1958). This was based on research I had done while on active duty in the navy, charged with learning to predict how any given group of men would work together.[32] The book presented the FIRO theory and several measuring instruments, including one called FIRO-B. This publication climaxed my first scientific phase.

These and the next five years appeared to be quite successful, but something was wrong. I was straining at the edges of academe. I wanted to try new, nontraditional techniques.

Outlaws

In the mid-1960s I was involved in studying clinical behavior in a hospital at the Albert Einstein Medical School, which is widely respected as an avant-garde institution. Under the supervision of an eminent psychoanalyst, I watched psychiatrists run psychotherapy groups. At the same time I began conducting T-groups (T for training) at Bethel, Maine. This activity was also being performed by many people who, from the traditional viewpoint, were "unqualified" and used "untested" methods for "too short a time" with "inadequate screening and follow-up." In short, they were outlaws.

I could not understand my reaction. I thought it must be due to my inexperience, but it seemed to me that the work done and the results obtained by the outlaws was more creative, more innovative, faster, and more effective than that done in the heart of the establishment. I was more attracted to the outlaws, partly due also to my growing unease with teaching.

Although I loved the classroom and the teaching process, I never felt fully adequate. I felt phony. I assigned my classes the second-best book in the field, while I read ahead in the best book and lectured from it. Until I became involved in groups—encounter groups—I did not feel that I *knew* anything. After being a member then a leader in groups I did not feel phony, because I was teaching what I personally had experienced. I was no longer repeating a textbook. I could now say something that I *knew* in a more complete, holistic, way rather than just having read about. I became fascinated with groups, and for the next twenty-five years I have been leading groups in one way or another all around the world.

My group experience inspired a whirlwind tour of seminars and meetings in New York to learn about the new techniques being practiced in the area of human behavior. I spent a year with Psychosynthesis, a spiritually oriented technique devised by an Italian contemporary of Freud named Roberto Assagioli. I learned of psychodrama, of bioenergetics, of rolfing, and of gestalt therapy. All these methods seemed rich and effective. I began to incorporate them into my own techniques of group leading, with wonderful results.

Consulting

At about this time I was also consulting with various organizations and corporations. I presented workshops on creativity, team building, communication, stress management, or whatever topic currently was popular. These workshops were usually successful, and I received high ratings on the post-workshop evaluations. I would read them, smile, and file them.

But again a discomfort: If I returned to the same corporation two weeks later and asked what they had learned from the workshop, I received answers like, "Wait just a minute till I find my notes." I smiled weakly, left, and rushed home to reread the post-workshop evaluations, trying to put the follow-up comments out of my head. But something was not working. I did not learn what that something was until about twenty years later.

Esalen

By this time, I had decided to leave the academic world. Even though I had just been promoted to associate professor in the Einstein Medical School—a coup for a nonmedical doctor—my heart was elsewhere. A man named Michael Murphy had started something called a growth center in California, and it seemed to provide an opportunity to experiment outside the confines of the traditional academic setting. In 1967, I resigned from Einstein, left New York and headed west.

From the group area I entered the human potential movement at the Esalen Institute in Big Sur, California. There I studied and experienced a variety of approaches to developing the full potential of each person and of the interaction between people.[2] These approaches came from many periods of history and from many countries. They included body methods, psychological approaches, and energy and spiritual orientations.

In my early years at Esalen I wrote a great deal. Before I moved in to live at Esalen I had written *Joy* (1967), which, fortunately, became a best seller and helped fill my workshops. *Here Comes Everybody* (1971) was a follow-up to *Joy*; it reflected my early experiences at Esalen. The principles of encounter groups were chronicled in *Elements of Encounter* (1973). *Leaders of Schools* (1977) was a final hurrah to the second scientific era: It reported a large (6,000 people) research study of school administrators done a few years before at Berkeley. *Body Fantasy* (1976) was a case study for a new bodymind therapy I had developed, combining rolfing and imagery.

In 1979 it was time to sum up the fascinating decade of the Esalen experience, which had so widened my perspective on what people and human interaction were about. I wrote of these experiences in *Profound Simplicity* (1979). The book is based on the realization that no matter where I began my investigation of human beings — whether with individual or interpersonal methods, such as encounter groups, imagery, gestalt therapy, or psychodrama; with body techniques, such as acupuncture, bioenergetics, rolfing, or Feldenkrais; with energy approaches, such as aikido or t'ai chi; or with spiritual orientations — if I understood what they were saying at a deep enough level, they were all saying about the same thing. In *Profound Simplicity,* I described the principles toward which I felt all approaches to human experiences were converging.

Integration

In 1975 I moved from Esalen to the San Francisco Bay Area. I intended to combine my experience from the previous decade with the scientific and theoretical work of my earlier years at Harvard and Berkeley, and to apply the result to established institutions. My first attempt was to establish the Holistic Studies graduate program at Antioch University, San Francisco[34] — an application of the principles to the institution of education. This program worked wonderfully. It continues to flourish, and it encouraged me to apply these methods to other aspects of establishment.

When I returned to organizational consulting to make a second application of the *Profound Simplicity* principles, I found that rather than directly addressing specific problems such as communications, turnover, motivation and stress management, I now preferred to help create an atmosphere of truth (one of the *Profound Simplicity* principles) in the organization. Once that atmosphere exists, other problems are relatively simple to solve. They become logical puzzles. What I discovered was that perhaps 80 to 90 percent of organizational problems dissolve if there is an atmosphere of truth. Truth is management's grand simplifier.

Further, the problem that had plagued me twenty years earlier — the ephemeral impact of highly rated workshops — seemed to be yielding a solution. If people were willing to tell the truth and if they understood themselves, the effect of workshops was far more likely to be permanent. The self-concept had become a central part of my work, and the difference in impact from my twenty-year-ago emphasis on behavior change was striking and dramatic.

After discoveries such as these, I decided to develop more systematically some materials based on my human potential experience and on the theoretical work with FIRO theory and the FIRO scales that I had developed many years before. Over the next four years I undertook the fascinating task of integrating the scientific with the experiential. After dozens of revisions based on administering the material to about 200 people from many organizations (including Kodak, Esso, Ampex, Mattel, United Biscuit, U.S. Army, and Apple Computer), modules emerged. These modules were called, collectively, "The Human Element." They were first published in 1981 in workbook form, to be administered by qualified trainers in a workshop setting.

Concurrent with my personal evolution, American organizations were becoming aware of the cost effectiveness of releasing more of the potential of their personnel. This awareness was spurred in part by the spectacular success of Japanese production—an achievement that usually is attributed to the Japanese treatment of personnel through such methods as quality circles and the creation of a family atmosphere in the organization. Japanese management uses many principles similar to those in *The Human Element,* partly because many of these principles were partially adopted from American approaches of the 1950s and 1960s—including T-groups, which were forerunners of the human potential movement.

Indirect support for the point of view of *The Human Element* came from several best-selling books. *In Search of Excellence, Megatrends, The One-Minute Manager, The Change Masters,* and *Theory Z* all agree that the organizations that succeed best are those that pay attention to people. The Human Element's organizational program is a *next step* after these books: It offers a program for dealing with the human side of organizations to develop employees' potential, to empower them, and to maximize their cooperation or fitting together for increased productivity and satisfaction.

Individuals

By combining my early experience with individual growth in a group context with The Human Element program for organizations, a similar program for individuals seemed a logical next step. This could provide a simple structure for more rapid growth, combining and harmonizing the virtues of experiential methods (such as group-process imagery and nonverbal methods) with those of scientific approaches (such as testing and experimentation). Thus The Human Element workbook was adapted for individuals. It has resulted in the present book.

This book is very satisfying to me because it accomplishes what I have held as an aim since university days. This aim is a philosophy of living, a theory of human existence, and a set of techniques to turn these ideas into avenues for more joyful and productive living. I have sided with those who feel that a philosophy or a theory remains an intellectual game unless it has practical and useful consequences; otherwise not only is it not useful but, if it does not work, it probably is wrong.

On the other hand, I also believe that a sound philosophy and theory makes practical applications simple to derive. It is tedious and inefficient to try to solve problems one at a time without looking for the underlying principles that generalize and simplify applications.

The Truth Option is a synthesis of East and West, of science and experience, of soft and hard, of yin and yang, of male and female. It is an integrated systems, or holistic, approach to the human problems of individuals, relationships, and families based on an overarching philosophy and theory.

I hope my mother likes it.

Appendix B
TRUTH AND MONEY

Let's apply these principles to the relation between you and me.

In this book I have presented several measures (Elements) and several forms that are sold commercially. Since they are printed in full, it is a simple matter for you to take them from the book and to make an indefinite number of copies at low cost. Even though these materials are copyrighted, in truth there is no way that I could prevent you from doing this, short of dropping my career and becoming a full-time policeman with a staff to guard every copying machine in the world all the time. I will not do that, and it would not be consistent with the principles of this book if I did.

This is my attitude toward the use of the materials printed in this book.

- I want these materials to be used as widely as possible. In my experience they are extremely valuable for a wide variety of users. They can help people and organizations to transform their lives in very positive ways. I feel good when people use them.

- If you want to use them for some local, modest purpose — for instance, for you and your mate, for your family, for a small committee or group of friends, or for charitable or community organizations — I encourage you to do so.

- If you feel that you do not have sufficient funds to pay the commercial price for the materials or for consultation services, I will take your word for it. If you wish, I will provide you with free supportive services. Call me or my staff at (415) 383-8275 and we shall give you advice and suggestions at no cost. For some groups we may provide an intern in training to help administer The Human Element, the organizational program, free of charge.

- Before deciding that you are not in a position to pay, I would like you to follow the spirit of this book by shutting your eyes and saying to yourself, "I am not able to pay anything for this service." If your body affirms the truth of this statement by feeling calm, clear, and good, that is all I need. I accept your decision and will provide you with all the cooperation at my disposal.

- If you feel that you are in a position to pay for this service, I would like you to pay for it. I want to make money from this work. I do not want you to use the copying machine to evade payment for the materials. I think you will feel better and I will feel better if you pay for the materials (sources are listed in back) or if you hire my company to provide consultation or a workshop for you.

- In summary, the spirit of this book implies that I trust you. If you feel that you are in a position to pay, I will provide you with the best materials and services. If you feel that you are not in a position to pay, I will provide you with free telephone consultation and possibly with trainees to help you administer these materials most effectively. I shall accept your judgment as to whether and how much you should pay. In this way we both win.

Appendix C
NEXT STEPS

There are several directions for you to go if you would like to follow up your experience with *The Truth Option*. If you would like to pursue any of these, please complete the enclosed form.

The Human Element Program for Organizational Effectiveness

Will Schutz Associates (WSA) offers a variety of programs for organizations, based on the principles used in this book. These programs include:

- One-day introductions.

- One- to three-day programs within organizations targeted at specific topics such as communication, team building, performance review, stress management, job fit, and decision making.

- One- and two-day workshops for learning to administer the Elements.

- Complete workshops of three and a half days covering all topics through the self-concept, presented as an integrated whole. This workshop is highly recommended for organizations and individuals who wish to explore this approach.

- Special workshops may be designed for your special circumstances.

Written Materials

Schutz Measures

The individual Elements presented in *The Truth Option* (B, F, R, S) are available for separate administration.

It is strongly recommended that people attend an Elements Training Workshop prior to administering these scales. The training workshop covers administration, scoring, interpretation, and theory behind each Element, and uses of the Elements.

Elements B, F, R, and S are published (under the name The Schutz Measures) separately by two publishers, and are targeted at different audiences.

For research and clinical purposes:
Consulting Psychologists Press
577 College Avenue
Palo Alto, CA 94306
(415) 857-1444

For training purposes:
University Associates
P.O. Box 26240
San Diego, CA 92126
(800) 854-2143

You may order directly from the publishers; or you may order from WSA.

Books

Books by Will Schutz are also available through WSA. They include: *The Interpersonal Underworld (FIRO), Joy, Here Comes Everybody, Elements of Encounter, Body Fantasy, Leaders of Schools, Profound Simplicity,* and *The Truth Option.*

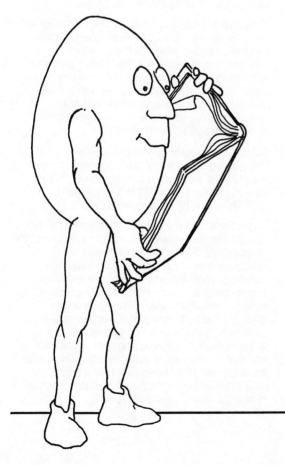

Other Instruments

Several instruments derived from the principles used in this book are also available from WSA.

- *Performance Review.* An instrument to appraise the relationship between supervisor and employee. It is unique in that it is a completely two-way communication based on the goal of improving and strengthening the relationship, thereby upgrading performance. It is designed to be used as a supplement to a performance appraisal.

- *Job Forms* (see page 100).

- *Job-Fit Forms* (see page 103).

- Other instruments and packages designed for your specific purposes.

Newsletter

WSA publishes a newsletter periodically, describing: experiences using The Human Element in organizations and with individuals; research; and revisions of the concepts. It is intended to support a network of people who are interested in this approach to human issues.

NOTES

For those of you who would like to find the scientific and experiential foundation for this approach, here are some guidelines.

(The numbers in parentheses refer to the pages on which the notes are referenced.)

1 The G.I. Bill is a precedent for this approach. It is one of the most successful pieces of legislation of the last half-century. Veterans were financially supported until they attained their educational goal, then were presumed to be self-sufficient, and the support stopped. This legislation is often given a great deal of credit for the rise in American prestige on the world scene following World War II. (3)

2 The human potential movement, which was at the core of this development, has been chronicled in Anderson (1984). (4, 283)

3 Reconciliation of religious views, especially Judeo-Christian, with the principles of *The Truth Option* has been the object of much interest. See Feddon (1983), Oden (1972), and Steinberg (1975). (4)

4 The philosophical basis of this approach is discussed in some detail in *Profound Simplicity* (Schutz, 1979). Earlier statements of the principles stated in this book evolved through several books by the author (Schutz, 1958, 1971, 1973, 1976, 1977, 1979.) (7)

5 The literature on self-regard is vast. "Self-esteem" and "self-concept" are also terms used similarly. One of the pioneering efforts in this field was reported in Snygg and Combs (1949). See also Sherif (1968). (8)

6 "Joy" is defined as "the feeling that comes from the fulfillment of one's potential. Fulfillment brings to an individual the feeling that he [this was written in preliberation days] can cope with his environment; the sense of confidence in himself as a significant, competent, lovable person who is capable of handling situations as they arise, able to use fully his own capacities, and free to express his feelings. Joy requires a vital, alive body, self-contentment, productive and satisfying relations with others, and a successful relation to society." (Schutz, 1967). (8)

7 One of the most thorough historical and philosophical discussions of truth is presented in Bok (1978). Also see Wise (1973). (9)

8 This theme is common in literature. In *Wuthering Heights* (Bronte, 1847), for example, Heathcliff overhears a discussion by Kathy, which he interprets as rejecting him. He then leaves and spends the next twenty years of his life trying to prove himself. If he had checked with her he would have discovered that she was not rejecting him. Perhaps he could have spent twenty more years with her. (11)

9 Similar concepts of choice have been developing over the last few decades. Some of the clearest are: Roberts (1976, 1974, 1978); Ichazo (1980); Erhard (1975); Greenwald (1973); Reich (1975); and Perls (1951). (18)

10 The choice idea is in contrast to the most widely used theory of behavior, conditioning or stimulus response (S–R) theory. In that theory, a response is posited to follow a stimulus with a certain probability, depending on the rewards (reinforcers) and punishments (extinguishers) associated with the event. The choice idea changes the S-R model to S-O-R, where O is the organism. It states that the organism (in the present case, a human being) perceives and interprets the stimulus, and the organism chooses its response. This change in outlook allows for individual empowerment and places the person in charge of his or her own life. (19)

[11] *The American Psychologist,* the house organ for the American Psychologist Association, published an article on responsibility (Brickman, *et al.,* 1982). The authors did an excellent job of delineating the various approaches to responsibility; but unfortunately, in describing the present approach, they completely misunderstood the nonjudgmental nature of this position, calling it "The Moralistic Model." (20)

[12] Workshops on stress management typically emphasize "stressors" as the basic ingredient of stress. There is a popular list of life events (divorce, death of a child, being fired from a job, going on vacation, etc.) that are assigned points, and a certain total indicates stress to the point of illness (Benson, 1980). This is an excellent example of a stimulus-response approach. The implication is that these stimuli "caused" the illness response. There is little consideration that the person interprets the stimulus and chooses how he or she will respond. (23)

[13] For the basis of this theory — including a summary of about twenty studies of psychoanalytic categories, empirical studies of group behavior, studies of delinquency, etc. — see Schutz (1958), Chapter 2. This review attempts to establish that many approaches to human behavior come to essentially the same three dimensions. (28)

[14] The dimension of openness was originally called "Affection" in Schutz (1958) and other publications. The reasons for the change are described in Schutz (1982, 1983). (29)

[15] The imagery technique used throughout this book is based on a long history of development in the psychological literature. The modern antecedents are Freud's "dream analysis" and Jung's "active imagination." The modern practitioners who have most influenced the present approach are Leuner (1965) and Desoille (1965). (32)

[16] Element B is an extension and refinement of the FIRO-B questionnaire. It has been revised to conform to the changes in theory and to produce more information in a short time. The changes are described in Schutz (1982, 1983) and this information and the other Elements are available. See Appendix C for detailed information on how to obtain them. (39)

[17] This definition of lovability or likeability is similar to that of Kelly (1955). (53)

[18] In organizational applications, jobs are defined by a number of people. Typically, the supervisor or the personnel office has that task, but it may also be performed by organization policy, peers, subordinates, or clients. For the present purpose, the job holder defines his or her own job. (71)

[19] For an excellent description of the area of job fit, see Bolles (1972). (81)

[20] Forms and manuals based on these principles for use in job selection, job placement and also for performance review are available. See Appendix C. (81)

[21] "Presence" and "Awareness" may have as a rough physiological counterpart exteroceptors and interoceptors, the nerve cells that allow us awareness of the outside and the inside. "Spontaneity" may correspond to motor cells that control the contraction and relaxation of the muscle cells. (114).

[22] There is an impressive literature on defense mechanisms or coping mechanisms. The first major work was by A. Freud (1946). One of the most comprehensive analyses of these mechanisms is given in Waxler (1960). This work was summarized and extended in Schutz (1976). (145)

[23] Prediction of political attitudes from a person's interpersonal orientations has been done with considerable success. See Schutz (1966, pp. 69–72). (146)

[24] The concept of choosing one's own illness is highly controversial. A small number of members of the holistic health movement plus some spiritual traditions are strong advocates of this position, while the medical profession in general is opposed. For some excellent statements of supportive positions, see Dunbar (1939) and Wolf (1968). (161)

[25] Michael Murphy has made a study of psychic phenomena in sports and of the control of the body. See Murphy and White (1978). This approach is related to the popular series of books by Gallwey (1974) and by Gallwey and Kriegel (1977). (163)

26 Feldenkrais (1970) has written brilliantly on the topic of body awareness. Several of the ideas and exercises presented here are based on his work. The work of Reich (1949) and elaborations made by his students, particularly Lowen (1976) and Baker (1980), is very important in the development of the areas of the relations between body and mind. (163)

27 There has been only spotty research of these ideas of specific illness choice, partly because research does not typically look for these factors. Borst (1984) has done a study of the theory with very positive results. (175)

28 It goes without saying that this technique is *not* offered as a replacement for standard medical treatment. Generally, the method that you believe will work has the best chance of working. If you prefer standard medical practice, by all means pursue it. The following method is offered for those of you who would like to try it. If you find it useful, you may wish to use it. If not, you can always return to whatever methods you now use. Remember, it is your choice. You may also find that *this* method works better the more you believe it works. If you resist—if you want to show that it is worthless—you are very likely to succeed. (180)

29 This technique is described in detail in Schutz (1966). (186)

30 Many people find that they feel better to the degree that their imagery was successful. Simonton's (1978) work on cancer uses a similar technique. He found that when the imagery (he used the image of white blood cells overcoming cancer cells) was unsuccessful, there was little physical improvement. (186)

31 This approach, used in Hong Kong with Chinese and British nationals, had a surprising result. Cultural stereotypes indicate that the Chinese are not open. Face-saving and indirection are important values. However, after a day and a half of a workshop it became obvious that the Chinese were more open than either the British or the Americans. One explanation is that *The Truth Option* deals with people as human begins rather than as cultural representatives; hence cultural differences dissolve. We are all people dealing with our fears, wishes, and defenses, regardless of our cultural heritage. (191)

32 The work on compatibility has been developed over the last several decades. The first publication appeared in a journal article (Schutz, 1955) and was later published in book form (Schutz, 1958). The original work was done in the navy and was created for the purpose of composing navy groups that would be productive together. (195, 210, 281)

33 This theory of group development recently has been offered as a framework for organizing approaches to family therapy. Doherty and Colangelo (1984) have proposed the theory as a way of organizing therapeutic approaches to families and to give direction for the order of problems to deal with. Bell (1984) has elaborated this idea to apply to movement family therapy. (244)

34 This project has been described in Schutz (1978a, 1979a). (283)

REFERENCES

Anderson, W. *The Upstart Spring.* Menlo Park, CA: Addison-Wesley, 1983.

Baker, E. *Man in the Trap.* New York: Macmillan, 1980.

Bell, J. "Family Therapy in Motion: Observing, Assessing and Changing the Family Dance," in Bernstein, P. (ed), *Vol. II. Theoretical Approaches to Dance Movement Therapy.* Dubuque, IA: Kendall/Hunt, 1984.

Benson, H. *Mind-Body Effect.* New York: G.P. Putnam's Suns, 1980.

Blanchard, K. and Johnson, S. *The One Minute Manager.* New York: William Morrow, 1982.

Bok, S. *Lying: Moral Choice in Public and Private Life.* New York: Vintage, 1979.

Borst, L. "Patterns That Connect Emotion and Disease." Master's thesis, Antioch University (San Francisco), 1983.

Brickman, P., Rabinowitz, V., Karuza, J., Coates, D., Cohn, E., and Kidder, L. "Models of Helping and Coping," *American Psychologist* (1982): 368–384.

Bronte, E. *Wuthering Heights.* London: Newby, 1847.

Canter, R. *The Change Masters.* New York: Simon and Schuster, 1983.

Desoille, R. *The Directed Daydream.* New York: Psychosynthesis Research Foundation, 1965.

Doherty, W. and Colangelo, N. "The Family FIRO Model: A Modest Proposal for Organizing Family Treatment," *Journal of Marital and Family Therapy* 10 (1984): 19–29.

Dunbar, F. *Psychomatic Medicine.* New York: Hoeber, 1939.

Erhard, W. From est (Erhard Training Seminars) seminar. 1975.

Feddon, J., "Toward a Holistic Spirituality." Master's thesis, Antioch University (San Francisco) 1983.

Feldenkrais, M. *Awareness Through Movement.* New York: Harper & Row, 1973.

Freud, A. *The Ego and Mechanisms of Defense.* New York: International Universities Press, 1946.

Gallwey, T. *Inner Tennis.* New York: Random House, 1974.

Gallwey, T. and Kriegel, B. *Inner Skiing.* New York: Random House, 1977.

Greenwald, H. *Direct Decision Therapy.* New York: Knapp, 1973.

Ichazo, O. "Arica Training Materials." New York: Arica Institute, 1980.

Kelly, G. *The Psychology of Personal Constructs.* New York: Norton, 1955.

Leuner, H. *Initiated Symbol Projection.* New York: Psychosynthesis Research Foundation, 1965.

Lowen, A. *Bioenergetics.* New York: Penguin Books, 1976.

Murphy, M. and White, R. *The Psychic Side of Sports.* Reading, PA: Addison-Wesley, 1978.

Naisbett, J. *Megatrends.* New York: Warner, 1982.

Oden, T. *The Intensive Group Experience.* Philadelphia: Westminster, 1972.

Ouchi, F. *Theory Z: How American Business Can Meet the Japanese Challenge.* Reading, PA: Addison-Wesley, 1981.

Perls, F., Goodman, P., and Hefferline, R. *Gestalt Therapy.* New York: Dell, 1951.

Peters, T. and Waterman, R. *In Search of Excellence.* New York: Harper & Row, 1983.

Reich, W. *Character Analysis*. New York: Orgone Press, 1949.

———. *Listen Little Man*. London: Penguin, 1975.

Roberts, J. *Seth Journal*. New York: Bantam, 1974.

———. *The Seth Material*. New York: Bantam, 1976.

———. *The Nature of Personal Reality*. New York: Bantam, 1978.

Schutz, W. "What Makes Groups Productive?" *Human Relations* 8 (1955): 429–465.

———. *The Interpersonal Underworld*. Palo Alto, CA: Science and Behavior Books, 1966 (original publication 1958).

———. *Joy*. New York: Grove Press, 1967.

———. *Here Comes Everybody*. New York: Irvington, 1983 (original publication 1971).

———. *Elements of Encounter*. New York: Irvington, 1982 (original publication 1973).

———. *Body Fantasy*. New York: Irvington, 1984 (original publication 1976).

———. *Leaders of Schools*. San Diego: University Associates, 1977.

———. "Antioch University Center for Holistic Studies." *AHP Newsletter (for the Association for Humanistic Psychology,* November 1978a.

———. *Profound Simplicity*. San Diego: Learning Concepts, 1979.

———. "Antioch University's Experiment with Holistic Education: Center for Holistic Studies." *AHP Newsletter (for the Association for Humanistic Psychology),* May 1979a.

———. *Trainer's Manual for Schutz Measures*. San Diego: University Associates, 1982.

———. *Professional Manual for Schutz Measures*. Palo Alto, CA: Consulting Psychologists Press, 1983.

Sherif, M. "Self-Concept" in *International Encyclopedia of the Social Sciences*. New York: Crowell, Collier and Macmillan, 1968.

Simonton, O., Simonton, S., and Creighton, J. *Getting Well Again*. Los Angeles: J. P. Tarcher, 1978.

Snygg, D. and Combs, A. *Individual Behavior*. New York: Harper, 1949.

Steinberg, R. "Encounter, Christian Enthusiasm and Mysticism." Ph.D. dissertation, York University, Ontario, Canada, 1975.

Waxler, N. "Defense Mechanisms and Interpersonal Behavior." Ph.D. dissertation, Harvard University, 1960.

Wise, D. *The Politics of Lying*. New York: Random House, 1973.

INDEX

atmosphere, 196, 230. *See also* Atmosphere
   compatibility
and compensation, 153, 267, 271
cf. competence, 51
defined, 27–28
and distortion, 233–35
and Element S, 126
and Human Element Job Form, 78–79
and human elements of job description,
   72–73
and identification, 266, 271
illnesses of, 173, 175, 177, 180–83, 184,
   185. *See also* Illness
and Job-Fit Form, 82–85
and Job-Satisfaction Form, 90–94, 97–99,
   102–104
measuring, via Element B, 39–48
physical-space dimension of, 30
projection, 265, 271
in relationships, 191, 211–30, 245–46, 256
and role compatibility, 208, 211–29. *See also*
   Role compatibility
and role incompatibility, 207
self, 113. *See also* Spontaneity
and self-congruence summary, 260–61
and self-descriptions, 274–75
Coping, 145–59. *See also* Mechanisms
   and awareness, 145
   defined, 145
   effect of choice on, 19
   improving, 19
   mechanisms. *See* Mechanisms
   with unconscious conflicts via the body, 162.
     See also Illness
C-P effect, 243, 252
Creativity, increasing, 26

D

Deafness, 177. *See also* Illness
Decision making. *See also* Problem solving
   and competence, 52
   consensus, 248–51, 256
   cooperation, 248–51
Defenses. *See also* Coping; Mechanisms
   coping mechanisms as, 145–60; 231–56;
     264–73; 289. *See also* Mechanisms
   and distortion, 148–49, 232–41, 256. *See*
     also Distortion

Descriptions, self. *See* Self-descriptions
Development
   compatibility, 247
   group, 246
   of relations, 244–46, 247, 252, 256
Digestive system, illness of, 176, 177, 185. *See*
   also Illness
Dimensions
   awareness, 144–15. *See also* Awareness
   behavior, 72–73
   feelings, 74–75
   presence, 114. *See also* Presence
   spontaneity, 114–15. *See also* Spontaneity
Displacement. *See also* Mechanisms
   and compensation, 157
   defined, 145
   as distortion, 232
   mechanisms, 153
   summary, 256, 266, 270, 271
   table, 234
Dissatisfaction. *See also* Satisfaction
   Do, and role compatibility, 220–29
   Get, and role compatibility, 212–17
   identifying and measuring, 192–230
   sources of, 220
Distortion, 139–60, 232–41. *See also* Lens;
   Mechanisms; Self-concept
   atmosphere, 238–41
   and awareness, 139
   and blame, 139
   compensation as, 232, 235, 238, 239, 256
   and coping mechanisms, 145–53, 232–41.
     256. *See also* Mechanisms
   due to denying conflict, 145
   and feelings, 160
   and feelings of competence, 148
   forms of, 146
   identification as, 145, 153, 157, 232, 234,
     256
   of perceptions, 148–49
   projection as, 145, 150–52, 157, 232, 233,
     256
   reflection as, 146, 153, 157, 232, 256
   in relationships, 232–41
   due to repressing conflict, 145
   and self-concept, 231–39

and feelings, 74–76
Form, 89
Is-Want, as aspects of, 90–91
job fit as key to, 69. *See also* Job fit
and job performance, 89
and Job-Satisfaction Form, 89, 90–94,
    97–99, 102–104
measuring types of, 89
and present job, 89
truth telling as key to, 26
Job-Satisfaction Form, 89, 90–94, 97–99,
    102–104, 287
Joy, 284, 288
Joy, 283, 286
Judgment. *See* Blame

K, L

Key, self-concept as. *See* Self-concept
Leaders of Schools, 283, 286
Lens, 139–60, 162, 231. *See also* Blame;
    Distortion; Mechanisms
Likeability. *See also* Competence; Feelings;
    Significance
    and aspects of feelings, 58–65
    and atmosphere distortion, 239
    and compensation, 153, 267, 271
    cf. competence, 53
    defined, 53, 289
    and Element S, 127
    feelings of, 26, 49, 51, 54
    feelings of, effect on body, 56
    and Human Element Job Form, 78–79
    and human elements of job description,
        72–73
    and identification, 266, 271
    and illness, 181–83, 185
    and Job-Fit Form, 82–85
    and job satisfaction, 75–76
    and Job-Satisfaction Form, 90–94, 97–99,
        102–104
    and joy, 288
    cf. openness, 53
    and projection, 265, 271
    in relationships, 191, 211–30. *See also*
        Relationships
    and role compatibility, 211–29. *See also*
        Role compatibility
    and self-concept, 109, 112, 119–22, 138

and self-congruence summary, 260–61
and self-descriptions, 274–75
cf. significance, 53
Love, and illness, 181, 184

M

Measurement. *See* Elements B, F, R, and S
Measures, Schutz, 287. *See also* Elements B, F,
    R, and S; Forms
Mechanisms, 145–60, 231–56, 264–73, 289.
    See also Coping; Defenses
    and choice, 157
    compensation, 147, 153, 154–59, 232, 235,
        238, 256, 267, 270, 271. *See also*
        Compensation
    displacement, 145, 146, 153, 157, 232, 234,
        256, 266, 270, 271. *See also* Displacement
    distortion, 145–53, 232–41, 256. *See also*
        Distortion
    identification, 146, 153, 157, 232, 256, 270.
        See also Identification
    illness as coping, 147
    projection, 145, 150–52, 157, 232, 233,
        256, 264, 265, 270, 271. *See also*
        Projection
    in relationships, 191, 193, 231–56. *See also*
        Relationships
    summary, 264–73
    understanding, 258, 278
Motivation, 109, 110–11
Mouth, illnesses of, 176. *See also* Illness
Muscular system, illnesses of, 175, 180, 185.
    See also Illness

N, O

Nearsightedness, 176. *See also* Illness
Nervous system, illnesses of, 175, 180, 185. *See
    also* Illness
Nose, illnesses of, 176. *See also* Illness
Open/closed. *See* Openness
Openness. *See also* Behavior; Control;
    Inclusion
    activity, 33
    and aspects of control, 35
    and atmosphere compatibility, 197, 198,
        230. *See also* Atmosphere compatibility

and compensation, 267, 271
defined, 27–29, 289
and distortion, 233–35
and Human Element Job Form, 78–79
and human elements of job description, 72–73
and identification, 266, 271
illnesses of, 173, 175, 181–83, 184, 185. *See also* Illness
and Job-Fit Form, 82–85
and Job-Satisfaction Form, 90–94, 97–99, 102–104
cf. likeability, 51
measuring, via Element B, 39–48
in organizations, 15
physical-space dimension of, 30
and projection, 265, 271
in relationships, 191, 211–30, 245–46, 256
and role compatibility, 209, 211–29
self-, 114, *See also* Awareness
and self-concept, 112, 114. *See also* Self-concept
and self-congruence summary, 260–61
and self-descriptions, 274–75
in work situation, 71
Opportunity, illness as, 161, 182
Organizations. *See also* Job; Work situation
and effectiveness, 284
Human Element program for, 283–84, 286
human side of, 7, 284
and motivation, 109, 110
openness in, 15
and productivity, 109
relationships as basis of, 191, 193
self-awareness and optimal functioning in, 139
and truth telling, 15
Orgasm, 184

P

Payoff
for choosing illness, 172, 173
for making choices, 20, 130
for understanding illness, 161
Perceptions, distorted. *See* Distortion; Mechanisms
Performance review, 287

Personal meaning
of behavior, 47
of health and illness, 188
of job and career fit, 107
of the key, 137
of the lens, 159
of a look back, a look forward, 280
of relations: expression, 228–29
of relations: understanding, 254
Physical symptoms and truth telling, 11. *See also* Body
Political context. *See* Social context
Potency, dysfunctions, 184. *See also* Illness
Presence
activity, 116
and atmosphere distortion, 239
and body response, 116
and compensation, 153
defined, 113, 114
and Element S, 126
physiology of, 289
and self-concept, 120, 138
Present job
activity, 95–96
satisfaction with, 89, 92–96
Problems. *See also* Conflicts; Problem solving
and feelings, 49
interpersonal, 7, 193–94
job, 9, 70, 139
Problem solving
via atmosphere, 239
and choice principle, 20
and competence, 52
difficulties and, 141
disagreements about, in relationships, 195–206. *See also* Atmosphere compatibility
and letting go, 242
via truth, 7, 9, 13
Productivity. *See also* Effectiveness
and C-P effect, 243, 256
effect of truth telling on, 11, 15
and feelings, 49
increasing, 26, 27
problems in organizations, 109
and stress, 243, 256
Profound Simplicity, 283, 286, 288

Projection. *See also* Mechanisms
 activity, 150–52
 and compensation, 157
 defined, 145
 and distortion, 232
 mechanisms, 153
 summary, 256, 264, 265, 270, 271
 table, 233

Q

Questions
 aspects of behavior, 36
 aspects of feelings, 59
 atmosphere compatibility, 200
 behavior, 31, 73
 Do, 221
 feelings, 54, 76
 Get, 213
 group development, 246
 mechanisms, 153
 role situations, 208–209
 self-concept, 120

R

Rashes, 176. *See also* Illness
Reactions, choosing, 18
Reality, and satisfaction, 272–73
Relations. *See* Relationships
Relationships, 191–230, 231–56
 and atmosphere compatibility, 195–206. *See also* Atmosphere compatibility
 blaming in, 140, 142–44
 changing, 247, 252
 choice as key to improved, 18
 competence in, 191, 211–30
 control in, 191, 211–30, 245–46
 coping mechanisms in, 191, 193, 231. *See also* Mechanisms
 development of, 244–46, 247, 252
 Do, 210, 220–29
 Get, 210–19
 inclusion, 191, 211–30
 incompatibility in, 192–230
 levels of truth in, 191, 193, 231
 likeability in, 191, 211–30

openness in, 191, 211–30, 245–46
 personal, as job problem, 71
 and role compatibility, 191, 207–29. *See also* Role compatibility
 and self-awareness, 139
 and self-concept, 109, 231
 significance in, 191, 211–30
 truth as key to improved, 9, 11, 191
 understanding, 231–56, 278
Reproductive system, illnesses of, 185. *See also* Illness
Respiratory system, illnesses of, 176, 177, 185. *See also* Illness
Responsibility. *See also* Blame
 vs. blame, 140, 142–44
 and self-concept, 141
Role compatibility, 191, 207–29, 230. *See also* Compatibility
 control and, 208, 230
 defined, 207
 and Do relations, 210, 220–29
 feelings and, 210, 211
 and Get relations, 210–19
 inclusion and, 208, 230
 openness and, 209, 230

S

Satisfaction. *See also* Dissatisfaction
 job. *See* Job satisfaction
 and reality, 272–73
Schutz Measures, 287
Self-acceptance, 26. *See also* Self-concept
Self-competence, 119. *See also* Competence
Self-concept, 109–38, 288
 awareness and, 114, 115, 120, 138, 148
 behavioral aspects of, 112–18, 120, 138, 257. *See also* Control; Inclusion; Openness
 changing the, 130–37, 258, 283
 and coping ability, 145–59. *See also* Coping
 defined, 112
 distortion and, 139–60. *See also* Distortion; Lens
 and Element S, 115, 123–27
 feelings aspect of, 112, 119–22, 278
 and feelings of competence, 109, 112, 119–22, 138. *See also* Competence
 and feelings of likeability, 109, 112, 119–22, 138. *See also* Likeability

WILL SCHUTZ ASSOCIATES
INFORMATION FORM

Mail to: Will Schutz Associates
Box 259
Muir Beach, CA 94965

Please send me information about the following:

____ The Human Element (THE) organization program for application to my organization or my clients.

____ Public workshops in THE organization program.

____ Training program for people interested in becoming certified trainers for THE organizational program (Phase I and Phase II).

____ I would like to order some books listed in Appendix C. Please send a book-order form.

____ The other instruments: Performance Reviews, Job Form, Job-Fit Form (specify interest).

____ Newsletter

____ Please place me on your mailing list.

Name _____

Address _____ Age _____ Sex ____

City _____ State _____ Province ____

Phone (   ) _____

Organization _____

Title _____

This is my reaction to this book:

You (may) (may not) quote me in your promotional materials.

   Signed _____

*May we introduce other Ten Speed Books you may find useful . . .
over three million people have already.*

What Color Is Your Parachute? by Richard Bolles
The Three Boxes of Life by Richard Bolles
Finding Money for College by John Bear, Ph.D.
Who's Hiring Who by Richard Lathrop
Finding Facts Fast by Alden Todd
Mail Order Moonlighting by Cecil Hoge
How to Get the Degree You Want by John Bear, Ph.D.
Computer Wimp by John Bear, Ph.D.
The Moosewood Cookbook by Mollie Katzen
The Enchanted Broccoli Forest and other timeless delicacies by Mollie Katzen
Sailing the Farm by Ken Neumeyer
Better Letters by Jan Venolia
Write Right! by Jan Venolia
The Wellness Workbook by Regina Sara Ryan and John W. Travis, M.D.
How to Grow More Vegetables by John Jeavons
Anybody's Bike Book by Tom Cuthbertson

You will find them in your bookstore or library;
or you can send for our *free* catalog:

TEN SPEED PRESS
BOX 7123 ● BERKELEY, CALIFORNIA 94707

NOTES

NOTES

NOTES

SCORING SUMMARY

Scale Code	Element	Page	Name
63	_____ R	222	You are open with me.
64	_____ R	222	I want you to be open with me.
Δ63	_____ R	222	You are more open with me than I want you to be.
65	_____ R	214	I like you.
66	_____ R	214	I want to like you.
Δ65	_____ R	214	I like you more than I want to.
67	_____ R	222	You like me.
68	_____ R	222	I want you to like me.
Δ67	_____ R	222	You like me more than I want you to.
71	_____ J	90	In my job I include people.
72	_____ J	90	In my ideal job I include people.
Δ71	_____ J	90	In my job I include people more than I want to.
73	_____ J	90	In my job people include me.
74	_____ J	90	In my ideal job people include me.
Δ73	_____ J	90	In my job people include me more than I want them to.
75	_____ J	90	In my job I feel that people are significant.
76	_____ J	90	In my ideal job I feel that people are significant.
Δ75	_____ J	90	In my job I feel that people are more significant than I want them to be.
77	_____ J	90	In my job people feel that I am significant.
78	_____ J	90	In my ideal job people feel that I am significant.
Δ77	_____ J	90	In my job people feel that I am more significant than I want them to feel.
81	_____ J	90	In my job I control people.
82	_____ J	90	In my ideal job I control people.
Δ81	_____ J	90	In my job I control people more than I want to.
83	_____ J	90	In my job people control me.
84	_____ J	90	In my ideal job people control me.
Δ83	_____ J	90	In my job people control me more than I want them to.
85	_____ J	90	In my job I feel that people are competent.
86	_____ J	90	In my ideal job I feel that people are competent.
Δ85	_____ J	90	In my job I feel that people are more competent than I want them to be.
87	_____ J	90	In my job people feel that I am competent.
88	_____ J	90	In my ideal job people feel that I am competent.
Δ87	_____ J	90	In my job people feel that I am more competent than I want them to feel.
91	_____ J	90	In my job I am open with people.
92	_____ J	90	In my ideal job I am open with people.
Δ91	_____ J	90	In my job I am more open with people than I want to be.
93	_____ J	90	In my job people are open with me.
94	_____ J	90	In my ideal job people are open with me.
Δ93	_____ J	90	In my job people are open with me more than I want them to be.
95	_____ J	90	In my job I like people.
96	_____ J	90	In my ideal job I like people.
Δ95	_____ J	90	In my job I like people more than I want to.
97	_____ J	90	In my job people like me.
98	_____ J	90	In my ideal job people like me.
Δ97	_____ J	90	In my job people like me more than I want them to.
10	_____ S	124	I am present (include myself).
19	_____ S	124	I want to be present.
Δ10	_____ S	124	I am more present than I want to be.
40	_____ S	124	I feel significant.
49	_____ S	124	I want to feel significant.
Δ40	_____ S	124	I feel more significant than I want to feel.
20	_____ S	124	I control myself.
29	_____ S	124	I want to control myself.
Δ20	_____ S	124	I control myself more than I want to.
50	_____ S	124	I feel competent.
59	_____ S	124	I want to feel competent.
Δ50	_____ S	124	I feel more competent than I want to feel.
30	_____ S	124	I am aware (am open with myself).
39	_____ S	124	I want to be aware.
Δ30	_____ S	124	I am more aware of myself than I want to be.
60	_____ S	124	I like myself.
69	_____ S	124	I want to like myself.
Δ60	_____ S	124	I like myself more than I want to.

TABLE 19.

Here's the way you have chosen to be right now. Date _____

IP	ID	IT	CP	CD	CT	OP	OD	OT	SP	SD	ST	MP	MD	MT	LP	LD	LT	GP	GD	GT	RP	RD	RT	JP	JD	JT	EP	ED	ET	OVERALL
Project	Displace	Compensate	Project	Displace	Compensate	Project	Displace	Compensate	Project	Displace	Compensate	Project	Displace	Compensate	Project	Displace	Compensate	Project	Displace	Compensate	Project	Displace	Compensate	Project	Displace	Compensate	Project	Displace	Compensate	
0	0	0	0	0	0	0	0	0	0	0	0	0	0	0	0	0	0	0	0	0	0	0	0	0	0	0	0	0	0	0
1	1	1	1	1	1	1	1	1	1	1	1	1	1	1	1	1	1	2	2	2	2	2	2	2	2	2	6	6	6	18
2	2	2	2	2	2	2	2	2	2	2	2	2	2	2	2	2	2	4	4	4	4	4	4	4	4	4	12	12	12	36
3	3	3	3	3	3	3	3	3	3	3	3	3	3	3	3	3	3	6	6	6	6	6	6	6	6	6	18	18	18	54
4	4	4	4	4	4	4	4	4	4	4	4	4	4	4	4	4	4	8	8	8	8	8	8	8	8	8	24	24	24	72
5	5	5	5	5	5	5	5	5	5	5	5	5	5	5	5	5	5	10	10	10	10	10	10	10	10	10	30	30	30	90
6	6	6	6	6	6	6	6	6	6	6	6	6	6	6	6	6	6	12	12	12	12	12	12	12	12	12	36	36	36	108
8	8	8	8	8	8	8	8	8	8	8	8	8	8	8	8	8	8	16	16	16	16	16	16	16	16	16	48	48	48	144
10	10	10	10	10	10	10	10	10	10	10	10	10	10	10	10	10	10	20	20	20	20	20	20	20	20	20	60	60	60	180
●	●	●	●	●	●	●	●	●	●	●	●	●	●	●	●	●	●	●	●	●	●	●	●	●	●	●	●	●	●	●
4	4	4	4	4	4	4	4	4	4	4	4	4	4	4	4	4	4	8	8	8	8	8	8	8	8	8	4	4	4	32
7	7	7	7	7	7	7	7	7	7	7	7	7	7	7	7	7	7	13	13	13	13	13	13	13	13	13	7	7	7	49
10	10	10	10	10	10	10	10	10	10	10	10	10	10	10	10	10	10	18	18	18	18	18	18	18	18	18	10	10	10	66
13	13	13	13	13	13	13	13	13	13	13	13	13	13	13	13	13	13	23	23	23	23	23	23	23	23	23	13	13	13	83
16	16	16	16	16	16	16	16	16	16	16	16	16	16	16	16	16	16	28	28	28	28	28	28	28	28	28	16	16	16	100
19	19	19	19	19	19	19	19	19	19	19	19	19	19	19	19	19	19	33	33	33	33	33	33	33	33	33	19	19	19	117
22	22	22	22	22	22	22	22	22	22	22	22	22	22	22	22	22	22	38	38	38	38	38	38	38	38	38	22	22	22	134
25	25	25	25	25	25	25	25	25	25	25	25	25	25	25	25	25	25	43	43	43	43	43	43	43	43	43	25	25	25	151
28	28	28	28	28	28	28	28	28	28	28	28	28	28	28	28	28	28	48	48	48	48	48	48	48	48	48	28	28	28	168
INCLUSION			CONTROL			OPENNESS			SIGNIFICANCE			COMPETENCE			LIKEABILITY			PEOPLE			PARTNER			JOB			SELF			OVERALL

Interpretation

The bottom part of the chart represents the degree of discrepancy between what IS and what I WANT. As I become what I want to be, the bottom reaches upward toward the row of circles. When I am fully what I want to be, the bottom of the chart will be totally filled up to the circle row. Each vertical segment represents the IS–WANT discrepancy in one area (inclusion, job, and so on).

The top half of the chart represents the coping mechanisms I may be using in various circumstances. The further down the bar goes, the less I use copers and the more clearly I see reality. My reality grounds me and helps my self-satisfaction rise.

I measure the degree of clarity and satisfaction by counting the number of numbers (e.g., "7") that show in each column. The larger the number of numbers, the more likely it is that I am not satisfied with myself and the more I distort my reality. A totally filled chart indicates that I am the way I want to be and that I see the world without distortion.

I assume that the less I distort the world, the more likely it is that I will achieve contentment or satisfaction. Below are interpretations for each of the columns in Table 19. Interpretations are appropriate only if there is a large gap (numbers in the column). The larger the gap, the more likely the interpretation is to be true.

In any case, the interpretation is simply a probability, it is only one interpretation. It is up to me to test it out and see if it makes sense to me and if I can make use of it.

The way I am is not the way I want to be in the area of:			Without being aware of it, I may be distorting reality by:
IP	Inclusion	:	Imagining that people do not include me when actually I feel that I am not including myself.
ID	Inclusion	:	Not including people because I do not include myself and I do not want to give them an advantage.
IT	Inclusion	:	Trying to get other people to include me to compensate for me not including myself.
CP	Control	:	Imagining that people are controlling me when actually I feel that I am controlling myself **or** imagining that people are not controlling me when actually I feel that I am not controlling myself.
CD	Control	:	Controlling others because I control myself and I do not want to give them an advantage **or** not controlling others because I do not control myself and I do not want to give them an advantage.
CT	Control	:	Trying to get you to control me to compensate for my lack of self-control **or** trying to prevent you from controlling me because I already control myself.
OP	Openness	:	Imagining that people are not open to me when actually I feel that I am not open to myself.
OD	Openness	:	Not being open to people because I am not open to myself and I do not want to treat them better than I treat myself.
OT	Openness	:	Trying to get people to be open with me to compensate for my lack of self-openness.
SP	Significance	:	Imagining that people feel that I am insignificant when actually I am the one who feels insignificant.
SD	Significance	:	Not feeling that you are significant because I do not feel significant and I do not want to feel inferior.
ST	Significance	:	Trying to get you to feel that I am significant to compensate for my feeling of insignificance.
MP	Competence	:	Imagining that you feel that I am incompetent when actually I am the one who feels incompetent.
MD	Competence	:	Not feeling that you are competent because I feel incompetent and I do not want to feel inferior.
MT	Competence	:	Trying to get you to feel that I am competent to compensate for my feeling of incompetence.
LP	Likeability	:	Imagining that you do not like me when I actually do not like myself.
LD	Likeability	:	Not liking you because I do not like myself and I do not want to feel inferior.
LT	Likeability	:	Trying to get you to like me to compensate for my not liking myself.
GP	People in General	:	Imagining that people in general relate (that is, act and feel) toward me in certain ways when actually I relate toward myself in those ways.
GD	People in General	:	Relating the same toward other people as I relate to myself.
GT	People in General	:	Trying to get other people to relate to me in ways that compensate for the ways that I do not relate to myself.
RP	Partner ("you")	:	Imagining that you relate toward me in certain ways when actually I relate to myself in those ways.
RD	Partner	:	Relating to you the same as I relate to myself because I do not want to give you any advantage.
RT	Partner	:	Trying to get you to relate to me in ways that compensate for the way that I relate to myself.
JP	Job	:	Imagining that people relate to me in certain ways when actually I relate to myself in those ways.
JD	Job	:	Relating to people on the job the way I relate to myself because I do not want them to have an advantage.
JT	Job	:	Trying to get people on the job to relate to me in ways that compensate for the way I relate to myself.
EP	Self	:	Imagining that people in general, people on the job and you relate to me in certain ways when actually I relate to myself in those ways.
ED	Self	:	Relating the same toward you, people on the job and people in general the same as I relate to myself because I do not want to give them an advantage or feel inferior.
ET	Self	:	Trying to get you, people, job and people in general to relate to me in ways that compensate for my lack of relating that way to myself.
OV	Everything	:	Being dissatisfied with myself in all areas and using all three distortions in all areas.

SCORING SUMMARY

Scale Code	Element	Page	Name
11	_____ B	40	I include people.
12	_____ B	40	I want to include people.
Δ11	_____ B	40	I include people more than I want to.
13	_____ B	40	People include me.
14	_____ B	40	I want people to include me.
Δ13	_____ B	40	People include me more than I want them to.
15	_____ F	62	I feel that people are significant.
16	_____ F	62	I want to feel that people are significant.
Δ15	_____ F	62	I feel that people are more significant than I want to feel.
17	_____ F	62	People feel that I am significant.
18	_____ F	62	I want people to feel that I am significant.
Δ17	_____ F	62	People feel that I am more significant than I want them to feel.
21	_____ B	40	I control people.
22	_____ B	40	I want to control people.
Δ21	_____ B	40	I control people more than I want to.
23	_____ B	40	People control me.
24	_____ B	40	I want people to control me.
Δ23	_____ B	40	People control me more than I want them to.
25	_____ F	62	I feel that people are competent.
26	_____ F	62	I want to feel that people are competent.
Δ25	_____ F	62	I feel that people are more competent than I want to feel.
27	_____ F	62	People feel that I am competent.
28	_____ F	62	I want people to feel that I am competent.
Δ27	_____ F	62	People feel that I am more competent than I want them to feel.
31	_____ B	40	I am open with people.
32	_____ B	40	I want to be open with people.
Δ31	_____ B	40	I am more open with people than I want to be.
33	_____ B	40	People are open with me.
34	_____ B	40	I want people to be open with me.
Δ33	_____ B	40	People are more open with me than I want them to be.
35	_____ F	62	I like people.
36	_____ F	62	I want to like people.
Δ35	_____ F	62	I like people more than I want to like them.
37	_____ F	62	People like me.
38	_____ F	62	I want people to like me
Δ37	_____ F	62	People like me more than I want them to.
41	_____ R	214	I include you. (You = Partner for 41–68)
42	_____ R	214	I want to include you.
Δ41	_____ R	214	I include you more than I want to.
43	_____ R	222	You include me.
44	_____ R	222	I want you to include me.
Δ43	_____ R	222	You include me more than I want you to.
45	_____ R	214	I feel that you are significant.
46	_____ R	214	I want to feel that you are significant.
Δ45	_____ R	214	I feel that you are more significant than I want to feel.
47	_____ R	222	You feel that I am significant.
48	_____ R	222	I want you to feel that I am significant.
Δ47	_____ R	222	You feel that I am more significant than I want you to feel.
51	_____ R	214	I control you.
52	_____ R	214	I want to control you.
Δ51	_____ R	214	I control you more than I want to.
53	_____ R	222	You control me.
54	_____ R	222	I want you to control me.
Δ53	_____ R	222	You control me more than I want you to.
55	_____ R	214	I feel that you are competent.
56	_____ R	214	I want to feel that you are competent.
Δ55	_____ R	214	I feel that you are more competent than I want to feel.
57	_____ R	222	You feel that I am competent.
58	_____ R	222	I want you to feel that I am competent.
Δ57	_____ R	222	You feel that I am more competent than I want you to feel.
61	_____ R	214	I am open with you.
62	_____ R	214	I want to be open with you.
Δ61	_____ R	214	I am more open with you than I want to be.